Contents

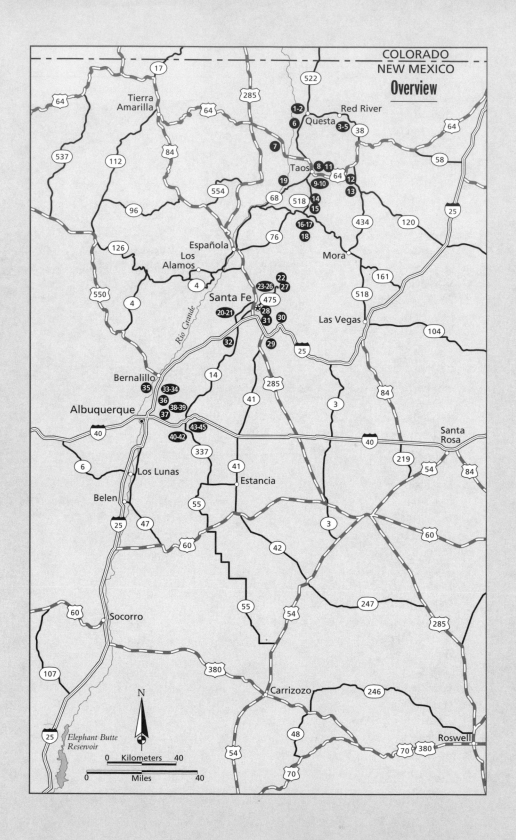

Mountain Biking
Northern New Mexico

A Guide to the Taos, Santa Fe, and Albuquerque Areas'
Greatest Off-Road Bicycle Rides

Bob D'Antonio

FALCON®

GUILFORD, CONNECTICUT
HELENA, MONTANA
AN IMPRINT OF THE GLOBE PEQUOT PRESS

AFALCONGUIDE®

A fat/trax book

All photographs except those in Repair and Maintenance
by Bob D'Antonio

Maps created by XNR Productions, Inc. © The Globe
Pequot Press

Library of Congress Cataloging-in-Publication Data is
available.

ISBN 0-7627-2802-7

Manufactured in the United States of America
First Edition/First Printing

Mountain Biking Northern New Mexico

Help Us Keep This Guide Up to Date

Every effort has been made by the author and editors to make this guide as accurate and useful as possible. However, many things can change after a guide is published—trails are rerouted, regulations change, techniques evolve, facilities come under new management, etc.

We would love to hear from you concerning your experiences with this guide and how you feel it could be improved and kept up to date. While we may not be able to respond to all comments and suggestions, we'll take them to heart and we'll also make certain to share them with the author. Please send your comments and suggestions to the following address:

The Globe Pequot Press
Reader Response/Editorial Department
P.O. Box 480
Guilford, CT 06437

Or you may e-mail us at:

editorial@GlobePequot.com

Thanks for your input, and happy travels!

Albuquerque Area

Introduction

This book describes forty-five mountain bike rides in north-central New Mexico. The rides run in a north to south direction, with Ride 1 in the northern part of the state near the village of Questa and Ride 45 just south of Albuquerque.

The state of New Mexico, and in particular the northern part of the state, is an area of great natural beauty and cultural diversity. From the sprawling city of Albuquerque, situated in a beautiful river valley, to Wheeler Peak, the highest point in New Mexico near Taos, north-central New Mexico has it all. In fact, five of the seven life zones are in northern New Mexico.

This book describes mountain bike trails in three different areas of north-central New Mexico: Taos, Santa Fe, and Albuquerque. Each area has its own distinct type of riding and feel. Each city is quite different from the other and each will offer a different feel and experience. Taos is a small city with a high population of Native Americans and Hispanics. Their influences are at the heart and soul of the town. If Santa Fe is the heart of northern New Mexico, Taos is its soul. In a state that is considered very laid-back, Taos is the most laid-back of the three cities. In fact, very little has changed in Taos in the thirty years I have been going there and, naturally, I hope it stays that way.

Next up is trendy and eclectic Santa Fe. A beautiful and ever-growing state capital that seems to always be changing, yet it still somehow clings to and retains its past—a past that is rich in history, culture, and architecture!

Moving farther south you come upon the sprawling city of Albuquerque—a city of 700,000 people (the largest in the state) nestled below the rugged Sandia Mountains and along the lazy-flowing Rio Grande. Albuquerque is the crossroads for two major interstate highways, I–40 running east and west and I–25 traveling north and south. The town is at a major crossroads and is poised to make the leap into major city status in the not-so-distant future.

Here in northern New Mexico, you can easily do an early-morning ride in the Upper Sonoran life zone near Albuquerque, take a short break, hop in the car, drive to Santa Fe, and cruise down the Windsor Trail located in the Hudsonian zone at 10,000 feet above sea level all in the same day. With this great topography comes a variety of trails and scenery. Smooth, tight singletrack will take cyclists through stands of cacti and desert junipers onto doubletrack trails that cut through miles of sage and piñon trees with the beautiful Rio Grande 1,000 feet below and Wheeler Peak 4,000 feet above. You can cruise on tight, rocky singletrack along soothing mountain streams, through meadows filled with vibrant wildflowers to crystal-clear mountain lakes below towering high peaks. This is the beauty and variety of mountain biking in northern New Mexico.

The preferred mode of transportation in Taos

When discussing the land of northern New Mexico, you cannot overlook its people. The varieties of people who call New Mexico home are as diverse as the topography. In fact, three different cultures (Anglo, Hispanic, and Native American) blend together to create a unique and colorful heritage found in few places elsewhere in the United States. The common bond that brought the first Native Americans here some 10,000 years ago continues to attract newcomers. It's a land that has for years attracted artists, writers, jewelry makers, weavers, potters, spiritual seekers, hippies, and photographers all inspired and seduced by this "land of enchantment."

As you ride your bike along the following trails, remember there is much more to northern New Mexico than mountain biking. Do yourself a favor and, after your ride, go out and explore the streets, the small villages, the Indian pueblos, and the museums, and speak to the people of this extraordinary land. You are guaranteed a wonderful journey regardless of your way of getting around.

How to Use This Book

Mountain Biking Northern New Mexico features forty-five mapped and cued rides, as well as everything from advice on getting into shape to tips on mountain bike camping and getting the most out of cycling with your dog. It is divided into three

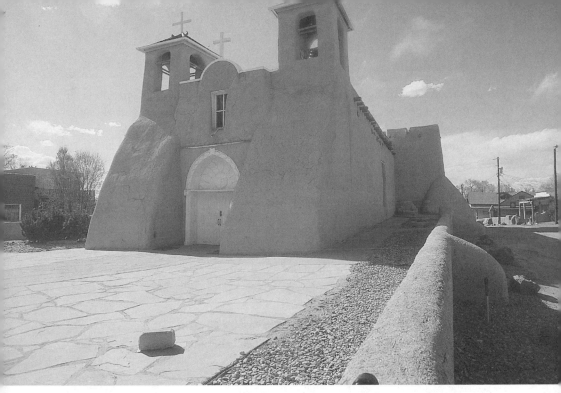

The beautiful and historic St. Francis of Assisi Mission Church in Rancho de Taos

sections, each representing distinct riding areas near northern New Mexico's three most-visited cities. Within each section you'll find featured rides found in each of these regions. Each chapter is then subsequently divided into a variety of components. The ride specs are fairly self-explanatory. Here you'll find the quick, nitty-gritty details of the ride: where the trailhead is located, the nearest town, ride length, approximate riding time, difficulty rating, type of trail terrain, if dogs are permitted, and what other trail users you may encounter. You will also find information on maps for the area, park schedules and fees, as well as information for contacting the trail managers. The Finding the Trailhead section gives you directions from a nearby city right down to where you'll want to park. The ride description is the meat of the chapter. It's the author's carefully researched impression of the trail. In the Miles and Directions section, mileage cues are provided to identify all turns and trail name changes, as well as points of interest. Between this and the route map, you should have enough information to keep from getting lost. The Ride Information section contains more useful information, including where to stay, what to eat, and what else to see while you're riding in the area.

How to Use These Maps

We don't want anyone, by any means, to feel restricted to just the routes and trails that are mapped here. We hope you will have an adventurous spirit and use this guide as a platform to discover new routes for yourself. One of the simplest ways to begin this is to just turn the map upside down and ride the course in reverse. The change in perspective is fantastic and the ride should feel quite different. With this in mind, it will be like getting two distinctly different rides on each map. Not to mention that if you ride the same trails in the dark, the rides become completely different. Like night and day! Pun intended!

For your own purposes, you may wish to copy the directions for the course onto a small sheet to help you while riding, or photocopy the map and cue sheet to take with you. Otherwise, just slip the whole book in your pack and take it all with you. Enjoy your time in the outdoors and remember to pack out what you pack in.

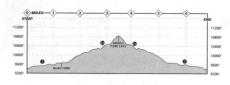

Elevation Profile

This helpful profile gives you a cross-sectional look at the ride's ups and downs. Elevation is labeled on the left, and mileage is indicated on the top. Landmarks and points of interest are labeled on the routes. There are also difficulty-rating numbers included in black circles on the profiles, with one being the easiest and five being the hardest.

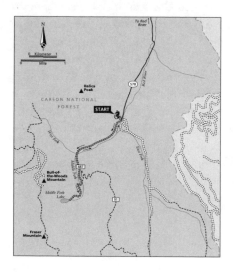

Route Map

This is your primary guide to each ride. It shows all of the accessible roads and trails, points of interest, water, towns, landmarks, and geographical features. It also distinguishes trails from roads, and paved roads from unpaved roads. The selected route is highlighted, and directional arrows point the way.

Map Legend

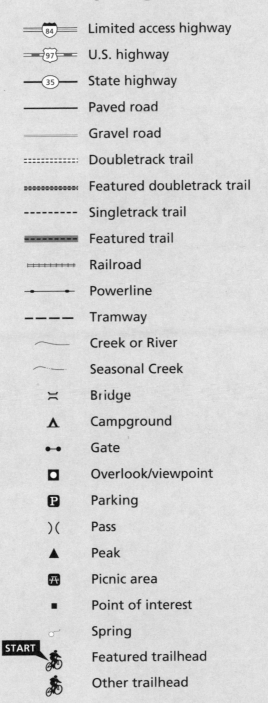

84	Limited access highway
97	U.S. highway
35	State highway
	Paved road
	Gravel road
	Doubletrack trail
	Featured doubletrack trail
	Singletrack trail
	Featured trail
	Railroad
	Powerline
	Tramway
	Creek or River
	Seasonal Creek
⋈	Bridge
⛺	Campground
	Gate
◻	Overlook/viewpoint
P	Parking
)(	Pass
▲	Peak
⛩	Picnic area
■	Point of interest
	Spring
START	Featured trailhead
	Other trailhead

Taos Area

aos sits in a beautiful, lush valley below the towering snowcapped peaks of the Sangre de Cristo Mountains. It is surrounded on the north, east, and south by mountains and on the west by the dramatic Rio Grande Gorge; Taos is one of the most beautiful areas in all of New Mexico. Wheeler Peak, New Mexico's highest point at 13,161 feet, and the sacred Taos Mountain dominate the skyline to the east and north. Mesas filled with piñon, sagebrush, cacti and desert junipers stretch far west to the Rio Grande and beyond. This is a place of profound beauty and varied topography. The tall and beautiful Sangre de Cristo Mountains provide a sensational and varied landscape that changes with each season. In winter the peaks are covered in white champagne powder that has made Taos Ski Valley a legend among ski fanatics. Winters can be quite cold and snow can fall from late October to early April. Only a few trails (West Rim Trail and Rio Grande del Rancho) in the Taos area can be ridden during the cold winter season. Spring brings longer days and warmer temperatures. April and early May can be wet with late-season snow showers and rain. The trails at lower elevations begin to dry out and excitement builds for the oncoming summer season. The arrival of summer brings long days and warm sunshine, and the mountains around Taos turn a lush, vibrant green. Mountain streams, swollen with summer runoff, burst into steep cut canyons and open meadows filled with colorful wildflowers, willows, and tall, green grasses. This is a time of spectacular beauty in the high mountain area and the best time to explore the rugged, high mountain trails. Summer temperatures can be quite warm during the day, but nights are refreshingly cool. Fall brings the changing of the aspens and very stable weather. This is my favorite time to ride a mountain bike in the Taos area. The trails are dry, temperatures are cool, and pockets of gold light up the mountainsides around each turn of the trail.

West of Taos lies the Rio Grande and miles of high, open mesas and endless vistas. The Rio Grande flows down the 800-foot-deep Rio Grande Gorge on its journey to the south. This is a place of dramatic beauty. Volcanic hills dot the plateaus, and the gorge is lined with vertical basalt cliffs. Coyotes, pronghorn antelope, rattlesnakes, jackrabbits, and various other creatures of the high desert call this place home. Mountain biking through this environment is unlike anywhere else in New Mexico and should be experienced by every cyclist who visits the Taos area.

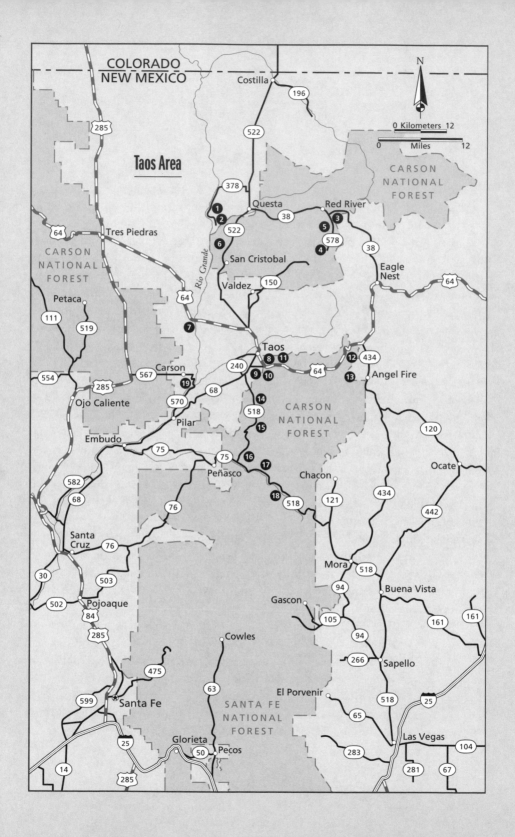

A few notes about the mountain biking in this area. Taos lies at 7,100 feet above sea level. Most of the rides start at this elevation or higher. This could be a cause for concern for those traveling from lower elevations. Take time to acclimate and try one of the rides at a lower elevation (Talpa Traverse or the West Rim Trail). Those who venture into the high county have a whole different set of concerns. Most rides in the high country have huge elevation gains and rugged terrain. Weather can and does change very rapidly. Summer storms roll in very quickly and can be quite violent and dangerous. What starts out to be a very wonderful day at 7,100 feet can turn into your worst nightmare at 11,000 feet above sea level. Be prepared and pack extra food, water, and clothing. If riding alone, let friends know of your route and destination. Bring proper tools and extra tubes. There is nothing worse than having to walk your bike out from a long mountain ride. Deer, elk, bears, wild turkeys, and mountain lions all live in the mountains high above Taos. It has been my pleasure on two occasions to come across the path of black bears. It is quite an experience to see these great animals in the wild, but it can also be very dangerous. I literally ran into a mother black bear and her two cubs high on the South Boundary Trail near the Ojitos Trail junction on a late spring day. The mother, not so happy with my arrival, growled at me several times. Luckily after several tense moments (seemed like hours to me), the cubs ran into the woods with Mother right behind. I was lucky and the outcome could have been a lot worse. Almost all the public lands around Taos are hunted in the fall and spring. If you venture out into the woods during these seasons, wear bright-colored clothing and make your presence obvious. Most of the public lands around Taos are multiuse. You are bound to see other trail users (hikers, dirt-bikers, and four-wheelers). Show a little friendliness and take the time to say hi. Some of my best encounters and conversations on the trails have been with these folks. Who knows, you might meet a new friend. So enjoy and relish your time riding in the Taos area; very few places in the United States offer the culture, topography, and beauty that this spectacular area does!

1 Red River Fault Loop

Start: At the trailhead, 11.5 miles from New Mexico Highway 552.
Distance: 4.8-mile loop.
Approximate riding time: 45 minutes to 1.5 hours.
Difficulty: Easy with a few short hills.
Trail surface: Well-groomed doubletrack trail.
Lay of the land: Great doubletrack riding on a piñon- and juniper-covered mesa near the wild and scenic Red River and Rio Grande.
Other trail users: This trail is popular with hikers, tourists, and joggers.
Canine compatibility: Dog friendly, but they must be kept on a leash at all times.

Wheels: Front suspension will work just fine on this ride.
Land status: Bureau of Land Management.
Nearest town: Questa.
Fees and permits: $3.00 a day per vehicle.
Schedule: 6:00 A.M. to 10:00 P.M. for day use.
Maps: Rio Grande Wild Rivers Map available from the visitor center; USGS maps: Taos County.
Trail contacts: Bureau of Land Management, Taos Resource Area Office, 226 Cruz Alta Road, Taos, NM 87571; (505) 758-8851; www.nm.blm.gov.
Rio Grande Wild Rivers Visitor Center, Cerro, NM 87519; (505) 770-1600.

Finding the trailhead: From Questa: Go north out of town on NM 552 for 3 miles to New Mexico Highway 378. Turn left onto NM 378 and travel 10.5 miles, passing through the village of Cerro and into the Rio Grande Wild Rivers Recreation Area. The ride starts at the Red River Fault trailhead 1 mile before the visitor center. *DeLorme: New Mexico Atlas & Gazetteer:* Page 16, C-3.

The Ride

This is one of my favorite areas in the northern part of New Mexico. The Wild Rivers Recreation Area offers up a multitude of outdoor pursuits for those willing to go off the beaten track. There are several excellent hiking trails that lead down to the Rio Grande where there's beautiful camping and good fishing. The hike up to Guadalupe Mountain travels through stands of beautiful ponderosa pine trees and offers great views to the surrounding mountains and north to Colorado, especially Blanca Peak (14,345 feet) and Little Bear Peak (14,037 feet). The campgrounds are well maintained and rarely, if ever, fill up. The Wild Rivers Recreation Area has five developed campgrounds and picnic areas. Each campground has bathrooms, drinking water, picnic sites, and tables. A fee of $7.00 is charged per vehicle, per night for camping. This is a great deal, and I suggest that you spend a few days hiking, fishing, or mountain biking in the area.

▶ In World War II, from the years 1939 to 1945, Native Americans from the Navajo Nation used their native language to send secret codes and confuse the Japanese army. The Navajo "code talkers" used their language for top-secret messages that the Japanese never decoded.

Northern New Mexico lawn ornaments

The visitor center has been remodeled and offers several visual displays on geology, fauna, and flora of the area. The staff at the center is very friendly and can answer any questions that you may have and offer things to do while staying in the area. If camping, this is a perfect spot to use as a base while exploring the many activities in this beautiful area of northern New Mexico.

From the trailhead just off NM 378, pedal through the gate and follow the signs for the well-marked Red River Fault Loop Trail. The trail travels in a northern direction through stands of piñon and juniper trees with great views of the surrounding landscape and Guadalupe Mountain. Reach the first trail junction and make a mental note: You will complete the loop from this trail junction. Continue to the north on a nice doubletrack trail. Pass under some power lines and reach a trail junction at the 1.5-mile mark. Continue straight up to a trail junction at the 1.8-mile mark. Here the ride goes right and heads into thick stands of beautiful piñon and juniper trees. The trail becomes a little rougher and climbs up a short, steep hill and then begins to lose elevation as you travel down to a marked trail junction.

The ride goes right at the 3.5-mile mark and climbs ever so gently to under the power lines. At the 3.7-mile mark and just past the power lines, the trail veers to the right and heads in a western direction back to a familiar trail junction and the end

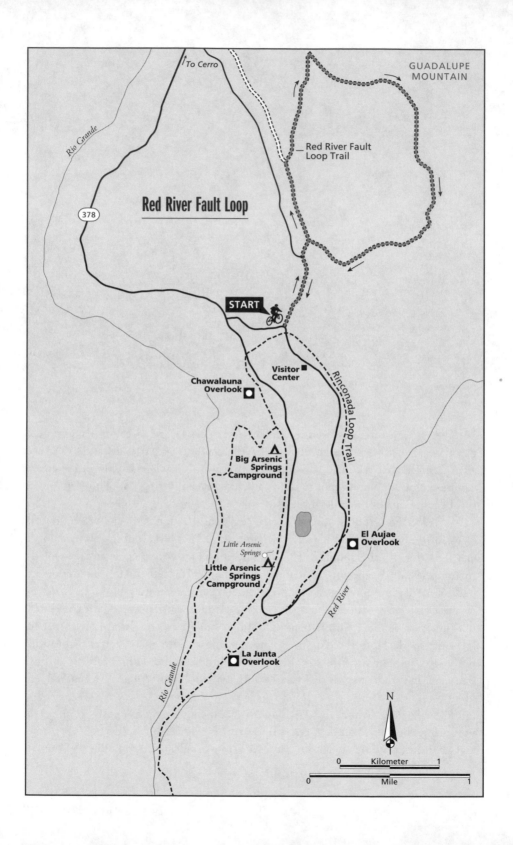

Red River Fault Loop

GUADALUPE MOUNTAIN

To Cerro

Rio Grande

378

Red River Fault Loop Trail

START

Visitor Center

Chawalauna Overlook

Rinconada Loop Trail

Big Arsenic Springs Campground

Little Arsenic Springs

El Aujae Overlook

Little Arsenic Springs Campground

Red River

La Junta Overlook

Rio Grande

N

0   Kilometer   1

0   Mile   1

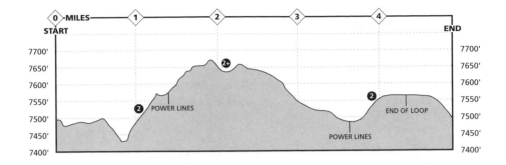

of the loop. Go left at the 4.3-mile mark and head south back to the trailhead. Complete the ride at the 4.8-mile mark or, if you are up to it, do another loop, this time in the opposite direction.

Miles and Directions

0.0 START at the trailhead on NM 378. Go through the gate, following the well-marked Red River Fault Loop Trail.

0.5 Arrive at a trail junction. Go left.

1.3 Pass under the power lines heading north to a trail junction.

1.5 Continue straight to a trail junction.

1.8 Go right, following the Red River Fault Loop Trail into thick stands of piñon and juniper trees.

2.3 Climb a short, steep hill.

3.5 The trail goes right at a marker.

3.6 Pass under the power lines again.

3.7 Bear right, heading up to a familiar trail junction.

4.3 Go left back to the trailhead.

4.8 Arrive back at the trailhead, or do another loop.

Ride Information

Local Information

Taos Chamber of Commerce, P.O. Drawer I, Taos, NM 87571; (505) 758-3873 or (800) 732-8267; www.taoschamber.com.

Restaurants

El Deville Restaurant, NM 522 & NM 38, Questa; (505) 586-0300.

2 Rinconada Trail

Start: At the Rio Grande Wild Rivers Recreation Area visitor center.
Distance: 5.3-mile loop.
Approximate riding time: 1.0 to 1.5 hours.
Difficulty: Easy with a few short hills.
Trail surface: Well-groomed singletrack trail.
Lay of the land: Great singletrack riding on a piñon- and juniper-covered mesa overlooking the Rio Grande Wild and Scenic River.
Other trail users: This trail is popular with hikers, fishermen, tourists, and joggers.
Canine compatibility: Dog friendly, but they must be kept on a leash at all times.
Wheels: Front suspension will work just fine on this ride.

Land status: Bureau of Land Management.
Nearest town: Questa.
Fees and permits: $3.00 a day per vehicle.
Schedule: 6:00 A.M. to 10:00 P.M. for day use.
Maps: Rio Grande Wild Rivers Map available from the visitor center; USGS maps: Taos County; *Trails Illustrated* number 730 Taos.
Trail contacts: Bureau of Land Management, Taos Resource Area Office, 226 Cruz Alta Road, Taos, NM 87571; (505) 758-8851; www.nm.blm.gov.
Rio Grande Wild Rivers Visitor Center, Cerro, NM 87519; (505) 770-1600.

Finding the trailhead: From Questa: Go north out of town on New Mexico Highway 552 for 3 miles to New Mexico 378. Turn left onto NM 378 and travel 12.6 miles, passing through the village of Cerro to the Rio Grande Wild Rivers Visitor Center. The ride starts here. *DeLorme: New Mexico Atlas & Gazetteer:* Page 16, C-3.

The Ride

The Rinconada Loop Trail is a must-stop for any mountain bikers visiting northern New Mexico. The trail is located on a mesa high above the Rio Grande and Red River. On this ride you are rewarded with views out to the Rio Grande, the Latir Peak Wilderness Area, and the Red River. The trails are user friendly, the campgrounds are well maintained, and the surrounding landscape is absolutely breathtaking. These attributes alone merit a visit to the area; throw in mountain biking and you have a great outdoor experience. Do this ride!

The Rio Grande, at 1,900 miles long, is the second-longest river in the United States. Originating high in the San Juan Mountains of southwestern Colorado, the river heads southeast, twisting its way through the San Luis Valley to the New Mexico state line. Below the volcanic plug of Ute Mountain, the Rio Grande flows through an 800-foot-deep canyon below the snowcapped peaks and piñon-studded plains of northern New Mexico. This part of the Rio Grande and the Canon Del Rio Grande has been designated as a wild and scenic river to protect the free-flowing state of the river and the natural beauty of the area. To me, beauty abounds everywhere in this part of New Mexico.

Your ride starts at the visitor center below Guadalupe Mountain and goes in a southern direction to the confluence of the Red River and the Rio Grande at La

Looking north up the Rio Grande Gorge

Junta Point. The trail is well marked and crosses NM 378 several times before reaching the overlook. Use caution when crossing the highway. Take time at the overlook to enjoy the views down to the rivers and the basalt-rimmed cliffs of the gorge. A steep hiking–only trail leads down to the rivers from La Junta Point and is a popular trail with fishermen to access the gold-medal waters of the Rio Grande and the Red River.

From La Junta Point the Rinconada Loop Trail bends to the right and heads north along the rim above the Rio Grande. The trail cuts through several campgrounds and day-use areas, so be on the lookout for other trail users and keep a low profile.

At the 4.2 mark the trail passes near the Chawalauna Overlook. This is another great place to stop and enjoy the views down to the Rio Grande and north to Ute Mountain and beyond Ute Mountain to the state of Colorado. Looking down to the river from Chawalauna Point, you will notice several river campsites. These sites are accessed only by hiking trails, at a cost of $5.00 per night. These campsites are popular with fishermen, but my son Jeremy and I made the descent down to the river and spent a wonderful, star-studded night along the Rio Grande, and I recommend this to anyone willing to make the 1.5-mile descent to the river. It is 800 feet from the rim to the river, and this has created a unique ecosystem from piñon and juniper

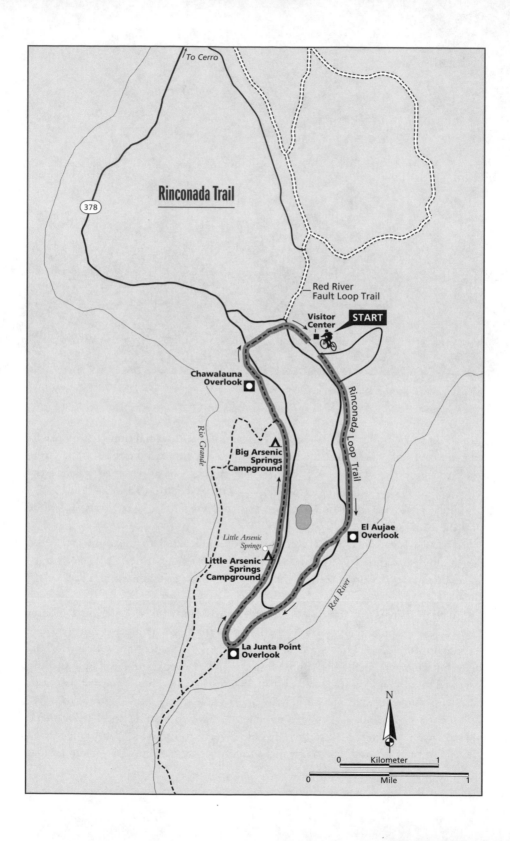

Rinconada Trail

378

To Cerro

Red River
Fault Loop Trail

Visitor
Center START

Chawalauna
Overlook

Rio Grande

Big Arsenic
Springs
Campground

Rinconada Loop Trail

Little Arsenic
Springs

Little Arsenic
Springs
Campground

El Aujae
Overlook

Red River

La Junta Point
Overlook

N

0   Kilometer   1

0   Mile   1

forest on the top of the mesa to the northern pike–, native brown trout–, and German brown trout–filled river below.

The Wild Rivers Recreation Area has five developed campgrounds and picnic areas. Each campground has bathrooms, drinking water, picnic sites, and tables. A fee of $7.00 is charged per vehicle, per night for camping. This is a great deal, and I suggest that you spent a few days hiking, fishing, or mountain biking in the area.

After the Chawalauna Overlook the trail heads north back to the parking area. To the northeast you can see the high peaks of the Latir Peak Wilderness Area and the 14,000-foot summits of Little Bear and Blanca Peaks in Colorado. Once back at the visitor center, take time to enjoy all the information that the center has on display. The rangers are more than willing to spend time with you to make your visit a more enjoyable one.

Miles and Directions

0.0 START from the visitor center and head south on the well-marked Rinconada Loop Trail. This is a one-way trail.

0.9 Come to the El Aujae Overlook and day-use area.

1.1 Go right.

1.2 Cross NM 378.

1.7 Cross NM 378 and head to the La Junta Point Overlook.

2.0 Arrive at the La Junta Point Overlook. Hop off your bike and walk left to the overlook and spectacular views down the gorge to the confluence of the Rio Grande and the Red River.

2.8 The trail passes through Little Arsenic Springs.

3.6 Go right.

3.7 Go left.

4.2 Chawalauna Overlook. Spectacular views down to the Rio Grande.

4.3 Cross NM 378. Enjoy views out to the Latir Peak Wilderness Area.

4.7 Cross NM 378. The Red River Fault Loop Trail goes straight. You go right, following the Rinconada Loop Trail back down to the visitor center.

5.3 Arrive at the visitor center.

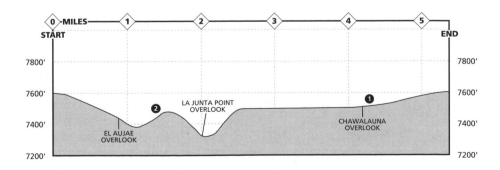

Ride Information

Local Information

Taos Chamber of Commerce, P.O. Drawer I, Taos, NM 87571; (505) 758-3873 or (800) 732-8267; www.taoschamber.com.

Accommodations

Try one of the many campsites within the Rio Grande Wild Rivers Recreation Area.

Restaurants

El Deville Restaurant, NM 522 & NM 38, Questa; (505) 586-0300.

3 Fourth of July Canyon and Red River Pass

Start: At the trailhead, 11.5 miles from New Mexico Highway 552.
Distance: 11.4-mile loop.
Approximate riding time: 2.0 to 3.5 hours.
Difficulty: Moderate with a steep climb up Fourth of July Canyon.
Trail surface: Well-groomed dirt roads, paved roads, and rough doubletrack.
Lay of the land: Good riding in the hills east of Red River.
Other trail users: Be aware of four-wheelers and car traffic on New Mexico Highway 578.
Canine compatibility: Leave the dog at home on this one.

Wheels: Front suspension will work just fine on this ride.
Land status: Carson National Forest.
Nearest town: Red River.
Fees and permits: No fees or permits required.
Schedule: Early May to early November.
Maps: USGS maps: Taos County.
Trail contacts: Questa Ranger District, Carson National Forest, P.O. Box 110, Questa, NM 87556; (505) 586–0520; www.fs.fed.us/r3/carson.

Finding the trailhead: From Red River: The mileage starts at the intersection of NM 578 and New Mexico Highway 38 in Red River. *DeLorme: New Mexico Atlas & Gazetteer:* Page 16, C-5.

The Ride

From the intersection of NM 578 and NM 38, travel southeast on NM 578 up into Red River Canyon on a nice paved road. The road gains altitude at a pleasant grade and passes the turnoff for Goose Lake (Forest Road 486) on the right at the 0.7-mile mark. At around the 1.6-mile mark, pass the Goose Creek trailhead on the right. The next 2 miles of riding are quite pleasant with excellent views up the Red River Canyon toward the high peaks and the surrounding mountains. I did this ride in the middle of October and the aspens were at their peaks, with gold pockets of trees lighting up dark green forest.

At the 3.9-mile mark you arrive at the marked turnoff for Fourth of July Canyon and Forest Road 490. Turn left here, pass the fire station on the left, and begin a steep climb up Fourth of July Canyon on a sometimes rocky and rutted jeep road. Climb steeply on the aspen-and-pine-tree-lined road up to a nice small meadow where the road veers to the left. Past the meadow the road becomes extremely rutted and very steep. Gain a level section at a road intersection at the 4.9-mile mark. Go left here and climb up on good tread with spectacular views down the Red River Canyon and up to Gold Hill and Wheeler Peak, the highest point in New Mexico at 13,161 feet.

Around the 5.1-mile mark the road veers to the right and heads into the woods and an old cut area. Drop down to a trail junction and the large open meadow of

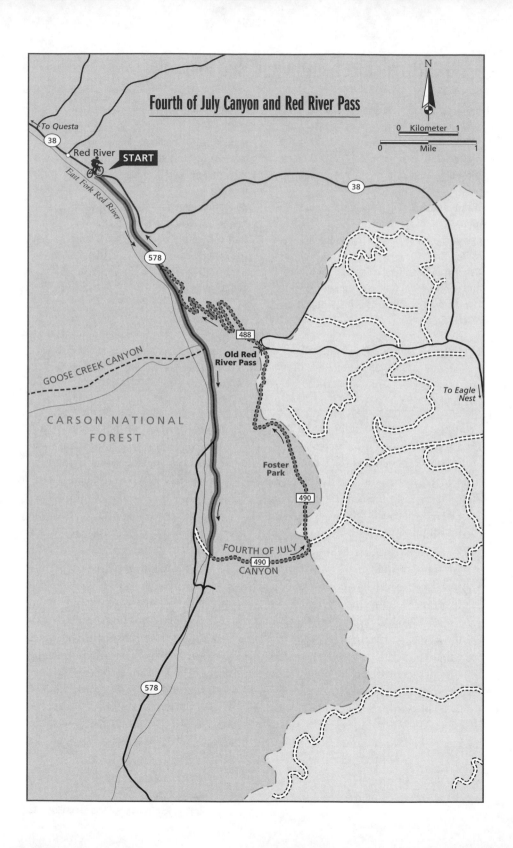

Fourth of July Canyon and Red River Pass

N

0   Kilometer   1

0   Mile   1

To Questa

38

Red River   START

East Fork Red River

38

578

488

Old Red
River Pass

GOOSE CREEK CANYON

To Eagle
Nest

CARSON NATIONAL
FOREST

Foster
Park

490

FOURTH OF JULY

490

CANYON

578

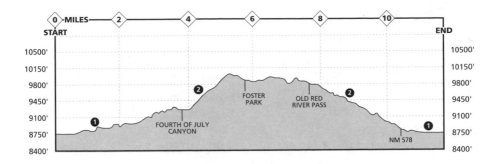

Foster Park. Continue straight on FR 490, cruising on a nice dirt road lined with pretty aspen and pine trees.

About the 6.5-mile mark the road climbs up some rocky tread near a fence. On the other side of the fence is private property and what looks to be the start of a new housing development. Reach the crest of the hill and drop steeply down a rocky loose hill. The road becomes narrower and dips and climbs, reaching a junction with Red River Pass at the 7.5-mile mark. Turn left onto Forest Road 488 and begin an extended fast downhill on sometimes loose and rocky tread. Be careful on the fast downhill, as a few switchbacks are quite sharp and loose. Also be careful of oncoming four-wheel traffic that uses this popular road during the summer and early fall months. After an exhilarating downhill of almost 3 miles, you reach a junction with NM 578 and the end of the loop. Turn right onto NM 578 and cruise back down to the intersection with NM 38 and the end of the ride.

Miles and Directions

0.0   START at the intersection of NM 578 and NM 38. Travel southeast on NM 578 heading south through Red River Canyon.

0.7   FR 486 to Goose Lake on the right.

3.9   Reach Fourth of July Canyon. Go left, passing the fire station on the left.

4.9   Reach a trail junction. Go left.

5.2   Pass through an old cut area with many downed trees.

5.9   Reach the open meadow of Foster Park.

6.7   Steep downhill, be careful.

7.5   Arrive at old Red River Pass (FR 488). Go left.

10.3   Arrive at NM 578. Go right toward Red River.

11.4   Back at the intersection of NM 578 and NM 38 and the end of the ride.

Ride Information

Local Information

Red River Chamber of Commerce, P.O. Box 870, Red River, NM 87558; (505) 754–2366 or (800) 348–6444; www.redrivernewmex.com.

Local Events and Attractions

Chili Cook-off, late August.

Top of the World Mountain Bike Race, early September.

Enchanted Circle Century Bike Tour, early September.

Accommodations

The Lodge at Red River, P.O. Box 189, Red River, NM 87558; (800) 91-LODGE.

Restaurants

El Deville Restaurant, NM 522 and NM 38, Questa; (505) 586–0300.

La Pomloma Coffee Shop, NM 522, Questa.

4 Middle Fork Lake

Start: From the intersection of New Mexico Highway 578 and Forest Road 487 (Middle Fork Lake Road).
Distance: 6.8-mile out-and-back.
Approximate riding time: 1.5 to 2.5 hours.
Difficulty: Strenuous with a steep climb up to the lake.
Trail surface: Rough doubletrack roads.
Lay of the land: Steep riding along the Middle Fork through dense pine forests.
Other trail users: Be aware of four-wheelers and car traffic on NM 578.
Canine compatibility: Good ride to bring the pooch on.

Wheels: Front suspension will work just fine on this ride.
Land status: Carson National Forest.
Nearest town: Red River.
Fees and permits: No fees or permits required.
Schedule: Early May to late October.
Maps: USGS maps: Taos County.
Trail contacts: Questa Ranger District, Carson National Forest, P.O. Box 110, Questa, NM 87556; (505) 586-0520; www.fs.fed.us/r3/carson.

Finding the trailhead: From Red River: Follow NM 578 east for 6 miles to FR 487 (Middle Fork Lake Road) and the end of the pavement. The mileage starts at the intersection of NM 578 and Forest Road 487 (Middle Fork Lake Road). *DeLorme: New Mexico Atlas & Gazetteer:* Page 16, D-5.

The Ride

From the town of Red River, feel free to bike up NM 578 for 6 miles to FR 487 and the start of the mileage for this ride. The road is paved and climbs a thousand feet to the start of FR 487. This will add another 12 miles to your ride.

From the intersection of NM 578 and Middle Fork Lake Road (FR 487), go right onto FR 487 and begin to climb gently along the Middle Fork River to the left. Ride past some beaver dams near the start of the road and tall stands of thick willows on the left. Travel through a wet area and climb on rocky tread past some nice camping spots along the Middle Fork on the left. Reach a parking area, bathrooms, and campsites at the 1-mile mark.

Past the parking the road forks at the 1.2-mile mark. Going straight leads to gated private property. Go left onto a bridge over the Middle Fork at a sign marked FR 91. FR 91 and FR 487 share the same road for the next mile. Travel through a very rocky, steep section (don't worry, not all the trail is like this) and climb up to the first switchback.

Climb past the first of several switchbacks on somewhat smooth tread through a dense pine forest with the Middle Fork on your right. The switchbacks are rutted out from four-wheel traffic and are hard to clean on your first go. I found going wide to the left helped a lot and made negotiating the switchbacks much easier. Around the 1.9-mile mark enjoy a stretch of nice smooth climbing with sounds of

Crossing Middle Fork at the waterfall

the Middle Fork tumbling down on your right. The riding is quite pleasant as you climb up to a crossing of the Middle Fork at a wooden footbridge. FR 91 goes up and left at the bridge and makes a steep climb up to Lost Lake and then on to Wheeler Peak, the highest point in New Mexico at 13,161 feet. FR 91 is best suited for foot travel, so don't attempt to ride this trail. This is a great spot to enjoy a short break and see and hear the tumbling water of the Middle Fork.

Cross the Middle Fork and begin to climb a series of steep, rocky switchbacks. You are gaining altitude at a rapid rate as you grunt your way through the trees. This is where the altitude kicks in for me and makes this section that much harder. The riding is strenuous, but keep spinning in a lower gear and you should be fine. Views open to the east and the scenery helps keep your mind off the strenuous riding. Around the 3.3-mile mark the road becomes very rocky and steep. This is the final grunt to the lake, so push hard and before you know it you are at a beautiful alpine lake situated in a beautiful alpine cirque at 10,845 feet.

Plan on spending some time at the lake walking around or just relaxing at the shore, looking at the beautiful scenery, the alpine flowers, and the crystal-clear waters of the lake. Hope you brought a camera, lunch, and even a small fly rod to do some great fishing for native cutthroat trout. After your stay at the lake, turn around and retrace your route back to NM 578 and your car. Keep your speed in check (for your own safety and the safety of others) and watch out for four-wheel traffic.

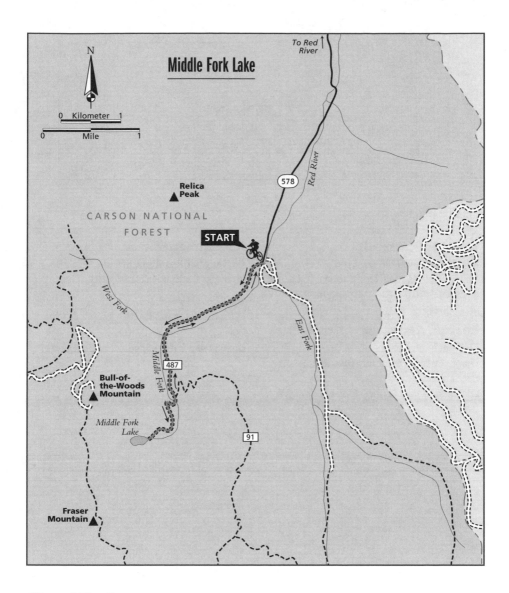

Miles and Directions

0.0 START at the intersection of NM 578 and FR 487. Follow FR 487 along the Middle Fork.

1.0 Parking area and bathrooms.

1.2 The road forks. Go left up FR 487 and FR 91.

2.3 Cross the Middle Fork at a wooden footbridge. FR 91 goes up and left.

3.4 Arrive at beautiful Middle Fork Lake.

6.8 Back at NM 578 and your car.

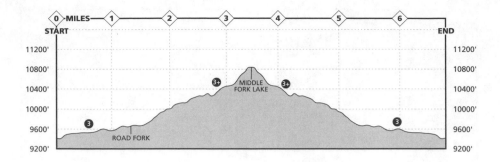

Ride Information

Local Information

Red River Chamber of Commerce, P.O. Box 870, Red River, NM 87558; (505) 754–2366 or (800) 348–6444, www.redrivernew mex.com.

Local Events and Attractions

Chili Cook-off, late August.
Top of the World Mountain Bike Race, early September.
Enchanted Circle Century Bike Tour, early September.

Accommodations

The Lodge at Red River, P.O. Box 189, Red River, NM 87558; (800) 91-LODGE.

Restaurants

El Deville Restaurant, NM 522 and NM 38, Questa; (505) 586–0300.
La Pomloma Coffee Shop, NM 522, Questa.

5 Goose Lake Loop

Start: From the trailhead just off New Mexico Highway 578 at Forest Road 486.
Distance: 14.2-mile loop.
Approximate riding time: 3 to 4 hours depending on how much time you spend at the lake. Plan on all day if you are going to hike to the summit of Gold Hill.
Difficulty: Strenuous with a long, long climb up to Goose Lake.
Trail surface: Doubletrack and singletrack trails.
Lay of the land: A beautiful ride in the pine- and aspen-covered mountains above Red River up to a splendid alpine lake.
Other trail users: The road up to the lake is popular with four-wheelers. The singletrack down from the lake sees little foot traffic

except for the last mile near NM 578.
Canine compatibility: Leave the dog at home.
Wheels: Front suspension will work just fine on this ride.
Land status: Carson National Forest.
Nearest town: Red River.
Fees and permits: No fees or permits required.
Schedule: Dawn to dusk, late May to late October.
Maps: USGS maps: Taos County.
Trail contacts: Questa Ranger District, Carson National Forest, P.O. Box 110, Questa, NM 87556; (505) 586-0520.
Carson National Forest Ranger Station, 208 Cruz Alta Road, Taos, NM 87571; (505) 758-6200; www.fs.fed.us/r3/carson.

Finding the trailhead: From Red River: From the center of town pedal or drive east to the intersection of NM 578 and FR 486. The mileage starts here. *DeLorme: New Mexico Atlas & Gazetteer:* Page 16, C-5.

The Ride

This ride really appeals to all-around mountain bikers. Right off the bat the rider is hit with a big hill climb. The climb follows an old mining road and lasts for almost 7 miles. The reward for that big climb is a beautiful alpine lake and a tremendous downhill run on beautiful singletrack. The climb up to Goose Lake is long, arduous, rocky, and steep. There is a fair amount of four-wheel traffic during the summer and early fall months. The downhill singletrack parallels Goose Creek through forests of dense, mature pines and tall, shimmering aspen trees. Early fall is a marvelous time to do this ride as brilliant pockets of golden aspen trees light up the dark green forest.

Start the ride by crossing Red River via a wooden footbridge. Begin a steep climb up extremely loose and rocky tread. This is the longest, steepest section of the climb and lasts for just under a mile. Reach a level area just before the mile mark and try to get some air back into your lungs. The road climbs at a modest grade up to a mine and old abandoned cabins on the left at the 1.8-mile mark. The town of Red River was established in the late 1800s as a mining town and saw a surge of growth into the early 1900s. A number of saloons, four hotels, a red-light district, and numerous other businesses flourished until the mining bust hit the town around

1910. The town lay dormant until the early 1920s when visitors from the flatland areas of Texas and Oklahoma discovered the area for recreation purposes. Hiking, hunting, fishing, and various other outdoor activities replaced the pick and shovel as the main attractions in the Red River Valley. The town really took off with the construction of the Red River Ski Area, which started in 1958 and turned Red River into a legitimate year-round resort.

Beyond the cabins the road continues to climb past several spur roads and through a couple of small meadows surrounded by beautiful aspen trees. Pass a cabin and the Jay Hawk Mine on the right at the 3.2-mile mark. Continue past the mine up a road junction. At the 4.1-mile mark the road forks, with Forest Road 486A leading right up to Bunker Hill. You follow FR 486 to the left and drop down a short hill through tall pines with views to towering Gold Hill (12,689 feet) straight ahead. The tread turns rocky and the road now climbs at a steady grade up to Goose Lake.

Arrive at Goose Lake at the 6.7-mile mark. Time to get off the bike and take a break at this picturesque alpine lake nestled tightly in a rocky cirque below the rocky summit of Gold Hill. The lake is stocked with cutthroat trout and a trail circles the lake, making for easy-access fishing. Bighorn sheep call the rocky slopes below Gold Hill home during the summer and early fall months. These agile rock climbers often can be seen climbing up and down the rocky cliffs near the lake. For an added treat bring a pair of hiking shoes so you can take the well-marked trail up to the summit of Gold Hill for spectacular views to Wheeler Peak and the surrounding mountains. It's a strenuous 1.2-mile hike to the summit, with an elevation gain of a thousand feet.

After your break look for a trail leading past the bathrooms and across Goose Creek. Just past the creek the trail goes left and down along the creek into the woods. Follow the trail down into the tall pines and the start of 6 miles of awesome singletrack. At the 7.3-mile mark reach Goose Creek, making the first of several water crossings. This section of the trail is just incredible! The trail snakes a thin line down through the tall pines and is sure to put a smile on the face of any mountain biker. At the 8.6-mile mark reach a fork in the trail and go right and down to Goose Creek. The trail slices through a beautiful aspen forest and soon reaches another fork. Take the right fork and enjoy beautiful singletrack through the aspen and pines trees. At the 10.5-mile mark reach a small, beautiful meadow surrounded by tall aspen trees. Continue straight through the meadow and arrive at another larger meadow. This is a good spot to take a short break and enjoy the beautiful wildflowers that fill the meadow during the summer months. Once you're back on your bike, continue downhill on tight singletrack. The trail clings to the side of a steep hill with Goose Creek on your right. The trail and the creek flow into a narrow canyon filled with tall, beautiful willows and cottonwood trees. Expect to see some hikers through this

◀ *Crossing Goose Creek at the beginning of the downhill*

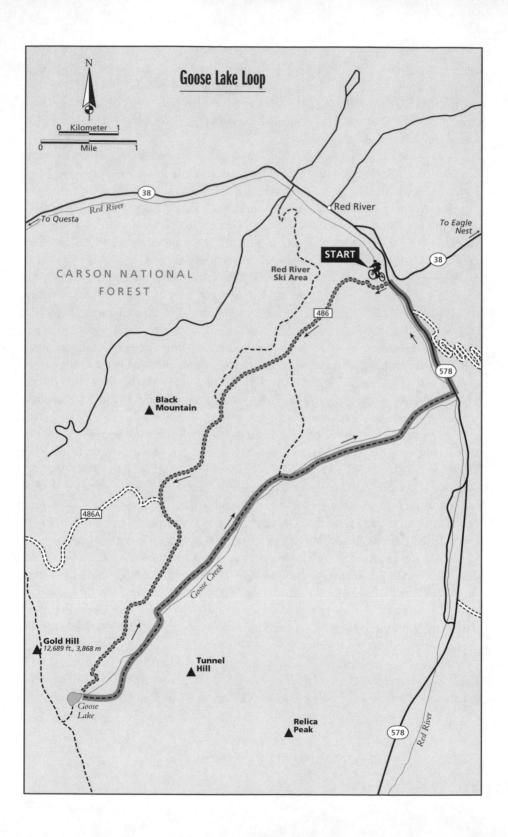

Goose Lake Loop

N

0 Kilometer 1
0 Mile 1

To Questa

38   Red River

Red River

To Eagle Nest

38

START

Red River Ski Area

486

578

CARSON NATIONAL FOREST

▲ **Black Mountain**

486A

Goose Creek

▲ **Gold Hill**
12,689 ft., 3,868 m

▲ **Tunnel Hill**

Goose Lake

▲ **Relica Peak**

578

Red River

Golden aspens near Goose Lake

section of the trail. Cross Goose Creek and reach a gate. Pass through the gate and follow tight singletrack along Goose Creek to the trailhead and NM 578. Cross a wooden bridge and turn left onto NM 578 and fly back down to your car at FR 486 or Red River and the end of a great mountain bike ride.

Miles and Directions

0.0 START from the intersection of NM 578 and FR 486. Turn right onto FR 486 and cross the Red River via a wooden bridge.

0.8 Level riding for the moment.

1.8 Old cabins and mine on the left.

2.2 The road forks. Continue straight.

3.0 Arrive at a trail junction. Continue straight.

3.2 Arrive at a cabin just off the road.

3.5 A spur road goes off to the left. You go up and right.

4.1 The road forks. FR 486A goes to the right. You go left onto FR 486.

6.7 Arrive at beautiful Goose Lake.

7.3 Cross Goose Creek.

8.6 The trail forks. Go right and down to Goose Creek.

9.4 Cross Goose Creek.

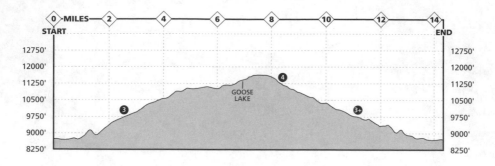

9.5 The trail forks. Take the right fork.

10.5 Reach a small, beautiful open meadow.

12.4 Cross Goose Creek.

12.5 Gate.

12.8 Reach the Goose Creek trailhead and NM 578.

14.2 Back at the junction of FR 486.

Ride Information

Local Information

Red River Chamber of Commerce, P.O. Box 870, Red River, NM 87558; (505) 754-2366 or (800) 348-6444; www.redrivernew mex.com.

Local Events and Attractions

Annual Fourth of July Parade and Celebration, Red River; (800) 348-6444; www.redrivernewmex.com.

Restaurants

Main Street Deli, 316 East Main Street, Red River; (505) 754-3400.

6 Cebolla Mesa

Start: From the parking area on New Mexico Highway 522 18 miles north of Taos.
Distance: 6.6-mile out-and-back with an optional steep 2-mile hike down to the Rio Grande and back.
Approximate riding time: 1.0 to 1.5 hours.
Difficulty: Easy with no hills or technical riding.
Trail surface: Dirt road and doubletrack trails.
Lay of the land: This ride is on mostly flat, piñon-, sage-, and juniper-covered mesa high above the Rio Grande.
Other trail users: Watch out for cars on the dirt road.
Canine compatibility: The mesa is wide open and hot during the summer months. Not a

good place for the pooch during these months.
Wheels: Front suspension will work just fine on this ride.
Land status: Carson National Forest and Bureau of Land Management.
Nearest town: Questa.
Fees and permits: No fees or permits required.
Schedule: The road can be ridden year-round.
Maps: USGS maps: Taos County.
Trail contacts: Carson National Forest Ranger Station, 208 Cruz Alta Road, Taos, NM 87571; (505) 758-6200; www.fs.fed.us/r3/carson.

Finding the trailhead: From Taos: Head north on U.S. Highway 64 for 5 miles to New Mexico Highway 522. Travel north on NM 522 for 11 miles to Forest Road 9 on the left. Park at the start of FR 9 at a cattle guard. The mileage starts here. *DeLorme: New Mexico Atlas & Gazetteer:* Page 16, D-3.

The Ride

This ride is a great ride to take the family and enjoy some nice flat, dirt road riding with beautiful views through a high piñon- and juniper-covered mesa on the fringe of the spectacular Rio Grande Gorge. There are a number of roads that lead south into Garrapata Ridge, where you could easily extend your mileage for a longer ride. The ride starts at the intersection of NM 522 and FR 9 just west of the small settlement of Lama.

Cross the cattle guard and follow FR 9 into Cebolla Mesa. Great views extend south to Taos and west toward the Rio Grande Gorge. At around the 0.9-mile mark, you will pass under some power lines. Views south toward the Sangre de Cristo Mountains are impressive, as are the views back north to the Latir Peak Wilderness Area. At the 1-mile mark turn right and head west toward the spectacular Rio Grande and Gorge. The riding is quite pleasant and flat, and you travel through stands of thick piñon and juniper trees. At the 1.8-mile mark turn right. If you want to increase your mileage, continue straight on a dirt road and explore the Garrapata Ridge area. There are many roads that crisscross Garrapata Mesa and make for some

The Rio Grande and gorge below Cebolla Mesa

interesting riding. It would be hard to get lost; when you want to turn around and head back to Cebolla Mesa, just head to the north.

Around the 1.9-mile mark you go right again over a cattle guard and take a straight line due west to the Cebolla Mesa campground and the Rio Grande Gorge. Pass a few cattle pens on the left and then travel directly into the campground.

Here are a few options to enhance your ride.

1. Lock your bike somewhere near the campground and take the hiker trail that drops steeply into the depths of the Rio Grande Gorge down to the river. The trail is steep and rocky in sections and travels past stands of tall ponderosa pine and steep volcanic rock walls down to the river. Once at the river huge black boulders cover the shore and make for a great place to fish, hang out, or swim.

2. Lock your bike and just explore the area near the campground. It is quite beautiful, with open views in all directions.

3. Ride back to your car and drive your car back to the campground. Cebolla Mesa campground is a beautiful place to camp and watch the sunrise or sunset.

4. Do all of the above. It's worth it!

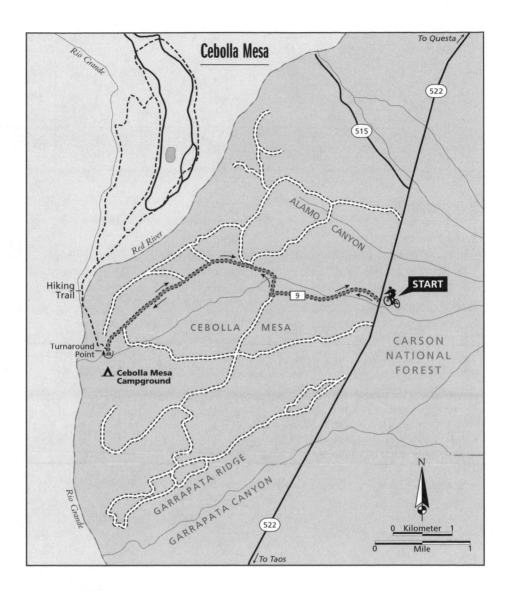

Cebolla Mesa

Miles and Directions

0.0 START from the parking area. Follow FR 9 into Cebolla Mesa.

0.9 Reach the power lines.

1.0 Go right at a road junction.

1.8 Go right at junction.

1.9 Go right over the cattle guard.

3.3 Reach the Cebolla Mesa campground.

6.6 Back at the parking area.

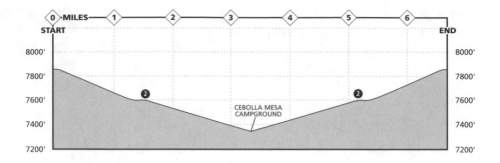

Ride Information

Local Information

Taos Chamber of Commerce, P.O. Drawer I, Taos, NM 87571; (505) 758-3873 or (800) 732-8267; www.taoschamber.com.

Local Events and Attractions

D. H. Lawrence Ranch, San Cristobal; (505) 776-2245; home and ranch of the author while he lived and wrote in the area during the early 1920s.

Accommodations

El Pueblo Lodge, 412 Paseo del Pueblo Norte, Taos; (505) 758-8700 or (800) 433-9612; a beautiful lodge on 3.5 cottonwood-shaded acres just north of the Plaza.

Restaurants

La Luna Ristorante, 223 Paseo del Pueblo Sur, Taos; (505) 751-0023; when, if ever, you get tired of green chile, head here for great Italian food. Dinner only!

Mountain Bike Tours

Native Sons Adventures, 1033-A Paseo del Pueblo Sur, Taos; (505) 758-9342 or (800) 753-7559; www.newmex.com/nsa.

7 West Rim Trail

Start: From the trailhead just off U.S. Highway 64.
Distance: 17.4-mile out-and-back.
Approximate riding time: 1.5 to 2.5 hours.
Difficulty: Easy, the ride is on mostly level tread.
Trail surface: Singletrack and doubletrack trails.
Lay of the land: Beautiful riding on a sage-covered plateau high above the Rio Grande.
Other trail users: This trail is popular with hikers.
Canine compatibility: It can get really hot on the mesa; leave the pooch at home.
Wheels: Front suspension will work just fine on this ride.

Land status: Bureau of Land Management.
Nearest town: Taos.
Fees and permits: No fees or permits required.
Schedule: Can be ridden year-round.
Maps: USGS maps: Taos County; BLM West Rim Trail.
Trail contacts: Southwest Regional Office of the Forest Service, 517 Gold Avenue, Albuquerque, NM 87102; (505) 842-3800; www.fs.fed.us/r3.
Carson National Forest Ranger Station, 208 Cruz Alta Road, Taos, NM 87571; (505) 758-6200; www.fs.fed.us/r3/carson.

Finding the trailhead: From Taos: From the intersection of US 64 and New Mexico Highway 522 just north of Taos, travel west on US 64 for 6.7 miles to a rest area and the trailhead on the west side of the Rio Grande Gorge Bridge. *DeLorme: New Mexico Atlas & Gazetteer:* Page 16, E-2.

The Ride

This is a beautiful ride that starts at the Rio Grande Gorge Bridge and travels south along the rim on fairly level double and singletrack trails. The riding is never that hard, and the miles seem to fly by. The views are spectacular, with several spots to stop to look at the lovely Rio Grande, a dizzy thousand feet below you. Access the trailhead across from the bathrooms, cross the cattle guard, and begin a slight descent with the bridge behind you. The trail is a little rocky and passes by several benches located right beside the trail. The trail is marked well with BLM markers and follows a fairly straight line along the west rim of the gorge. Take it easy on this ride and take in all the views. This is beautiful riding in a spectacular setting and the riding should not be hurried. Around the 2.7-mile mark there is a trail junction and an overlook on the

▶ Of the twenty Native American pueblos in the southwestern United States, nineteen are located in New Mexico. The Hopi Pueblo is located in Arizona.

left with great views down to the river. Bands of basalt cliffs line the gorge, a telltale sign of volcanic activity from long ago. This area is part of the Rio Grande Rift Valley. This is an area where the Earth has dropped between opposing faults, leaving a great depression open to running water. The Rio Grande took advantage of the

The Rio Grande Bridge and the beginning of the West Rim Trail

fault and took the easy path through this dramatic landscape. Enjoy smooth sailing for the next 1.5 miles and arrive at a trail junction at 4.2 miles. Continue straight through the sage and red-ant hills to an overlook at the 5.2-mile mark. Past the overlook the trail bends toward the gorge and heads to the imposing power lines. Reach the power lines and dismount your bike. This is a weird spot. You can feel and hear the electricity coming from the power lines. Quite a strange feeling!

Past the power lines the trail bends left through open land, passing an earth home on the right. The mesa is home to rattlesnakes, red ants, high-flying raptors, jackrabbits, and earth-dwelling humans. Around the 8.4-mile mark the trail turns to singletrack and makes a short downhill run to the trailhead on New Mexico Highway 567 and the turnaround point. Take a break, then enjoy the views again as you ride back to the trailhead and bridge.

Miles and Directions

0.0 START at the trailhead.

2.7 Trail junction and overlook. Continue straight.

4.2 Trail junction. Continue straight.

5.2 Overlook.

6.3 Overlook and power lines.

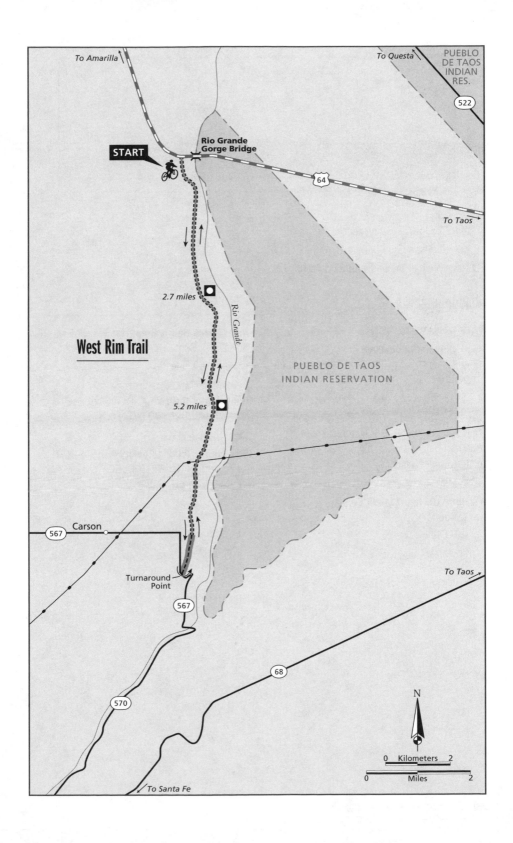

To Amarilla

To Questa

PUEBLO
DE TAOS
INDIAN
RES.

522

Rio Grande
Gorge Bridge

START

64

To Taos

2.7 miles

Rio Grande

West Rim Trail

PUEBLO DE TAOS
INDIAN RESERVATION

5.2 miles

567   Carson

To Taos

Turnaround
Point

567

68

570

N

0   Kilometers   2

0   Miles   2

To Santa Fe

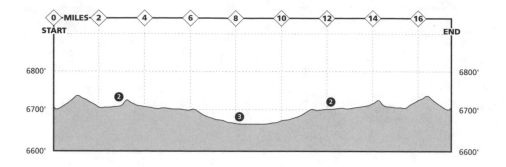

8.4 Trail turns to singletrack.

8.7 Trailhead and turnaround point.

17.4 Back at the bridge and trailhead.

Ride Information

Local Information
Taos Chamber of Commerce, P.O. Drawer I, Taos, NM 87571; (505) 758-3873 or (800) 732-8267; www.taoschamber.com.

Local Events and Attractions
Martinez Hacienda, 708 Ranchitos Road, Taos; (505) 758-8234; restored Spanish Colonial hacienda with displays of Hispanic culture and folklore.

Accommodations
La Dona Luz Inn, 114 Kit Carson Road, Taos; www.ladonaluz.com.

New Mexico Bed & Breakfast Association, P.O. Box 2925, Santa Fe; (505) 983-4554; www.nmhotels.com.

Restaurants
Guadalajara Grill, 1822 Paseo del Pueblo Norte, Taos; (505) 737-0816.

Organizations
New Mexico Touring Society, P.O. Box 1261, Albuquerque, NM 87103; (505) 237-9700; www.swcp.com/~nmts.

8 Devisadaro Peak

Start: From the parking area at the Devisadaro Peak trailhead.

Distance: 6.4-mile loop.

Approximate riding time: 1.5 to 2.5 hours.

Difficulty: This is a serious uphill grunt. There are several technical sections that will demand your best.

Trail surface: Singletrack trails.

Lay of the land: Tight singletrack riding up Devisadaro Peak in the piñon-covered foothills just east of downtown Taos.

Other trail users: This trail is popular with horseback riders and joggers.

Canine compatibility: Leave the pooch at home for this one.

Wheels: Front suspension will work just fine on this ride.

Land status: Carson National Forest.

Nearest town: Taos.

Fees and permits: No fees or permits required.

Schedule: Dawn to dusk, March to November.

Maps: USGS maps: Taos County; *Trails Illustrated* number 730 Taos.

Trail contacts: Carson National Forest Ranger Station, 208 Cruz Alta Road, Taos, NM 87571; (505) 758–6200; www.fs.fed.us/r3/carson.

Finding the trailhead: From Taos: Go southeast out of downtown Taos on U.S. Highway 64 for 4 miles to a pullout on the right at the El Nogal Picnic Area and Devisadaro Peak trailhead. The ride starts here. *DeLorme: New Mexico Atlas & Gazetteer: Page 16, F-4.*

The Ride

This ride is a true test of your technical riding skills. The riding is never easy! The uphill sections are quite grueling and will truly test the skills of most riders. The downhill sections are rocky, technical, and dangerous. With all that said, this is a short, rewarding ride for expert cyclists looking for a technical testpiece. Once you reach the top of Devisadaro Peak, relax on the cool man–made rock chairs. I can only guess that these stone chairs have been built over the years by various hikers and cyclists, each adding his or her stone to the ongoing project. The views out to Taos Valley and Taos Mountain are just spectacular and well worth the grunt up the steep slopes to the chairs.

The trailhead is right off US 64 and climbs immediately up to a trail junction on extremely rocky tread. This is just a glimpse of what lies ahead. Reach the junction at the 0.7-mile mark and go left to start the loop. The trail cuts across a steep slope and begins an extended climb on tight singletrack heading west through stands of beautiful juniper and piñon trees with good views out to the Taos Valley and the Rio Grande Gorge. The trail drops for a short distance and crosses a seasonal drainage. It then climbs up on rocky tread to a trail marker, a short rock cliff on the left, and an overlook with expansive views to the west. This is a good spot to take a short break and enjoy the views. After the overlook the trail veers to the north and climbs up through the piñon and juniper trees, gaining altitude on tight, rocky

An over-the-hill mountain biker taking a rest at the top of Devisadaro Peak

singletrack. Several rock steps must be negotiated and will test the best to stay on the bike. The trail enters a dense forest of tall pine trees and climbs steeply on smoother tread up to a junction with the North Boundary Trail. Reach the junction with the North Boundary Trail at the 3.3-mile mark and make a sharp right up to the summit of Devisadaro Peak and the stone chairs.

Time for a break here. Take a seat in one of the stone chairs and savor the moment of your accomplishment of climbing up to Devisadaro Peak. The true summit marker is just behind the chairs and to the east. Enjoy great views north up Taos Canyon and east over to Fernando Mountain where the South Boundary Trail cuts a line running east to west.

The trail drops steeply past the summit and the terrain becomes very rocky. Several technical sections will try to impede your progress back to the end of the loop. Be careful through these sections and be on the lookout for other trail users using this popular trail. Arrive at the end of the loop at the 5.7-mile mark and drop down extremely rocky tread to the trailhead, US 64, and the end of the ride. That was a tough 6.4-mile ride! I have seen John Nichols (a famous Taos author) hiking on the trail several times, so bring a copy of one of his books and maybe he will sign it!

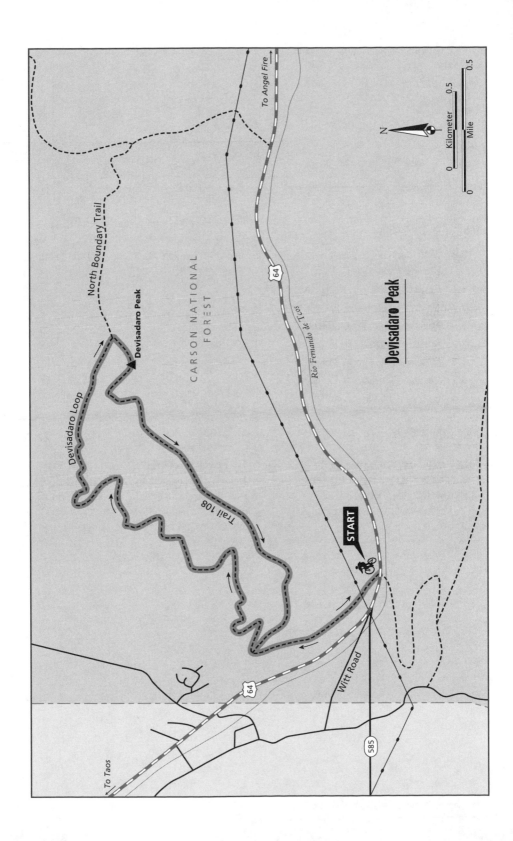

Devisadaro Peak

To Angel Fire

North Boundary Trail

Devisadaro Peak

Devisadaro Loop

Devisadaro Peak

CARSON NATIONAL FOREST

Trail 108

Rio Fernando de Teos

64

START

64

To Taos

Witt Road

585

N

Kilometer   0.5
0
Mile   0.5
0

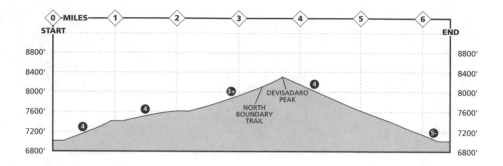

Miles and Directions

0.0 START from the parking area. Head up the marked Devisadaro Peak Trail and climb up to where the trail splits.

0.7 Go left up steep, tight singletrack tread.

3.3 Arrive at junction with the North Boundary Trail.

3.8 Reach the summit and the chairs.

3.9 Steep, rocky downhill.

4.3 More steep, technical downhill.

5.7 Back at a familiar trail junction.

6.4 Back at the trailhead.

Ride Information

Local Information

Taos Chamber of Commerce, P.O. Drawer I, Taos, NM 87571; (505) 758-3873 or (800) 732-8267; www.taoschamber.com.

Local Events and Attractions

Harwood Museum of Art of the University of New Mexico, 238 Ledoux Street, Taos; (505) 758-9826; museum filled with New Mexico-inspired images, with an admission fee of $5.00.

9 Ojitos Canyon Loop

Start: From the parking area at the Devisadaro Peak trailhead.
Distance: 10.5-mile loop.
Approximate riding time: 2.5 to 4.0 hours.
Difficulty: Strenuous with a long climb up to the Ojitos Trail junction. Expect loose, rocky sections on tight singletrack on the climb.
Trail surface: Paved roads, doubletrack and singletrack trails.
Lay of the land: The ride starts at the South Boundary trailhead just east of downtown Taos. The ride begins in the piñon-covered foothills and climbs more than 2,000 feet in a little more than 3 miles to an aspen and mixed-conifer forest.

Other trail users: This trail is popular with horseback riders, hikers, and joggers.
Canine compatibility: Bring the pooch, but watch out for the bears.
Wheels: Front suspension will work just fine on this ride.
Land status: Carson National Forest.
Nearest town: Taos.
Fees and permits: No fees or permits required.
Schedule: Late March to early November.
Maps: USGS maps: Taos County; *Trails Illustrated* number 730 Taos.
Trail contacts: Carson National Forest Ranger Station, 208 Cruz Alta Road, Taos, NM 87571; (505) 758-6200; www.fs.fed.us/r3/carson.

Finding the trailhead: From Taos: Travel southeast on U.S. Highway 64 for 4 miles to a pullout on the right at the El Nogal Picnic Area and Devisadaro Peak trailhead. The ride starts here. *DeLorme: New Mexico Atlas & Gazetteer:* Page 16, F-4.

The Ride

If you are an expert cyclist and you're looking for a hard technical ride with a big uphill, this is the ride for you. The first 3 miles of the ride gain more than 2,000 feet on mostly tight singletrack through stands of piñon and juniper trees in a beautiful high-desert environment. The first 3 miles also climb up the famous "South Boundary" (Forest Road 164) before reaching a junction with the Ojitos Canyon Trail. Along this ride you will be treated to spectacular views out to the Taos Valley, Taos Mountain and Wheeler Peak, and west to the Jemez Mountains.

From the trailhead at the El Nogal Picnic Area, pedal through a picnic area and cross a footbridge to the South Boundary Trail (FR 164). Go right onto the tight singletrack and begin an extended climb through the piñon and juniper trees to a trail junction at the 0.2-mile mark. Go left and climb up to the first of four switchbacks. This section is actually fun compared to what lies ahead. Enjoy some steep riding through the tight switchbacks up to a level section at the 1.5-mile mark. Enjoy a short section of level riding before reaching a steep rock garden at the 1.6-mile mark. I pushed through this section and felt no remorse whatsoever.

► Almost half of Taos County's 1,444,480 acres are public lands managed by Carson National Forest and the Bureau of Land Management.

A momma bear making sure her cubs are safe and giving me a last warning to back off

At the 2-mile mark you hit a level section that comes not a minute too soon. The level trail offers a brief reprieve from the steep climb and gives you a chance to regroup for the mile of climbing that lies ahead. It was back into low gear for me, and was I thankful for the views north to Wheeler Peak to help take my mind off the steep climbing. The trail cuts through a beautiful aspen forest and soon reaches the Ojitos Canyon Trail on the right at the 3.2-mile mark. This is a good spot to take a break.

Hop back on the bike and travel through the cut log on the wide trail through forests of pine and aspen trees. Beautiful level riding through this section is a welcome relief from the huge climbing of the previous miles. At the 4.7-mile mark the trail begins an extended downhill through Ojitos Canyon. This is great riding so hang on and enjoy. At the 6.9-mile mark you will reach the first of what seems to be a thousand berms. The only good thing these berms seem to offer the cyclist is a chance to catch some big air. Fly over the berms but be careful, you never know what's on the other side of them.

On the way back down Ojitos Canyon Trail at about the 5.5-mile mark, I had the pleasure of seeing two bear cubs right off the trail. Only being 20 to 30 feet away, I thought they were such darling little things, and then Mom appeared from behind the trees. Not having enough sense to be scared, I started clicking pictures, and then

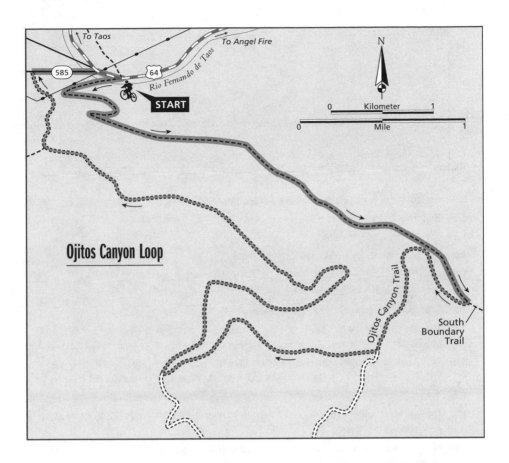

Ojitos Canyon Loop

I realized I was in big trouble. Mom started to snort and grunt and I started to look for a way out. Luckily, the cubs took off down the side of the trail and Mom soon followed. My heart rate was about 230 beats per minute as I waited a few seconds to recoup and make sure Mom was gone. I jumped back on the bike and took off like a bat out of hell down the fast doubletrack trail. I glanced back behind me a number of times just to make sure momma bear wasn't hot on my heels. Back at the trailhead and the safety of my car, I took stock of what had happened and realized what an incredible mountain bike experience I had just had!

Miles and Directions

0.0 START from the parking area. Go into the El Nogal Picnic Area (the ride starts here). Go over the bridge and make an immediate right onto a singletrack trail (FR 164). The trail climbs gently to a trail junction near a fence line.

0.2 Go left up the nice singletrack trail.

0.3 Hit the first switchback.

0.4 Hit the second switchback.

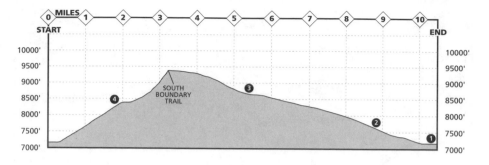

0.8 Go left at the third switchback. Here's where the real fun begins.

1.1 Steep, loose tread. Crank hard!

1.3 Steep, loose, rocky tread.

1.5 The grade eases for a moment. Don't be fooled.

1.6 Walk through the steep rock steps.

2.0 Hit a section of nice, level singletrack.

2.2 That didn't last long. Begin climbing again.

3.1 The trail enters an aspen forest. Spectacular views to the north to Wheeler Peak and Taos Mountain.

3.2 Come to a junction with the Ojitos Canyon Trail. The South Boundary Trail (FR 164) goes left. You go right onto the Ojitos Canyon Trail through the cut log on a wide dirt trail.

4.4 A road goes left. Continue straight.

4.7 The trail veers to the right down a very loose, rocky hill. Enjoy more than 2 miles of great riding before the "berms."

6.9 Hit the first of the "berms." Watch your speed through this section. You never know what's on the other side of those berms.

8.7 They never end.

9.3 The Talpa Trail goes left. You continue straight to the power lines.

9.7 Go left at the power lines down to the dirt road. At the road go right and down to New Mexico Highway 585.

9.9 Go right down NM 585.

10.2 Turn right onto US 64 to the parking area.

10.5 Arrive back at the parking area.

Ride Information

Local Information

Taos Chamber of Commerce, P.O. Drawer I, Taos, NM 87571; (505) 758-3873 or (800) 732-8267; www.taoschamber.com.

Mountain Bike Tours

Native Sons Adventures, 1033-A Paseo del Pueblo Sur, Taos; (505) 758-9342 or (800) 753-7559; www.newmex.com/nsa.

10 Talpa Traverse Trail

Start: From the parking area at the Devisadaro Peak trailhead.
Distance: 8.4-mile out-and-back.
Approximate riding time: 1.5 to 2.5 hours.
Difficulty: Moderate with a few short hills and rocky sections on tight singletrack.
Trail surface: Paved roads, doubletrack and singletrack trails.
Lay of the land: Tight singletrack riding through several arroyos in the piñon-covered foothills just east of downtown Taos.
Other trail users: This trail is popular with horseback riders and joggers.

Canine compatibility: Bring the pooch and some extra water.
Wheels: Front suspension will work just fine on this ride.
Land status: Carson National Forest.
Nearest town: Taos.
Fees and permits: No fees or permits required.
Schedule: March to November.
Maps: USGS maps: Taos County; *Trails Illustrated* number 730 Taos.
Trail contacts: Carson National Forest Ranger Station, 208 Cruz Alta Road, Taos, NM 87571; (505) 758–6200; www.fs.fed.us/r3/carson.

Finding the trailhead: From Taos: Drive or bike southeast out of downtown Taos on U.S. Highway 64 for 4 miles to a pullout on the right at the El Nogal Picnic Area and Devisadaro Peak trailhead. The ride starts here. *DeLorme: New Mexico Atlas & Gazetteer:* Page 16, F-4.

The Ride

The good folks at Gearing Up Bike Shop recommended this ride to me, and what a pleasant surprise it turned out to be. Sherry and Rey, the owners of Gearing Up, were more than happy to give me information and directions to rides and any other information I needed while in the Taos area. Local bike shops are really at the heart of the biking scene and deserve your support. Gearing Up Bike Shop is conveniently located just off the Plaza in downtown Taos, so if you are in the area and need any supplies, stop by and say hi to these fine folks.

Your ride takes in a combination of dirt roads, a short section of paved roads, and 6 miles of wonderful, tight singletrack in the piñon-studded foothills just outside town. The singletrack section is way too much fun as it takes a wandering line in and out of several arroyos on its way out to Talpa Reservoir. The Talpa Trail was first used by horseback riders and is still a popular trail with riders. If you come in contact with horseback riders, slow down, let them pass by, and show common courtesy. This is a great singletrack trail and the locals would like to keep it that way. Remember, stay on the singletrack and don't cut or make any new trails. This is a fragile, high–desert environment, and any unusual impact will leave long-lasting scars.

From the parking area at El Nogal Picnic Area, pedal west on US 64 back toward Taos and the junction with New Mexico Highway 585. Turn left onto NM 585 and

Cranking hard!

pedal up the paved road. At the 0.6-mile mark reach a gate on the left and a dirt road leading up to a large water tower. Turn left through the gate and pedal up to the water tower. Veer left at the water tower and pedal up to the power lines. Turn right onto a dirt road and pass a NO VEHICLE sign. Reach two large metal posts at the 1-mile mark and the start of the "berms." Count off eleven berms and turn right onto the Talpa Trail just after the eleventh berm. Drop down into a small drainage and begin 3 miles of excellent singletrack through the beautiful juniper- and piñon-covered hills heading southwest to the village of Talpa. The trail is easy to follow and travels in and out of several arroyos, arriving at a gate and the turn-around point.

At the turnaround point at the gate and as you head back to the parking area, you are rewarded with spectacular views of the Taos Valley and Taos Mountain. I rode this ride in the late afternoon on an early spring day and experienced one of the most beautiful sunsets I have ever seen. The hills around me took on a soft, mellow light, the green piñon trees stood out in contrast to the gold-colored dirt underneath my bike tires, and snowcapped Taos Mountain to the north was aglow in a deep hue of red. It is easy to understand how the effect of light and scenery leave a lasting impression on all people who live here or visit this very special area. Enjoying the moment, I was in no real hurry to get back to the parking area and

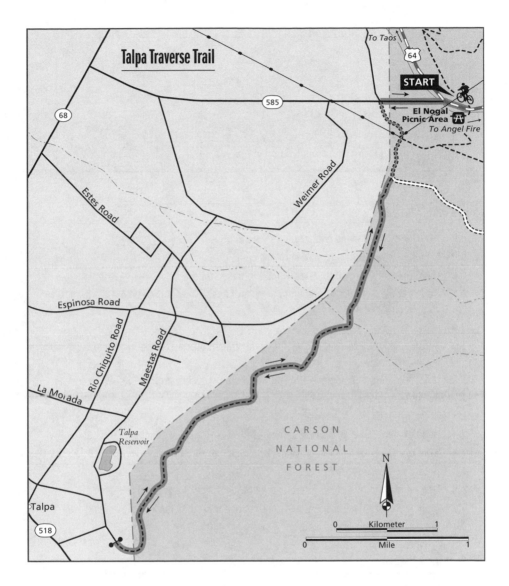

Talpa Traverse Trail

felt like this sunset was happening just for me. If you spend enough time in the area, you come to realize this is just another day in the "Land of Enchantment."

Once you are back on the doubletrack, the "berms" on the downhill offer a great chance to catch some big air. This is a fun section and a good spot to hang out and polish up on your BMX skills. Past the "berms" the trail drops back to the highway. Be on the lookout for car traffic as you pedal back to the parking area and the end of a sweet singletrack ride through the beautiful piñon-covered foothills southeast of downtown Taos.

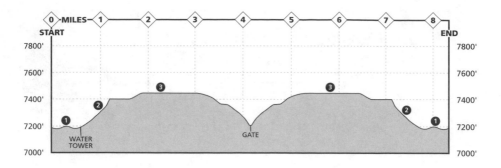

Miles and Directions

0.0 START from the parking area. Go back toward town on US 64.

0.2 Go left onto NM 585 and up a short hill.

0.6 Go left past a gate and up a gravel road to the water tower.

0.7 Go left at the water tower and up to the power lines. Make a right onto a dirt road. Go straight on this road.

0.9 NO VEHICLE sign. Continue straight.

1.0 Pass through double metal posts. Continue straight over eleven berms to the Talpa Trail on the right.

1.2 Here is where the fun begins. Go right down the tight, singletrack Talpa Trail.

1.5 Rocky, tight tread.

1.7 Short, steep hill.

2.4 Bear left into an arroyo at a small rock garden.

2.7 Start of a nice downhill run on tight singletrack.

2.9 Great views back to Taos Mountain.

3.5 Drop in and out of a steep arroyo and follow tight singletrack down to a gate.

4.2 Stop at the gate. Take a short break and retrace tour route back to the parking area.

8.4 Arrive back at the parking area.

Ride Information

Local Information
Taos Chamber of Commerce, P.O. Drawer I, Taos, NM 87571; (505) 758-3873 or (800) 732-8267; www.taoschamber.com.

Local Events and Attractions
Ernest L. Blumenschein Home and Museum, 222 Ledoux Street, Taos; (505) 758-0505; home of one of the first eastern United States artists to visit and then live in Taos.

Restaurants
Eske's Brew Pub and Eatery, 106 Des Georges Lane, Taos; (505) 758-1517; great pub food located just behind the Gearing Up Bike Shop.

11 Capulin Trail

Start: From the parking area on U.S. Highway 64.
Distance: 11.1-mile out-and-back.
Approximate riding time: 1.5 to 2.5 hours.
Difficulty: Moderate with a good climb to start the ride. The upper loop has a moderate climb on loose tread.
Trail surface: Dirt road, doubletrack and singletrack trails.
Lay of the land: The ride follows a dirt road up Capulin Canyon along the Rio Capulin. The ride then climbs through aspen and pine forests to Palo Encebado Peak on good tread with fantastic views out to Taos Canyon and Garcia Park.
Other trail users: This trail is popular with horseback riders and four-wheelers on the lower section.
Canine compatibility: Bring the pooch, but watch out for car traffic.
Wheels: Front suspension will work just fine on this ride.
Land status: Carson National Forest.
Nearest town: Taos.
Fees and permits: No fees or permits required.
Schedule: Late April to early November.
Maps: USGS maps: Taos County; *Trails Illustrated* number 730 Taos.
Trail contacts: Carson National Forest Ranger Station, 208 Cruz Alta Road, Taos, NM 87571; (505) 758-6200; www.fs.fed.us/r3/carson.

Finding the trailhead: From Taos: Go southeast out of downtown Taos on US 64 for 11.2 miles to a pullout on the right. The ride starts here. *DeLorme: New Mexico Atlas & Gazetteer:* Page 16, F-4.

The Ride

Your ride starts at a pull-off-parking area just off US 64, about 11 miles from downtown Taos. The first part of the ride is on a well-maintained forest road that takes an easy uphill grade through Capulin Canyon with the Rio Capulin on the right. At the 1.8-mile mark the road forks and the ride climbs up and into beautiful forests of aspen and pine. This is where you really feel like you are high in the mountains. You are surrounded by steep forest slopes and small, clear mountain streams. At the 3.5-mile mark the road opens up into a flat area. Look left for the start of Forest Road 494 and the upper-loop portion of the ride. Here's where the real fun begins. The trail starts out as doubletrack, then turns to narrow, tight singletrack as you climb to Palo Encebado Peak and close to the boundary of Taos Pueblo Indian Land.

The Taos Indians have called the mountain lands of northern New Mexico home for more than 1,000 years, and history seems to permeate from the land around Taos Pueblo. The present site of Taos Pueblo was first settled sometime in the early 1300s. Here the Indians planted corn, squash, and beans that grew easily in the lush, green valley nestled below Taos Mountain. They hunted deer and small game in the surrounding hills and started to construct, mud brick by mud brick, what is

Beautiful golden aspen near Palo Encebado Peak

now Taos Pueblo. Taos Pueblo is the most famous of the northern New Mexico pueblos, and for good reason. The centuries-old five-story adobe structures are located 2 miles north of Taos at the base of sacred Taos Mountain and along the banks of the beautiful Rio Pueblo de Taos. The Taos Indians no longer live in the ancient adobe homes at the original pueblo. Few have left the Taos area and most live on land surrounding the original pueblo site.

The Taos Indians have remained fiercely independent from most modern pitfalls and have retained a powerful spiritual connection to their religion and the land. If you are fortunate enough to see one of their ceremonial dances or visit the pueblo during one of the feast days, you will be seeing ceremonies that have been a major part of their lives for centuries. You might want to call the pueblo ahead of time if you are going to visit, as certain ceremonial dances and feast days are for tribal members only.

Taos Pueblo is open to the public year-round except for one month in the late winter or early spring. There is an admission fee of $4.00 per person; if you bring a still camera, the fee is $10.00, and $20.00 for moving or video cameras. Keep a low profile when you visit the pueblo and remember that you are a guest in someone's home. Please show respect while you tour the Taos Pueblo and realize that you are visiting an area that has changed very little over the years.

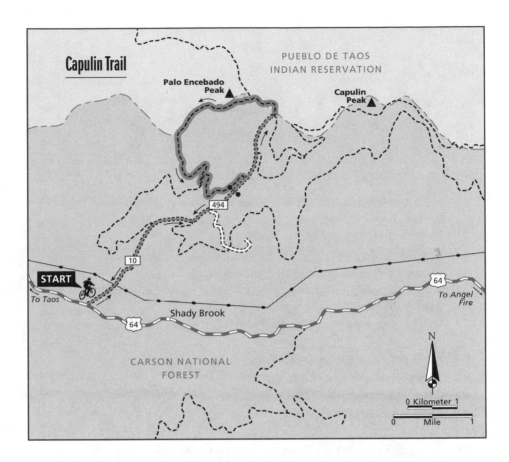

The views on the upper loop are just beautiful as you look east up Taos Canyon and south to Garcia Park and Valle Escondido. The downhill singletrack is just pure fun! The tight, narrow tread will put a smile on your face as you fly back down to the start of the loop. If you do this ride in late spring, be on the lookout for wild turkeys and elk that make this land their home. Once you're back on Forest Road 10, keep your speed in check and watch out for car traffic on your way back to the parking area.

Miles and Directions

0.0 START from the parking area. Cross US 64 and begin a gentle climb on FR 10.

0.1 Pedal over a cattle guard.

1.0 Notice the open meadow on the right and steep hills on the left.

1.8 The road forks; go right.

2.0 Pass through a gate and pedal up a gradual incline.

2.7 The hill becomes steeper through a beautiful aspen forest.

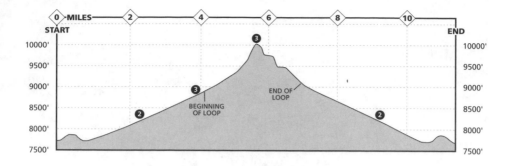

3.5 At the open area look left for FR 494. Go left onto FR 494 over a berm and then start climbing on somewhat loose tread.

3.8 Short, steep climb up to the trail junction.

4.0 Go right up to a gate.

4.2 The upper loop begins here. Go right onto a wide doubletrack trail.

4.5 Spectacular views out to Taos Canyon and Garcia Park. The trail is covered with many pine needles that give a sweet fragrance to the area.

5.1 Go left and up to where the trail quickly turns to singletrack. Climb on sweet tread up to a meadow.

5.7 A nice spot to take a break. Enjoy the downhill that lies ahead.

6.1 The trail takes a sharp left on tight singletrack.

6.4 Cross over a small stream.

6.9 The upper loop ends here. Go right.

7.1 Back at the gate.

7.6 Back at FR 10. Go right and retrace your route back to the parking area.

11.1 Arrive back at the parking area.

Ride Information

Local Information

Taos Chamber of Commerce, P.O. Drawer I, Taos, NM 87571; (505) 758-3873 or (800) 732-8267; www.taoschamber.com.

Restaurants

The Chow Cart, 402 Paseo del Pueblo Sur, Taos; (505) 776-2969; the best breakfast burrito in town.

Eske's Brew Pub and Eatery, 106 Des Georges Lane, Taos; (505) 758-1517; good pub food and Taos's only brewpub, located close to Gearing Up Bike Shop.

Mountain Bike Tours

Native Sons Adventures, 1033-A Paseo del Pueblo Sur, Taos; (505) 758-9342 or (800) 753-7559; www.newmex.com/nsa.

12 Elliot Barker Trail

Start: From the trailhead just off U.S. Highway 64.
Distance: 8.5-mile loop.
Approximate riding time: 1.5 to 2.5 hours.
Difficulty: Moderate with a few steep hills.
Trail surface: Singletrack and doubletrack trails.
Lay of the land: Singletrack and doubletrack riding up through the forested hills and meadows to Apache Pass.
Other trail users: This trail is popular with hikers.
Canine compatibility: Good ride to bring along a dog.

Wheels: Front suspension will work just fine on this ride.
Land status: Carson National Forest.
Nearest town: Taos or Angel Fire.
Fees and permits: No fees or permits required.
Schedule: April to early November.
Maps: USGS maps: Taos County; *Trails Illustrated* number 730 Taos.
Trail contacts: Carson National Forest Ranger Station, 208 Cruz Alta Road, Taos, NM 87571; (505) 758-6200; www.fs.fed.us/r3/carson.

Finding the trailhead: From Taos: Go southeast out of downtown Taos on US 64 for 19.4 miles to a pullout on the right and the Elliot Barker trailhead. The ride starts here. *DeLorme: New Mexico Atlas & Gazetteer:* Page 16, F-5.

The Ride

Elliot Barker, forest ranger, state game warden, conservationist, lover of wilderness, and one of New Mexico's biggest advocates of wild places, was born in 1886 and moved to New Mexico at the age of three, arriving in a covered wagon with his family from Texas. They settled near Pecos and thus began his love of northern New Mexico wild places.

He became a ranger in the Forest Service in 1909 and served a short stint near Cuba, New Mexico, before being transferred back to the Pecos region. He then moved north to Carson National Forest and began a lifelong friendship with fellow ranger and supervisor, Aldo Leopold. In 1919 Barker left the Forest Service to work his family ranch near Pecos. In 1931 he returned to public service as a state game warden and, literally, in the next twenty-two years of service changed wilderness and wildlife management for the betterment of all New Mexicans.

Barker especially loved the Pecos Wilderness Area near his ranch and spent many days throughout his long and productive life exploring that beautiful area.

The ride starts at the Elliot Barker trailhead just off US 64. Pass through a gate and follow the trail up into a small meadow. A trail shoots down from the left. Continue straight up through a larger meadow, passing a small, beautiful pond on the left. Time to start using those climbing legs. The trail turns steep and rocky and stays steep up to Palo Flechado Pass at the 1.1-mile mark. Pass through a gate with

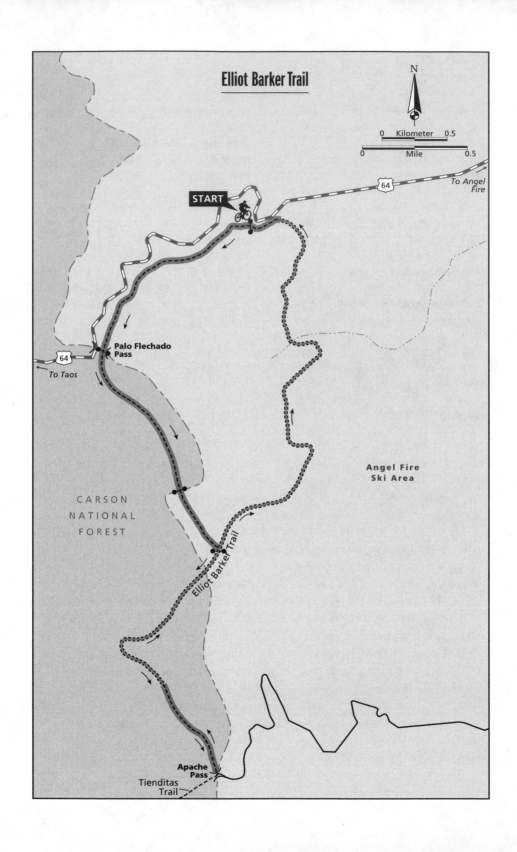

US 64 on your right. Follow the tight singletrack trail over several small berms into a beautiful pine and aspen forest. The trail weaves through the moss-draped pines up to a gate. This section of the ride offers beautiful riding on excellent singletrack through the tall pine trees. Pass through a gate, and then the trail drops down to a doubletrack trail. Go right onto the doubletrack up through a beautiful open meadow to a gate with a trail marker at the 2.9-mile mark. At the trail marker go left up into the trees toward Apache Pass. Here comes a section of tough riding on very rocky tread. At the 3.5-mile mark reach level tread and a singletrack trail that shoots through the pines and tall meadow grasses. Around the 3.7-mile mark the trail drops steeply down to the Apache Pass trailhead and the turnaround point for this ride. You can easily extend your ride by following the Elliot Barker Trail south and intersecting with the South Boundary Trail. It is 4.4 miles from the Apache Pass trailhead to the South Boundary Trail.

After a short rest at the Apache Pass trailhead, retrace your route back to the 2.7-mile mark. Instead of going left, continue straight and down on a wide doubletrack trail. Fast riding over several berms adds to the fun on this exciting downhill run. To your right are the Angel Fire ski runs and the village of Angel Fire. At the 7.9-mile mark you arrive at a hiker sign, where you bear right down to a doubletrack trail. Go left on the doubletrack and drop down close to US 64. Go left at the fence line on singletrack back to the trailhead and your car.

Miles and Directions

- **0.0** START from the gate and trailhead.
- **0.2** Trail junction. Continue straight.
- **1.0** Overlook on the left; go right on rocky tread.
- **1.1** Gate and Palo Flechado Pass.
- **2.2** Gate.
- **2.7** Go right.
- **2.9** Trail marker. Go left.
- **4.0** Apache Pass trailhead and turnaround point.

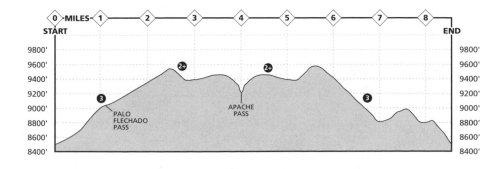

5.1 Go right.

5.3 Continue straight.

7.9 Hiker sign; bear right.

8.5 Back at the trailhead.

Ride Information

Local Information

Taos Chamber of Commerce, P.O. Drawer I, Taos, NM 87571; (505) 758–3873 or (800) 732–8267; www.taoschamber.com.

13 South Boundary Trail

Start: From the trailhead on Forest Road 76 near the town of Angel Fire.
Distance: 22.1-mile point-to-point.
Approximate riding time: 3 to 5 hours.
Difficulty: Moderate to strenuous with a few short hills and rocky sections on tight single-track.
Trail surface: Doubletrack and singletrack trails.
Lay of the land: Beautiful riding on mostly singletrack tread through mixed forest of aspens and pine trees.
Other trail users: This trail is popular with horseback riders and hikers.
Canine compatibility: Leave the pooch at home for this one.

Wheels: Front suspension will work just fine on this ride.
Land status: Carson National Forest.
Nearest town: Taos or Angel Fire.
Fees and permits: No fees or permits required.
Schedule: Late May to late October.
Maps: USGS maps: Taos County; *Trails Illustrated* number 730 Taos.
Trail contacts: Southwest Regional Office of the Forest Service, 517 Gold Avenue, Albuquerque, NM 87102; (505) 842-3800; www.fs.fed.us/r3.
Carson National Forest Ranger Station, 208 Cruz Alta Road, Taos, NM 87571; (505) 758-6200; www.fs.fed.us/r3/carson.

Finding the trailhead: From Taos: Follow U.S. Highway 64 east toward Angel Fire. Turn right onto New Mexico Highway 434 for 6.9 miles to FR 76 on the right. Turn right onto FR 76 and travel 4.4 miles to the signed South Boundary Trail on the right. The ride starts here. *DeLorme: New Mexico Atlas & Gazetteer:* Page 16, F-5 to F-4.

The Ride

On a scale of one to five, I would give this ride a ten. This is without a doubt one of the best mountain bike rides in New Mexico. Hands down! Believe me when I tell you this is one of the best mountain rides you will ever do around here! For logistics, time, and convenience, a shuttle from Taos to the trailhead is the best way to do the ride. Native Sons Adventures in Taos runs a shuttle to the trailhead at $20 per person. This is a good deal and eliminates the hassle of car shuttling.

The ride is a beautiful tour along the north flank of Fernando Mountain through stands of tall aspen and pine trees on mostly tight singletrack trails. Begin the ride from FR 76 and the trailhead. Climb into the woods on tight singletrack. The trail climbs at a steep grade up to Osha Mountain. This is the steepest climb on the ride and lasts for about 2 miles. The tread is rocky and will demand your attention to stay on the bike. At around the 2-mile mark, the trail turns to doubletrack and drops down into an open meadow. Look for a hiker sign on the right at around the 2.4-mile mark and get ready for 5 miles of exceptional riding through tall stands of mature aspens and pine trees. This section of trail will put a huge smile on any mountain biker's face and is just a taste of what lies ahead. The trail will lose some

elevation for the next 2 miles and then make a gentle climb up to Quintana Pass. After the pass more singletrack riding takes you through a mature pine forest with a steep gully on your right.

Around the 8.1-mile mark you reach Forest Road 437 and Garcia Park. Go straight on Forest Road 437 and travel a little less than a mile on a smooth dirt road to a cattle guard. Just past the cattle guard, turn left over some berms (back on Forest Road 164) and follow the tight singletrack trail up to a trail on the right. Go right at the junction, climbing up past a trail marker into an open meadow. Past the meadow the trail goes left on tight singletrack and reaches another trail on the left at the 11.8-mile mark. Go left at this junction over a berm and enjoy 3 miles of beautiful singletrack riding that takes you to an open, flower-filled meadow at the 14.9-mile mark. This is a great spot to hang out and take a break before the next 6 miles of technical downhill riding.

Past the meadow the trail becomes somewhat rockier and starts to lose elevation. Numerous flowers line the trail and views open to the west. Reach a small spring at the 17.3-mile mark and drop down on rocky tread to a junction with the Ojitos Trail at the 18.3-mile mark. This is a good spot to take a break before tackling the intense downhill that lies ahead. Strap on the helmet, check your brakes, and get ready for some wild downhill riding on technical singletrack. Several rock stairs will challenge the best of riders. Stay cool and dismount if things don't feel right. You could get hurt through this section. Past the rock stairs things mellow somewhat and you begin losing elevation at a rapid rate. Stay left at a trail junction at the 21.1-mile mark and descend quickly to the El Nogal Campground and the end of an incredible mountain bike ride.

Miles and Directions

0.0 START from the trailhead and follow the signed South Boundary Trail west into the woods.

0.4 Reach a trail marker.

0.7 Go left.

0.9 Reach a gate and views to the east.

1.2 Reach a trail marker and the beginning of a steep climb.

1.5 Bear right.

1.6 Cross over a small stream at a trail marker.

2.4 Go right on a tight singletrack trail marked with a hiker sign. Get ready for 5 miles of beautiful singletrack riding.

4.5 Trail slices through a beautiful aspen forest.

4.9 Trail slices through a mixed-conifer forest.

◄ *Singletrack on the South Boundary Trail*

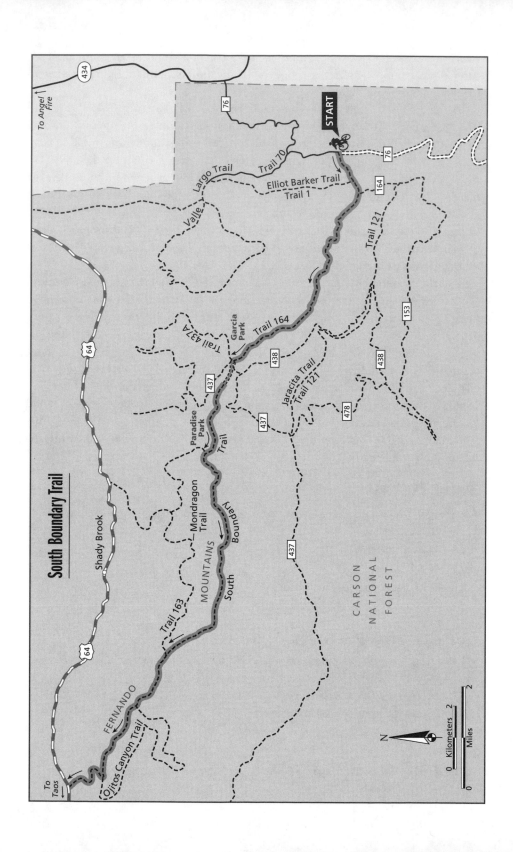

South Boundary Trail

START

To Angel Fire

To Taos

CARSON NATIONAL FOREST

Largo Trail
Trail 70
Elliot Barker Trail
Trail 1
Valle

Trail 164
Garcia Park
Trail 437A
Paradise Park
Mondragon Trail
South Boundary Trail
FERNANDO MOUNTAINS
Trail 163
Shady Brook
Ojitos Canyon Trail

Jaracita Trail
Trail 121

N

0 Kilometers 2
0 Miles 2

434
76
76
164
153
121
437
438
438
478
437
437
64
64

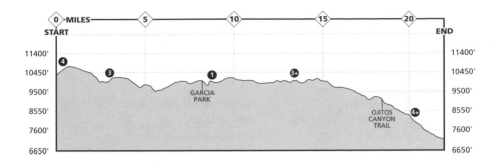

6.3 Small stream crossing.

8.1 Reach a junction with FR 437. Follow FR 437 to a cattle guard.

8.9 Reach a cattle guard.

9.0 Turn left onto FR 164 over several berms.

9.7 Go right up a tight singletrack trail into the pines.

10.0 Pass a trail marker.

10.3 Go right onto tight singletrack.

10.6 Pass a sign and reach an open meadow.

10.8 Go left onto singletrack.

11.8 Bear left onto a tight singletrack trail. This is the start of more than 9 miles of singletrack riding.

14.9 Pass through a small, open meadow.

17.3 Cross a small stream with a spring on the left.

18.3 Arrive at a junction with Ojitos Canyon Trail.

19.2 *Caution!* Extremely rocky tread.

19.7 Another section of rocky tread.

21.1 Go left at a tight switchback.

21.9 Bear left at a fence and travel down to El Nogal Campground.

22.1 Reach El Nogal Campground.

Ride Information

Local Information

Taos Chamber of Commerce, P.O. Drawer I, Taos, NM 87571; (505) 758-3873 or (800) 732-8267; www.taoschamber.com.
Angel Fire Chamber of Commerce, P.O. Box 274, Angel Fire; (800) 446-8117.

Local Events and Attractions

DAV Vietnam Veterans Memorial, US 64 between Angel Fire and Red River.

Mountain Bike Tours

Native Sons Adventures, 1033 Paseo del Pueblo Sur, Taos; (505) 758-9342 or (800) 753-7559; www.newmex.com/nsa; bike rentals and shuttle service.

14 Rio Grande del Rancho Trail

Start: At the trailhead on New Mexico Highway 518.
Distance: 12.2-mile out-and-back.
Approximate riding time: 1.5 to 2.5 hours.
Difficulty: Easy with a few hills and a rocky section.
Trail surface: Doubletrack and a short section of singletrack riding.
Lay of the land: Fantastic doubletrack riding in the piñon- and juniper-covered foothills just south of downtown Taos.
Other trail users: This trail is popular with horseback riders and joggers.
Canine compatibility: This is a great ride for the pooch, just bring water.

Wheels: Front suspension will work just fine on this ride.
Land status: Carson National Forest.
Nearest town: Taos.
Fees and permits: No fees or permits required.
Schedule: Dawn to dusk, March to November.
Maps: USGS maps: Taos County; *Trails Illustrated* number 730 Taos.
Trail contacts: Southwest Regional Office of the Forest Service, 517 Gold Avenue, Albuquerque, NM 87102; (505) 842–3800; www.fs.fed.us/r3.
Carson National Forest Ranger Station, 208 Cruz Alta Road, Taos, NM 87571; (505) 758–6200; www.fs.fed.us/r3/carson.

Finding the trailhead: From Taos: Go south out of town on New Mexico Highway 68 for 7 miles to NM 518. Go south on NM 518 for 2.8 miles to a parking-pullout on the right directly across from the trailhead. *DeLorme: New Mexico Atlas & Gazetteer:* Page 16, F-3 to G-4.

The Ride

This is by far one of the finest novice rides in the area. After the first initial singletrack section, the trail mellows out and takes a traversing line across the piñon- and juniper-studded foothills below Tetillas Peak. The riding is never really difficult and there is only a short section of rocky tread. Strong beginners in good shape will definitely enjoy this ride, and the intermediate cyclists will like the fact that they can push hard in the middle chain ring. The expert cyclists can really rack up the mileage on this one. The views are wonderful, so go out and enjoy what is one of the best mountain bike rides in the Taos area.

I just love this ride! It is a just a short distance from downtown Taos and the Plaza. You drive through Ranchos de Taos and Talpa, two small villages that seem to resist the influences of modern times and hopefully will continue to do so.

Your ride starts at the trailhead 2.8 miles from the junction of NM 68 and NM 518. Be on the lookout for a pullout on the right at the start of a guardrail on the left. Locating the start of the ride is a little tricky, so keep your eyes open and follow the directions. The beginning of the ride is the most difficult, and most novice cyclists will want to walk this section. Thankfully this section is short-lived, and the trail mellows out to wonderful doubletrack riding that parallels NM 518 and the

Cruising along on a wonderful spring day in northern New Mexico

Rio Grande del Rancho to the west. The riding is never very difficult, and the trail passes through several arroyos on its way to Forest Road 438. The trail is well marked and easy to follow. There are several roads and trails that shoot off from the main trail. Follow the mileage cues and you will have no problem enjoying this great ride. This is a fairly long ride, so novices should take it easy and keep a nice, mellow pace.

While you are in this neck of the woods, make a point to stop and see the San Francisco de Asis Church located just off NM 68 in the village of Ranchos de Taos. The church was built in 1850 and is a magnificent example of classic adobe architecture. The thick adobe walls, the blue sky, and the soft rounded lines of the church have attracted photographers and painters from around the world, who try to capture the beauty of this impressive structure. You can click all daylong outside the church, but no photographs are allowed inside the church. During the early-morning and late-evening light are the best times to photograph the church, as the soft light creates an illuminating image.

The church was not always in its present state! By 1966 the condition of the church had deteriorated considerably and something had to be done to preserve the beauty of the church. The 4- to 6-foot-thick adobe walls were in need of dire repair, as were the old vigas inside the church, and the roof was leaking badly. Under the guidance of Father Manuel Alvarez and John Gianardi, who specializes in the restoration of old adobes, the church is back to its original condition, if not better.

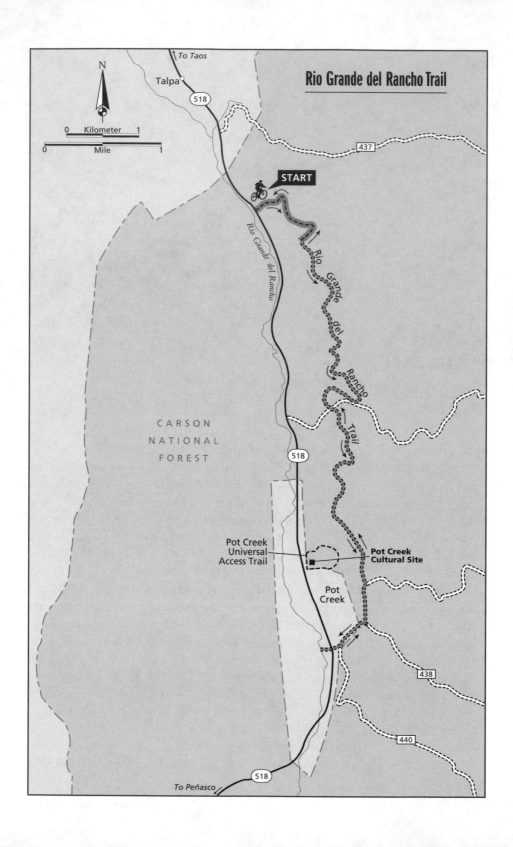

Rio Grande del Rancho Trail

N

0 Kilometer 1

0 Mile 1

To Taos

Talpa

518

437

START

Rio Grande del Rancho

Rio Grande del Rancho Trail

CARSON NATIONAL FOREST

518

Pot Creek Universal Access Trail

Pot Creek Cultural Site

Pot Creek

438

440

518

To Peñasco

While you're at the church, stop by the rectory hall directly across from the church to check out the puzzling *Shadow of the Cross* painting by Henri Ault. The painting is of Christ on the shore of the Sea of Galilee when it is first viewed in daylight or artificial light. Here comes the strange part: After about fifteen minutes in the dark, the painting becomes a different one altogether. The figure of Christ changes posture, a cross appears over his left shoulder, and a halo appears over his head. Hit the lights and the figure of Christ by the sea reappears. The painting was completed two years before the discovery of radium, and the artist himself has no explanation for the changes the painting goes through in different light. The painting has becomes quite famous, and for years it toured the galleries of Europe and North America before being purchased by Mrs. Herbert Sydney Griffin of Wichita Falls, Texas, for the Ranchos mission church, its permanent home.

Miles and Directions

0.0 START from the pullout-parking area and cross NM 518 to the marked trailhead at the start of a guardrail. Crank up the steep, loose, rocky singletrack trail. Take heart, the trail eases off in just a bit and the riding becomes mellow.

0.2 Go right onto the wide doubletrack trail.

0.9 The trail swings right across a drainage.

1.6 Cross the drainage.

1.7 Drop down a hill and begin a nice downhill run. I know you're having fun now.

2.2 Cross another drainage. Have you noticed how green the area is around these drainages?

3.1 The Tetillas Peak Trail goes right. You continue straight on Forest Road 18.

3.3 Trail junction. Continue straight.

3.7 The trail bends right.

4.3 Great views and a nice downhill. Enjoy!

5.5 NO VEHICLE sign at berms.

5.6 Nice open meadow. Continue straight.

5.7 Junction with FR 438 and the Rito de la Olla stream. Go right over the bridge to a gate.

6.1 Arrive at the gate. Take a rest and retrace your route back.

12.2 Back at the car.

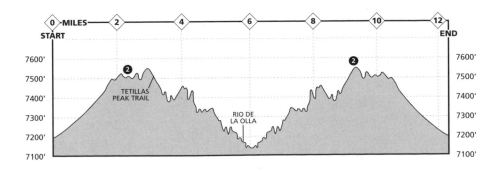

Ride Information

Local Information

Taos Chamber of Commerce, P.O. Drawer I, Taos, NM 87571; (505) 758-3873 or (800) 732-8267; www.taoschamber.com.

Accommodations

San Geronimo Lodge, 1101 Witt Road, Taos; (505) 751-3776 or (800) 894-4119.

New Mexico Bed & Breakfast Association, P.O. Box 2925, Santa Fe; (505) 983-4554; www.nmhotels.com.

Restaurants

Orlando's New Mexican Café, 114 Don Juan Valdez Lane, El Prado; (505) 751-1450; my choice for the best green chile in town.

15 Bernardin Lake

Start: From the trailhead 17 miles southeast of Taos.
Distance: 10-mile out-and-back.
Approximate riding time: 2 to 3 hours with time spent at the lake.
Difficulty: Moderate with a stiff climb up to the lake.
Trail surface: Singletrack and doubletrack trail.
Lay of the land: Beautiful riding up the Rio de la Olla Canyon and along the stream of the same name.
Other trail users: Hikers and hunters.
Canine compatibility: Dog friendly.
Wheels: Front suspension will work just fine on this ride.

Land status: Carson National Forest.
Nearest town: Taos.
Fees and permits: No fees or permits required.
Schedule: Late April to early November.
Maps: USGS maps: Taos County; *Trails Illustrated* number 730 Taos.
Trail contacts: Southwest Regional Office of the Forest Service, 517 Gold Avenue, Albuquerque, NM 87102; (505) 842-3800; www.fs.fed.us/r3.
Carson National Forest Ranger Station, 208 Cruz Alta Road, Taos, NM 87571; (505) 758-6200; www.fs.fed.us/r3/carson.

Finding the trailhead: From Taos: From the junction of New Mexico Highway 68 and NM 518 near Taos, drive 7 miles south on NM 518 to Forest Road 438 just past Pot Creek. Turn left onto FR 438 and follow it for 6 miles to the trailhead. The ride starts here. *DeLorme: New Mexico Atlas & Gazetteer:* Page 16, G-4.

The Ride

This is a wonderful ride up Rio de la Olla Canyon with the picturesque Rio de la Olla stream hugging the side of the trail for most of the ride. Wildflowers, tall stands of willows, small tarns, beaver ponds, and a beautiful small alpine lake are the highlights of this ride.

From the trailhead ride past the metal posts and through a few berms on a tight singletrack trail. After a short distance the trail becomes wider and skirts a rockfall that has blocked part of the trail. Past the slide area you arrive at a small, wooden bridge at the 0.7-mile mark. Cross the bridge and crank up a short hill to a second bridge. The second bridge is in dire need of repair and should not be trusted. Cross through the Rio de la Olla and continue up the obvious trail. After the second bridge the riding becomes quite pleasant and climbs at a gentle grade. You will pass by several small, open meadows that are filled with beautiful wildflowers during the summer months. When I did the ride, I didn't see any other trail users and felt it was one of the most peaceful mountain bike rides that I had ever done. It was a beautiful summer day, the sky was turquoise blue, the wildflowers were blooming everywhere, and the wind was blowing ever so gently through the trees. It was a wonderful place to be.

A flower-filled meadow along the Bernardin Lake Trail

At the 2.6-mile mark you arrive at a trail junction with a forest road on the right. This road climbs steeply up Diablo Canyon and eventually reaches Maestas Ridge. For this ride you continue straight on FR 438, passing several tarns, flower-filled meadows, and beaver houses on the right. At the 4.3-mile mark you reach the first of several berms. Start counting and at the fifth berm turn left over a large berm onto a rocky doubletrack trail. Climb the doubletrack and reach a large open meadow. Travel through the meadow and climb steeply to a ridge bearing to the right. The trail becomes level and winds around to just above the lake. Drop down to the shore and take a rest at this beautiful mountain lake.

I have done this ride twice, and the second time was in the summer of 2002. The lake was extremely low and not the same picturesque lake that I remember from the first time. Hopefully the next few years will bring more moisture and restore the lake to its previous state. The lake is a great place to just hang out, eat some lunch, and look at wildflowers during the summer months.

After a good rest retrace your route back to the trailhead. Enjoy the fast downhill and remember to keep your speed in check when encountering other trail users.

Miles and Directions

0.0 START from the trailhead and float over some berms.

0.4 Rock-slide area.

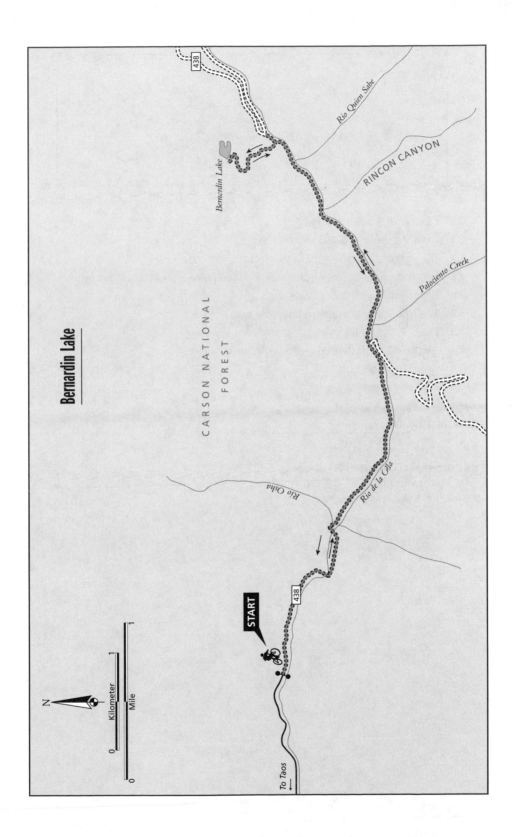

Bernardin Lake

N

Kilometer
0   1

Mile
0   1

To Taos

START

438

438

CARSON NATIONAL
FOREST

Rio Osha

Rio de la Olla

Bernardin Lake

Rio Quien Sabe

RINCON CANYON

Palociento Creek

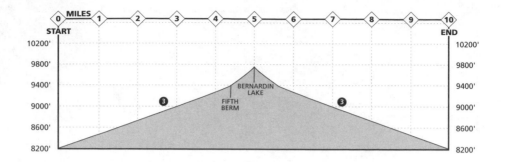

0.7   Cross a small wooden bridge.

0.8   Cross the stream at a dilapidated bridge.

1.7   The trail cuts through a stand of tall willows.

2.1   Reach an open meadow, which is filled with wildflowers during the summer months.

2.6   Reach a trail junction. Continue straight.

3.8   Beautiful tarns and beaver ponds on the right.

4.3   Reach the first of the berms.

4.4   Go left at the fifth berm up an old doubletrack road.

5.0   Reach Bernardin Lake.

10.0   Back at the trailhead.

Ride Information

Local Information

Taos Chamber of Commerce, P.O. Drawer I,
Taos, NM 87571; (505) 758–3873 or (800)
732–8267; www.taoschamber.com.

16 Gallegos Peak via Forest Road 442

Start: From the trailhead 14.3 miles south of Taos.

Distance: 14.4-mile out-and-back.

Approximate riding time: 2 to 3 hours.

Difficulty: Moderate. The elevation gain is spread out, and there are only a couple of short, steep climbs.

Trail surface: Dirt roads and doubletrack trails.

Lay of the land: Excellent riding on a mostly graded forest road along Apache Canyon and to just below Gallegos Peak (10,528 feet).

Other trail users: Four-wheelers and hunters.

Canine compatibility: Dog friendly.

Wheels: Front suspension will work just fine on this ride.

Land status: Carson National Forest.

Nearest town: Taos.

Fees and permits: No fees or permits required.

Schedule: Early April to early November.

Maps: USGS maps: Taos County; *Trails Illustrated* number 730 Taos.

Trail contacts: Southwest Regional Office of the Forest Service, 517 Gold Avenue, Albuquerque, NM 87102; (505) 842-3800; www.fs.fed.us/r3.
Carson National Forest Ranger Station, 208 Cruz Alta Road, Taos, NM 87571; (505) 758-6200; www.fs.fed.us/r3/carson.

Finding the trailhead: From Taos: From the junction of New Mexico Highway 68 and NM 518 near Taos, drive 14.3 miles south on NM 518 to Forest Road 442 on the left. The ride starts here. *DeLorme: New Mexico Atlas & Gazetteer:* Page 16, G-3 to G-4.

The Ride

This is a nice ride for the strong beginner or intermediate rider looking to get back into some beautiful country without a lot of hard riding. Forest Road 442 is a mostly graded road that cuts along Apache Canyon, passes below Gallegos Peak, and eventually winds to the north to join with the Rio Grande del Rancho. The views are beautiful along the road, and wildflowers grow on the steep slopes during the summer months.

From the trailhead at the junction of NM 518 and FR 442, follow FR 442 into the woods and up a short hill. The road drops down to a cattle guard and begins a gentle climb, passing several trails on the right that lead into the Amole Canyon Cross-country Ski Park.

Around the 1.8-mile mark you will reach a road on the left that drops steeply into Apache Canyon. You continue straight on FR 442 and at 2.2 miles you begin a steep climb up a rocky, rutted hill. The hill is short-lived and the tread soon becomes level. At the 3.2-mile mark begin another climb and pass a road on the right that leads to the Gallegos Peak Trail. The more-advanced riders might want to explore more trails by taking this road to the Gallegos Peak Trail. Several trails drop steeply to NM 518 and the Sipapu Ski Area.

Catching air on Forest Road 442

It's best to bring a map and remember that if you do drop down to NM 518, it's a long climb on the road back to your car. For this ride you continue straight on FR 442. Views open to the north, and the riding is quite pleasant through the tall pine and aspen trees. Reach the last of the big hill climbs at the 4.9-mile mark and enjoy almost 2 miles of nice cruising. Around the 6.7-mile mark a rough road on the right leads up to Gallegos Peak. You continue straight and drop down into a wide-open meadow at the 7.2-mile mark and the turnaround point.

This is a wonderful place to stop to enjoy the views and eat some lunch. There are awesome views to the south of Jicarita Peak and the Truchas Peaks. Wildflowers are numerous in the meadow during the summer months and make for some

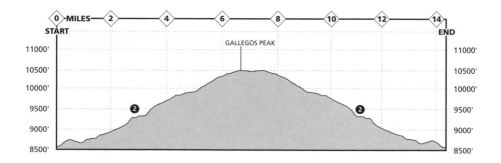

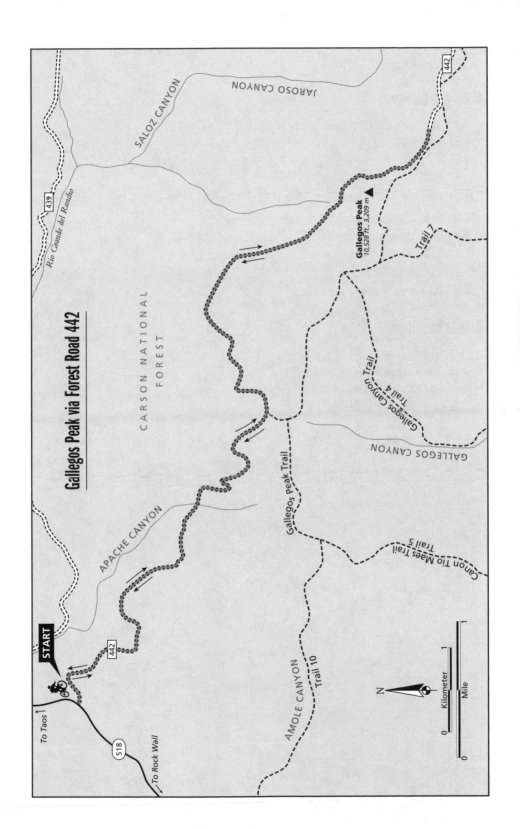

Gallegos Peak via Forest Road 442

CARSON NATIONAL FOREST

START

To Taos

518

To Rock Wall

442

APACHE CANYON

439

Rio Grande del Rancho

SALOZ CANYON

JAROSO CANYON

442

Gallegos Peak
10,528 ft., 3,209 m

Trail 7

Gallegos Canyon Trail
Trail 4

GALLEGOS CANYON

Gallegos Peak Trail

Canon Tio Maes Trail
Trail 5

AMOLE CANYON
Trail 10

N

0 — 1 Kilometer
0 — 1 Mile

very scenic photos. After your break retrace your route back to the trailhead and your car.

Miles and Directions

0.0   START at the NM 518 and FR 442 junction. Follow FR 442 into the woods.

0.8   Cattle guard.

1.8   A road on the left leads into Apache Canyon. Continue straight.

2.2   Climb up a steep, rutted, rocky hill.

3.2   Climb up another steep hill.

3.5   Road on the right leads to the Gallegos Peak Trail.

4.9   Climb up the last of the big hills.

6.7   Rough road on the right leads to the top of Gallegos Peak.

7.2   Reach a beautiful open meadow and the turnaround point.

14.4   Back at the trailhead and your car.

Ride Information

Local Information

Taos Chamber of Commerce, P.O. Drawer I,
Taos, NM 87571; (505) 758-3873 or (800)
732-8267; www.taoschamber.com.

17 Canon Tio Maes Trail

Start: From the parking area just off New Mexico Highway 518.

Distance: 6.8-mile out-and-back.

Approximate riding time: 2 to 3 hours.

Difficulty: This is a serious uphill grunt and an extremely technical downhill. There are several technical sections that will demand your best.

Trail surface: Singletrack and doubletrack trails.

Lay of the land: Tight singletrack riding up a narrow, rocky canyon below Gallegos Peak.

Other trail users: This trail is popular with horseback riders, hikers, and dirt bikers.

Canine compatibility: Bring the dog, maybe he can help push the bike up the steep section.

Wheels: Front suspension will work just fine on this ride, but full suspension will make the ride a lot smoother.

Land status: Carson National Forest.

Nearest town: Peñasco.

Fees and permits: No fees or permits required.

Schedule: Early April to late October.

Maps: USGS maps: Taos County; *Trails Illustrated* number 730 Taos.

Trail contacts: Carson National Forest Ranger Station, 208 Cruz Alta Road, Taos, NM 87571; (505) 758-6200; www.fs.fed.us/r3/carson.

Finding the trailhead: From Taos: From the junction of New Mexico Highway 68 and NM 518 near Taos, travel south on NM 518 for 18.7 miles to the trailhead on the left just past a guardrail. The ride starts here. *DeLorme: New Mexico Atlas & Gazetteer:* Page 16, H-3 to G-4.

The Ride

This ride is a true test of your technical riding skills. The riding is extreme for the most part and is quite demanding in several sections. You are going to push your bike up at the start of the ride, but after that the riding is hard but doable.

From the parking area, pedal up the gravel road to a gate. Pedal through the gate and into a narrow canon. This section is the uphill crux of the ride, and it is extremely difficult to maintain any sort of rhythm. After pushing for a short bit, the riding becomes doable. At the 0.7-mile mark cross a small stream and crank through a short rocky section up to level tread. At the 1-mile mark the tread becomes surprisingly smooth and level. This is quite a contrast to the riding below you. Nice riding leads you into a small, beautiful meadow filled with tall aspen and pine trees. The creek is now on your left and the riding is on narrow singletrack. Crank up to a second spectacular meadow, which is covered with tall, white aspen trees. It's a great place to take a short break. There is still some hard riding ahead. After resting, enjoy tight singletrack up to the fork in the trail. Either way will keep you going in the right direction. Going left is a little easier. Crank through a steep, rocky section up to a wide, open meadow. Follow the trail through the meadow up to a trail on the right. Go right at the 2.3-mile mark up to a sign. Continue straight up on the Tio Maes Trail on tight singletrack. The trail is rutted-out in sections due to dirt bike use. The trail levels out and then makes a quick left up a steep, rocky hill to level

Steep climbing and tight switchbacks on the Canon Tio Maes Trail

ground. Follow the trail to a doubletrack with a hiker's sign. Go left up the double-track to a gate. Make a right down to another trail junction at the 3.4-mile mark and the turnaround point.

There are several road and trails leading in all directions. Bring a map and feel free to explore. Forest Road 442 is a major road through the area and climbs close to the summit of Gallegos Peak. Several singletrack trails lead back down to NM 518 close to the trailhead. It's just a matter of finding them.

This ride description returns via your same route up. The downhill is extremely fast and technical, especially near the bottom. Use caution and ride in control. I could ride about 98 percent of the downhill by letting the bike go with the flow. Feather your brakes and keep your speed in control. I found this ride to be one of the harder rides in the area but felt quite satisfied once I was safely back at the trail-head.

Miles and Directions

0.0 START from the parking area and follow the gravel road up to a gate.

0.1 Pass through the gate and into the hard riding.

0.5 Level tread.

0.7 Stream crossing.

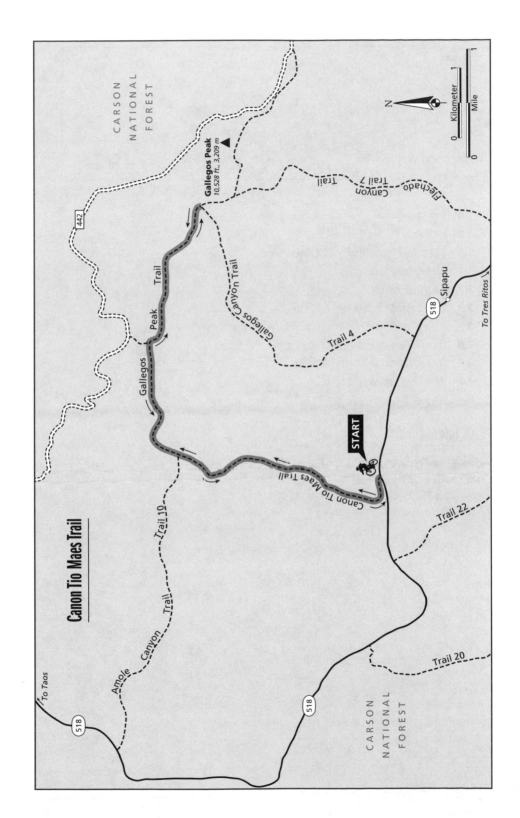

Canon Tio Maes Trail

Gallegos Peak
10,528 ft., 3,209 m

CARSON
NATIONAL
FOREST

Gallegos Peak Trail

Gallegos Canyon Trail

Flechado Canyon Trail 7

Trail 4

Trail 10

Amole Canyon Trail

START

Canon Tio Maes Trail

Trail 22

Trail 20

CARSON
NATIONAL
FOREST

442

518

518

518

To Taos

To Tres Ritos

Sipapu

N

0   Kilometer   1
0   Mile   1

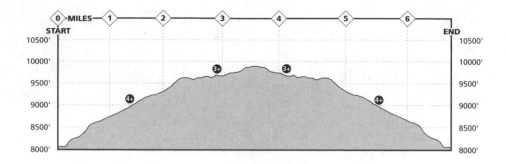

1.0 Level tread.

1.2 Meadow.

1.4 Open meadow with beautiful aspen trees.

1.7 Steep, rocky section.

2.2 Continue straight.

2.3 Go right and up to a sign.

2.7 Go left.

2.8 Go left at doubletrack and hiker's sign.

3.2 Go right and down to trail junction.

3.4 Reach the turnaround point.

6.8 Back at the trailhead.

Ride Information

Local Information

Taos Chamber of Commerce, P.O. Drawer I,
Taos, NM 87571; (505) 758–3873 or (800)
732–8267; www.taoschamber.com.

18 Angostura Trail

Start: From the trailhead just off New Mexico Highway 518.
Distance: 7.6-mile out-and-back.
Approximate riding time: 1.5 to 2.5 hours.
Difficulty: Moderate to strenuous with a big climb up to the Alamitos Trail.
Trail surface: Doubletrack and singletrack trails.
Lay of the land: The trail follows along Rito Angostura up through the steep hills near the Sipapu Ski Area.
Other trail users: This trail is popular with hikers and other trail users.

Canine compatibility: Bring the pooch. There is a lot of shade and water on this ride.
Wheels: Front suspension will work just fine on this ride.
Land status: Carson National Forest.
Nearest town: Peñasco.
Fees and permits: No fees or permits required.
Schedule: March to November.
Maps: USGS maps: Taos County; *Trails Illustrated* number 730 Taos.
Trail contacts: Carson National Forest Ranger Station, 208 Cruz Alta Road, Taos, NM 87571; (505) 758-6200; www.fs.fed.us/r3/carson.

Finding the trailhead: From Taos: From the intersection of New Mexico Highway 64 and NM 518, travel south on NM 518 for 27.6 miles to the trailhead on the right. The ride starts here. The trailhead is not marked. *DeLorme: New Mexico Atlas & Gazetteer:* Page 16, H-4.

The Ride

Numerous trails shoot off from NM 518 along the Rio Pueblo and climb steeply to various peaks and forest roads. The trails usually follow small streams and narrow canyons on extremely rough terrain. The Angostura Trail follows the beautiful Rio Angostura up a narrow canyon, and the trail, surprising enough, is very doable for expert cyclists.

The ride starts from the unmarked trailhead just off NM 518, follows a rough doubletrack road past some beautiful flower-filled meadows, and passes several summer homes to a trail marker. Continue straight past the marker over two berms and a stream crossing to a trail junction. The Agua Piedra Trail goes right. You continue straight and begin a steep climb on very rocky tread. At the 1.5-mile mark you reach another unmarked trail junction. Continue straight on the wide singletrack trail into the tall pine and aspen trees along the Rio Angostura. This is beautiful riding along this section with various wildflowers covering the steep hillsides during the summer months. Around the 1.8-mile mark you reach the crest of a hill, make a short downhill run to a small stream crossing, and begin a gentle climb up to a pleasant surprise at the 2.3-mile mark—a small, beautiful waterfall on the right. It's a great place for a short break to enjoy the sounds of the woods and the soothing waterfall. What a beautiful spot!

Near the top of the Angostura Trail

Past the waterfall the trail cuts through a small, open meadow and begins to gain altitude quickly. The trail becomes very rocky at the 3.3-mile mark and then levels out for a short distance before tackling a very short, steep, rocky hill. At the top of the hill, the trail meets Alamitos Trail and the turnaround point for this ride description.

Many options exist for the cyclists who want to explore the many trails that crisscross the hills in this area. I did a loop, hooking up with the Agua Piedra Trail (I got lost for an hour) and following that trail (extremely steep, loose, and rocky) back to the junction with the Angostura Trail at the 1-mile mark. I don't recommend this option, but go for it if you are up for a teeth-rattling, extreme, technical downhill. Bring a map and compass. You might need it. Remember that the Pecos Wilderness Area lies just to the south and no bicycles are allowed in the wilderness area.

Miles and Directions

0.0 START from the trailhead and follow the rough doubletrack road up along the Rio Angostura.

0.8 Reach a trail marker.

1.0 Reach a junction with Agua Piedra Trail.

1.5 Reach an unmarked trail junction. Continue straight.

2.3 Arrive at the waterfall.

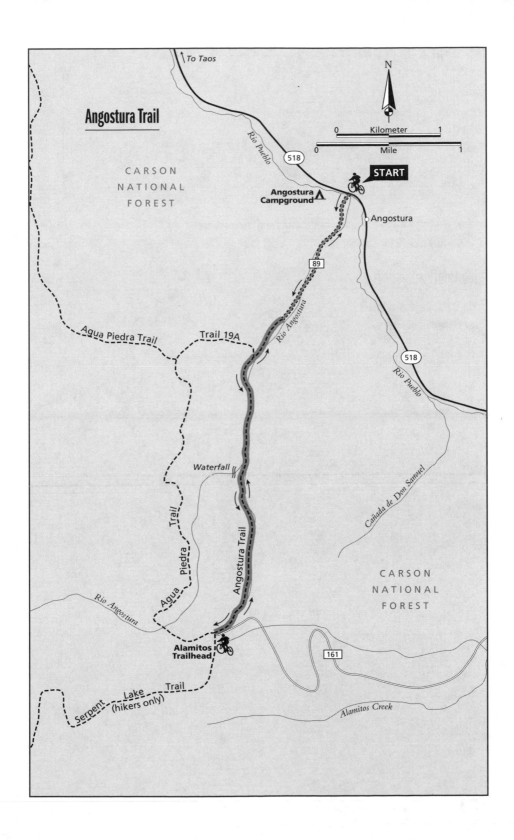

Angostura Trail

To Taos

Rio Pueblo

518

START

Angostura
Campground △

Angostura

CARSON
NATIONAL
FOREST

89

Rio Angostura

518

Rio Pueblo

Agua Piedra Trail

Trail 19A

Waterfall

Cañada de Don Samuel

Agua Piedra Trail

Angostura Trail

Rio Angostura

Agua

CARSON
NATIONAL
FOREST

Rio Angostura

Alamitos
Trailhead

161

Serpent Lake Trail
(hikers only)

Alamitos Creek

N

0   Kilometer   1
0   Mile   1

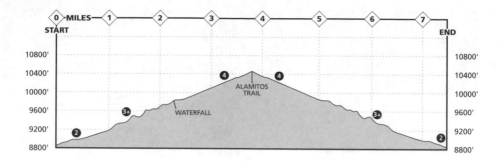

3.8 Reach the junction with Alamitos Trail and the turnaround point.

7.6 Arrive back at the trailhead.

Ride Information

Local Information

Taos Chamber of Commerce, P.O. Drawer I,
Taos, NM 87571; (505) 758–3873 or (800)
732–8267; www.taoschamber.com.

19 La Vista Verde Trail

Start: From the trailhead 20 miles southwest of Taos.
Distance: 2.4-mile out-and-back.
Approximate riding time: 30 minutes to 1 hour.
Difficulty: Easy.
Trail surface: Singletrack.
Lay of the land: A short, beautiful trail along the Rio Grande.
Other trail users: Hikers and anglers.
Canine compatibility: Dog friendly.

Wheels: Front suspension will work just fine on this ride.
Land status: Bureau of Land Management.
Nearest town: Pilar.
Fees and permits: $3.00 a day per vehicle.
Schedule: Dawn to dusk.
Maps: USGS maps: Taos County.
Trail contacts: Taos Resource Area Office, 226 Cruz Alta Road, Taos, NM 87571; (505) 758-8851.
Rio Grande River Visitor Center, 226 Cruz Alta Road, Taos, NM 87571; (505) 758-4060.

Finding the trailhead: From Taos: Travel 15 miles southwest on New Mexico Highway 68 to Pilar and New Mexico Highway 570. Turn right onto NM 570 and travel along the Rio Grande to the Taos Junction Bridge. Turn left over the bridge onto New Mexico Highway 567 and travel 1 mile to the trailhead and large parking area on the right. The ride starts here. *DeLorme: New Mexico Atlas & Gazetteer:* Page 16, F-2.

The Ride

This is a short, beautiful ride along the Rio Grande and the Rio Grande Gorge. The highlights of this ride are spectacular views of the Rio Grande Gorge, access to the Rio Grande for fishing, and an option to hook up with the West Rim Trail for added mileage. The camping along NM 570 is just wonderful, and you could spend a few days exploring the many outdoor activities in the area. River rafting is quite popular near the village of Pilar, and trips can be arranged with one of the many outfitters in the Taos area. Try Los Rios River Runners in Taos (800–544–1181) or Native Sons Adventures at (800–753–7559). These are two reputable river runners that offer wonderful trips in the Taos area. One of the more exciting runs is the 17-mile trip down the deep chasm of the Taos Box. This run starts just south of the Wild Rivers Recreation Area and offers many sections of class-IV rapids. The river drops 90 feet per mile through this section and is one of the most exhilarating river runs in the west. The best time to run the river is during spring runoff in the months of May and June. For more information on river running in the Taos area, contact the Bureau of Land Management at (505) 758–8851.

From the trailhead, ride through a short section of rocky steps. After the steps the trail becomes smooth and crosses a small arroyo at around the 0.4-mile mark.

Sweet singletrack on La Vista Verde Trail

Numerous basalt rocks line the trail, and if you look carefully you may stumble upon petroglyphs in some of the larger rocks. Look for geometric designs believed to be 5,000 years old (some of the oldest in the area) and handprints that are 600 years old. Good views are north up the gorge and east to the river. At the 0.6-mile mark a trail on the right leads down to the river. Continue straight through an open area of scattered piñon trees, cacti, and tall meadow grass. The trail cuts through a stand of old, beautiful piñon trees and soon reaches a bench and the turnaround point.

Enjoy this spot before heading back to the trailhead. The solitude of this place, the peaceful sound of the free-flowing Rio Grande, and the sweet smell of sage all add to the wonderful feeling you get from doing this ride. For you fishermen this is a great spot to access some excellent fly-fishing along a wild section of the Rio Grande.

For those looking to add mileage to their ride, you can easily access the West Rim Trail by riding up NM 567 from the trailhead for 2 miles to the West Rim trailhead on the right.

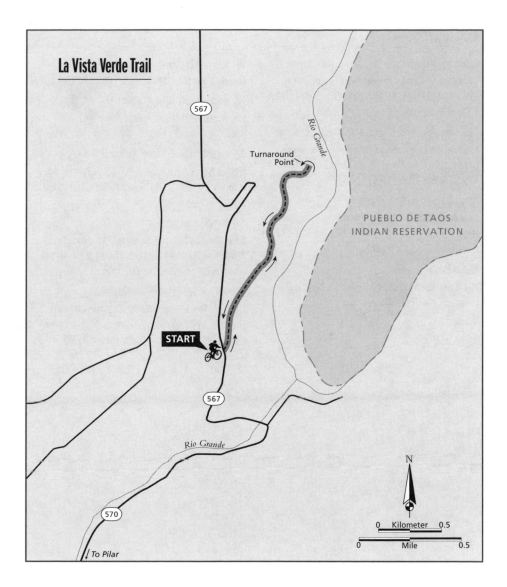

La Vista Verde Trail

567

Rio Grande

Turnaround
Point

PUEBLO DE TAOS
INDIAN RESERVATION

START

567

Rio Grande

N

570

To Pilar

0 Kilometer 0.5
0 Mile 0.5

Miles and Directions

0.0 START from the trailhead and pedal through a section of steep, rocky steps.

0.6 Trail on the right leads down to the river.

1.2 Arrive at a bench and the turnaround point.

2.4 Back at the trailhead.

Ride Information

Local Information

Taos Chamber of Commerce, P.O. Drawer I, Taos, NM 87571; (505) 758-3873 or (800) 732-8267; www.taoschamber.com.

Local Events and Attractions

Kit Carson Home and Museum of the West, East Kit Carson Road, 1 block off the Plaza, Taos; (505) 758-4741.

Accommodations

Sun God Lodge, 919 Paseo del Pueblo Sur, Taos; (505) 758-3162 or (800) 821-2437; nice, clean, and affordable.

Restaurants

The Pilar Yacht Club, NM 68 and NM 570, Pilar; (505) 758-9072.

Group Rides

Gearing up Bike Shop, Taos; (505) 751-0365.

River Running Trips

Big River Raft Trips; (800) River-GO; www.bigriverrafts.com.

Mountain Bike Tours

Native Sons Adventures, 1033-A Paseo del Pueblo Sur, Taos; (505) 758-9342 or (800) 753-7559; www.newmex.com/nsa.

Organizations

New Mexico Touring Society, P.O. Box 1261, Albuquerque, NM 87103; (505) 237-9700; www.swcp.com/-russells/nmts.

Recommended Reading

Horgan, Paul. *Great River: The Rio Grande River in North America History.* Middletown, Conn.: Wesleyan University Press, 1991.

Santa Fe Area

Nestled below the beautiful Sangre de Cristo Mountains at the southernmost point of the Rocky Mountains, Santa Fe is a city of rare beauty and diverse topography. This is where the high desert meets the Rocky Mountains, creating a unique physical environment. To the south and west of Santa Fe are the high-desert mesas covered with cacti, sagebrush, yucca, chamiso, and piñon and juniper trees. This is an open area with expansive views and dramatic terrain. To the north and east of Santa Fe, the towering high peaks of the Sangre de Cristo Mountains surround the city. Aptly named by Spanish colonists who arrived in the area in the early 1600s, the snowcapped peaks give off various hues of pink at sunset. Sangre de Cristo translates to "Blood of Christ" in English. These are beautiful mountains filled with crystal-clear mountain streams, quaking aspens, thick conifer forests, sharp-cut canyons, and meadows filled with colorful flowers during the summer months.

Santa Fe is situated at 7,000 feet above sea level, higher than any mountain east of the Mississippi. The highest point near Santa Fe is Santa Fe Baldy, at 12,622 feet above sea level. Santa Fe is blessed with more than 300 days of sunshine a year. Summer days can be hot, but the nights are refreshingly cool. This is the time to explore the trails at the higher elevations and enjoy the beauty of high-mountain riding. Winter brings snow, and most trails above 9,000 feet will be snowed in until spring. Late spring brings warmer temperatures and longer days. Most trails are free of snow and the trails at lower elevations are free of mud and moisture. Fall is a time of stable weather, mild temperatures, dry trails, and the changing of the aspens. Great for mountain biking!

The mountain biking around Santa Fe is different, like the city itself. You can ride on smooth doubletrack trails on the Caja Del Rio Plateau high above the Rio Grande, through rounded volcanic hills with spectacular views, to the Jemez and Sangre de Cristo Mountains. The Dale Ball Trails, a mere 2 miles from downtown, offer a plethora of excellent singletrack trails that wind through the piñon- and juniper-covered foothills. The Windsor Trail is a wonderful downhill singletrack that starts at 10,000 feet above sea level and loses a staggering 3,400 feet in 10 miles. There is an amazing amount of variety in trails and scenery around the Santa Fe area, and you would be hard-pressed to find a more spectacular place to ride in the southwestern United States.

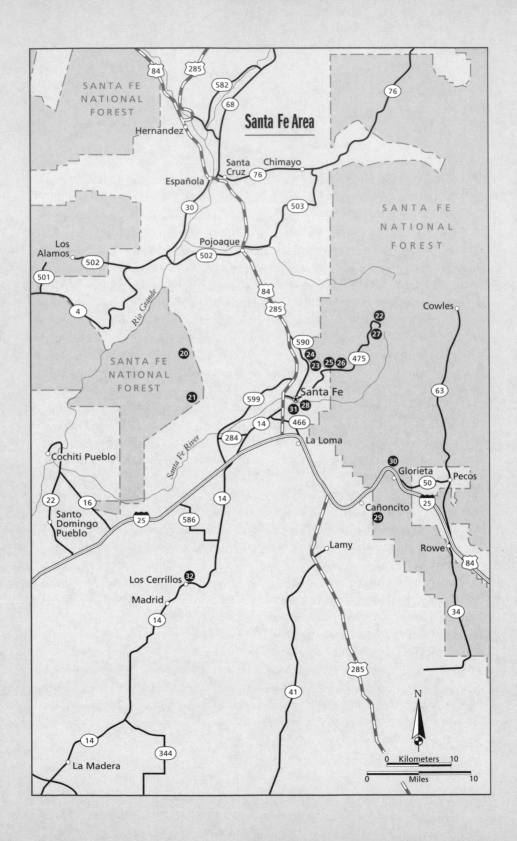

I first came to Santa Fe in 1971 to attend college. It was a mellow town of 50,000 diverse citizens. The city has since grown up and become quite cosmopolitan. Trendy restaurants, galleries, and hotels now line the area around "The Plaza," and million-dollar homes line the foothills. The city has become one of the most visited tourist spots in the world, and the once-empty foothills are now filled with trendy summer homes for the rich and famous and those who want to be. I have traveled almost around the world from South America to Indonesia, and I am still hard-pressed to find a city as beautiful as this one nestled at 7,000 feet above sea level below the spectacular Sangre de Cristo Mountains. Even though the city has changed much in the last thirty years and tensions sometimes run high between the different cultures, Santa Fe is a city of tolerance and acceptance. You really can be yourself, dress the way you want, and follow whatever spiritual path you wish, and still not feel out of place in this "City Different."

The mountain biking is as good as anywhere in the state, but when you add in the cultural aspects of the area, Santa Fe is in a class of its own. So explore the trendy restaurants (the variety of food is unsurpassed). Check out the wonderful galleries and museums (also unsurpassed for a city of Santa Fe's size). Go out and enjoy a walk along the tight, crooked streets lined with beautiful adobe homes and surrounded by tall cottonwood trees, and feel the essence that is this special city in a very special state.

20 Caja del Rio North

Start: At the junction of Forest Roads 24 and 2554.

Distance: 8.3-mile loop.

Approximate riding time: 1 to 2 hours.

Difficulty: Easy with a couple of short, steep climbs.

Trail surface: Mostly doubletrack trails and dirt roads.

Lay of the land: Through the gentle rolling hills just northwest of Santa Fe on the Caja del Rio Plateau.

Other trail users: Popular with bovines, woodcutters, and four-wheel-drive traffic.

Canine compatibility: Bring the pooch and plenty of water.

Wheels: Front suspension will work just fine on this ride.

Land status: Santa Fe National Forest.

Nearest town: Santa Fe.

Fees and permits: No fees or permits required.

Schedule: Can be ridden year-round.

Maps: USGS maps: Santa Fe County.

Trail contacts: Santa Fe National Forest, 1474 Rodeo Road, Santa Fe, NM 87501; (505) 438-7840; www.fs.fed.us/r3/sfe.

Finding the trailhead: From Santa Fe: From downtown Santa Fe take U.S. Highway 84 north to New Mexico Highway 599. Follow NM 599 southwest for 4 miles to County Road 62. Go right onto CR 62 and travel for 2 miles to the boundary of the national forest near the city disposal center and the start of FR 24. Follow FR 24 west for 6.1 miles to FR 2554. The ride starts here. *DeLorme: New Mexico Atlas & Gazetteer:* Page 23, C-9 to D-10.

The Ride

The Caja del Rio Plateau is a wild, seldom-used area filled with remnants of many ancient volcanoes just east of White Rock Canyon high above the Rio Grande. The area was once the site of intense volcanic activity from almost two million years ago. Numerous volcanic cones dot the rugged landscape and are now covered with piñon and juniper trees and scattered basalt rocks. The plateau has a long history of human influence and use, and many petroglyphs can be found along the basalt cliffs lining White Rock Canyon. Once the site of two large land grants dating from the late 1600s, the land is now under management of the Forest Service with the primary uses of cattle grazing and woodcutting. The plateau is crisscrossed with many forest and woodcutting roads, giving access to many easy and intermediate mountain bike tours. The plateau lies at an elevation of 7,000 feet and can be ridden almost year-round, especially in years of light snowfall. The area should be avoided during times of heavy moisture, as the roads become impassable due to thick, heavy mud.

From the junction of FR 24 and FR 2554, cross the cattle guard and travel southwest on FR 2554 with FR 24 on the other side of the fence on your left. Follow the

Near the overlook toward White Rock Canyon and the Rio Grande

nice doubletrack up to a junction at the 0.6-mile mark. Go straight, heading west on the smooth doubletrack through the piñon and juniper trees with the large volcanic cone, named Montoso Peak, dominating the landscape to your left. Good views west to Los Alamos and north to the Sangre de Cristo Mountains make the riding even more enjoyable. Around the 1.5-mile mark the trail crosses an old, dry arroyo filled with black, basalt rocks. Past the arroyo the trail drops a little and then crosses another rocky area, which soon leads to a fork in the road at a signed junction. Forest Road 2554 goes to the right, but you continue straight on Chino Mesa Road heading west toward White Rock Canyon and the Rio Grande. At the 2.9-mile mark you reach a junction with Pinabete Tank Road on the right. Enjoy beautiful views down to the Rio Grande and across White Rock Canyon. Continue straight on smooth singletrack to a trail junction at the 3.5-mile mark. Turn left onto a faint doubletrack surrounded by cacti and piñon and juniper trees. It's beautiful riding through this section. Pass through another cacti-filled field and reach a road junction at the 4.2-mile mark. Go right and turn right again at 4.3 miles, heading up to the power lines. Reach the power lines and spectacular views down to the Rio Grande and up and down White Rock Canyon. Take the road down and

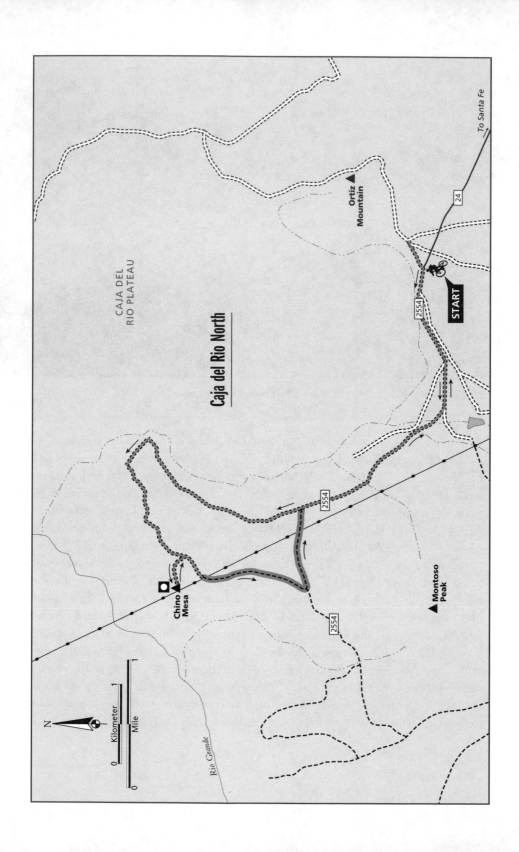

reach a small, open area at the 4.5-mile mark. Get off your bike and walk west a short way to a spectacular overlook to the Rio Grande. This is a great spot to just hang out and enjoy the splendor of this rugged and beautiful canyon. Back on the bike, head back up the steep road to the power lines. Bear right at the 4.8-mile mark and then again at the 5-mile mark. Reach the power lines again at the 5.1-mile mark and go left down the rocky doubletrack. Climb up a short, steep hill and come to a junction with FR 2554 on the left at the 6-mile mark. Go left onto FR 2554 and pedal to a familiar road junction with Chino Mesa Road. Turn right and follow FR 2554 back to FR 24 and your car.

Miles and Directions

0.0 START from the junction of FR 24 and FR 2554 at a fence and cattle guard. Cross the cattle guard and follow FR 2554 into the trees with FR 24 on your left.

0.6 A doubletrack goes left. Continue straight.

1.5 Short, rocky section across a dry arroyo.

2.1 Reach a junction with Chino Mesa Road. Continue straight.

2.9 Reach a junction with Pinabete Tank Road. Continue straight.

3.5 Go left onto a faint doubletrack trail. Lots of beautiful cacti line the side of the trail.

4.2 Veer right.

4.3 Veer right and up to the power lines.

4.4 Reach the power lines and great views. Drop down the steep, rocky road to an overlook on the left.

4.5 Overlook on the left with some fire rings. Good spot to enjoy the views.

4.6 Reach the top of the hill at the power lines. Continue straight.

4.8 Go right.

5.0 Bear to the right

5.1 Turn left at the power lines. Drop down a rough and rocky doubletrack.

6.0 Turn left onto FR 2554.

6.2 Back at the junction of FR 2554 and Chino Mesa Road. Go right.

8.3 Reach FR 24 and your car.

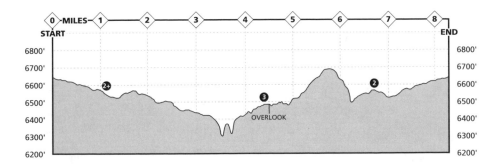

Ride Information

Local Information

Santa Fe Convention & Visitors Bureau, P.O. Box 909, Santa Fe, NM 87504-0909; (505) 984-6760 or (800) 777-2489; www.santafe.org.

Local Events and Attractions

Institute of American Indian Arts Museum, 108 Cathedral Place, Santa Fe; (505) 954-7205; houses the largest collection of contemporary Native American art in the world; admission is $4.00 for adults, $2.00 for seniors and students, and free for ages sixteen and younger.

Accommodations

Old Santa Fe Inn, 320 Galisteo Street, Santa Fe; (505) 995-0800 or (800) 745-9910; close to the plaza and easy on the wallet.

Restaurants

Plaza Café, 54 Lincoln Avenue, Santa Fe; (505) 982-1664; great spot for breakfast.

Mountain Bike Tours

Sun Mountain Bike Company, 107 South Washington Avenue, Santa Fe; (505) 820-2902; bike rentals and mountain bike tours.

21 Forest Road 24/Caja del Rio

Start: At the junction of Forest Road 24 and County Road 62.
Distance: 12.2-mile out and back.
Approximate riding time: 1 to 2 hours.
Difficulty: Easy with a few gradual climbs and big views.
Trail surface: Mostly doubletrack trails and dirt roads.
Lay of the land: Through the gentle rolling hills just west of Santa Fe on the Caja del Rio Plateau.
Other trail users: Popular with cattle, wood-cutters, and four-wheel-drive traffic.

Canine compatibility: Leave the pooch at home.
Wheels: Front suspension will work just fine on this ride.
Land status: Santa Fe National Forest.
Nearest town: Santa Fe.
Fees and permits: No fees or permits required.
Schedule: Can be ridden year-round.
Maps: USGS maps: Santa Fe County.
Trail contacts: Santa Fe National Forest, 1474 Rodeo Road, Santa Fe, NM 87501; (505) 438-7840; www.fs.fed.us/r3/sfe.

Finding the trailhead: From Santa Fe: From downtown Santa Fe take U.S. Highway 84 north to New Mexico Highway 599. Follow NM 599 southwest for 4 miles to CR 62. Turn right onto CR 62 and travel for 2 miles to the boundary of the national forest near the city disposal center and the start of FR 24. The ride starts here. *DeLorme: New Mexico Atlas & Gazetteer:* Page 23, D-10.

The Ride

FR 24 is a long, winding horseshoe-shaped road that makes for an excellent beginner's ride through Caja del Rio Plateau. This description takes in the first 6 miles of FR 24 from the junction with CR 62. FR 24 extends the whole length of the plateau and ends close to La Bajada Hill, in the southern part of the plateau. The road is fairly smooth for much of the distance and offers no technical obstacles except for a few cattle-guard crossings. This is a great ride for the novice cyclists to work on learning how to shift gears and put in some miles on the dirt. This is a beautiful area and extremely accessible from Santa Fe and Albuquerque.

From the junction of CR 62 and the boundary of Santa Fe National Forest marked by a cattle guard, head north on the dirt road. Pass a shooting range on the right and enjoy views to the Jemez and Sangre de Cristo Mountains. Pass an old cabin on the left at the 0.7-mile mark and reach a road on the right and a cattle guard at the 0.9-mile mark. Avoid the road on the right, cross over the cattle guard, and reach another cattle guard at the 1.1-mile mark. At the 1.6-mile mark Twin Hills Road comes in from the left. Continue straight and begin a mellow climb with good views to the surrounding hills and volcanic cones. The next major road you

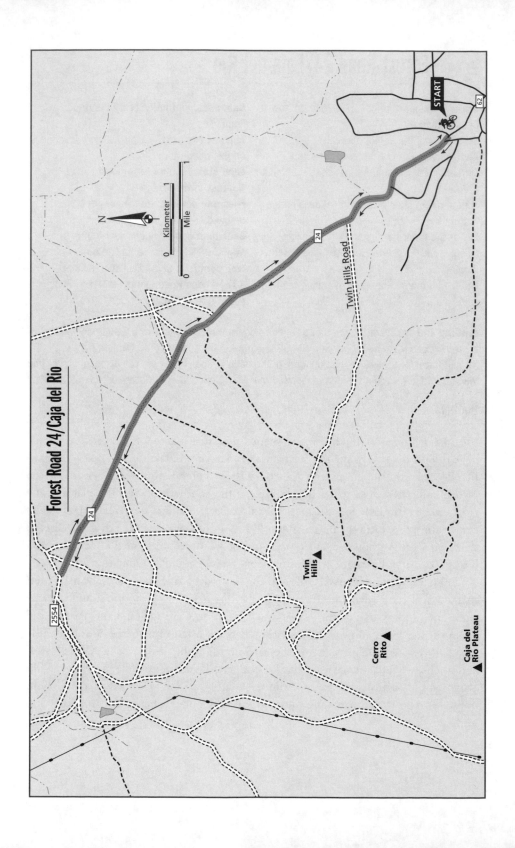

Forest Road 24/Caja del Rio

come to is Forest Road 2551 (Sagebrush Flats Road) at the 2.7-mile mark on the right. Continue straight and enjoy good riding on smooth doubletrack. The road becomes mostly level, and the views north to Sangre de Cristo are open and beautiful. The major cone on the right is Ortiz Mountain, one of the largest volcanoes in the area. At the 5.4-mile mark a road (Eleven Hundred Well) goes right to a holding pen and corral. Continue straight and you'll soon cross a cattle guard and reach Forest Road 2554 on the right at the 6.1-mile mark and the turnaround point. Turn around and retrace your route back to CR 62 and your car. Feel free to explore the many (and I mean many) roads that intersect FR 24. Just remember that there are many unmarked roads that shoot out in all directions, and it is very easy to become disoriented.

If you are going to explore, bring a map, extra water, and tools, and remember that the miles can add up quickly and you will still have to pedal back to CR 62.

Miles and Directions

0.0 START from the point where CR 62 and FR 24 meet. Follow FR 24 north over a cattle guard and into Santa Fe National Forest.

0.7 Pass an old cabin on the left.

0.9 Reach a road on the right. Continue straight over the cattle guard.

1.1 Pedal over a second cattle guard.

1.6 Twin Hills Road comes in from the left. Continue straight.

2.7 Pass Sagebrush Flats Road on the right. Continue straight.

5.4 Eleven Hundred Well Road comes in from the right and leads to a corral. Continue straight.

5.6 Cross a cattle guard.

6.1 Reach FR 2554 on the right and the turnaround point.

12.2 Back at CR 62 and your car.

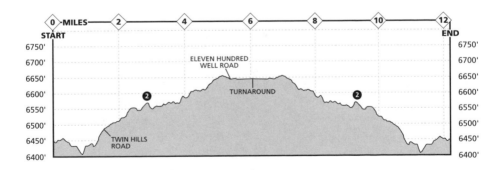

Ride Information

Local Information

Santa Fe Convention & Visitors Bureau, P.O. Box 909, Santa Fe, NM 87504-0909; (505) 984-6760 or (800) 777-2489; www.santafe.org.

Local Events and Attractions

Wheelwright Museum of the American Indian, 704 Camino Lejo, Santa Fe; (505) 989-7386 or (800) 607-4636; www.wheelwright.org.

Accommodations

Old Santa Fe Inn, 320 Galisteo Street, Santa Fe; (505) 995-0800 or (800) 745-9910; close to the plaza and easy on the wallet.

Restaurants

Plaza Café, 54 Lincoln Avenue, Santa Fe; (505) 982-1664; great spot for breakfast.

Mountain Bike Tours

Sun Mountain Bike Company, 107 South Washington Avenue, Santa Fe; (505) 820-2902; bike rentals and mountain bike tours.

22 Windsor Trail

Start: From the trailhead at the Santa Fe Ski Area.

Distance: 10-mile one-way.

Approximate riding time: 1.5 to 2.5 hours.

Difficulty: Moderate with a few short climbs.

Trail surface: Singletrack with a short section of dirt roads.

Lay of the land: A wonderful downhill adventure along the Tesuque Creek drainage.

Other trail users: This trail is popular with hikers and runners.

Canine compatibility: Leave the pooch at home for this one.

Wheels: Front suspension will work just fine on this ride.

Land status: Santa Fe National Forest.

Nearest town: Santa Fe.

Fees and permits: No fees or permits required.

Schedule: Dawn to dusk, late May to late October. Expect to see snow at the beginning of the ride well into late May or early June. I once encountered snow here in late September.

Maps: USGS maps: Santa Fe County; Map of the Mountains of Santa Fe, Drake Mountain Maps 2001.

Trail contacts: Southwest Regional Office of the Forest Service, 517 Gold Avenue, Albuquerque, NM 87102; (505) 842–3800; www.fs.fed.us/r3.
Santa Fe National Forest, 1474 Rodeo Road, Santa Fe, NM 87501; (505) 438–7840; www.fs.fed.us/r3/sfe.

Finding the trailhead: From Santa Fe: From Saint Francis Drive and Paseo de Peralta in Santa Fe, go east on Paseo de Peralta to Washington Avenue. Go north (left) onto Washington Avenue for 0.1 mile to New Mexico Highway 475 (Hyde Park Road). Turn right onto NM 475 and travel 14 miles to the lower parking area for the Santa Fe Ski Area. Look left (west) for the Windsor Trail sign. The mileage starts here. *DeLorme: New Mexico Atlas & Gazetteer: Page 24, C-2.*

The Ride

A highly touted and very popular ride, the Windsor Trail is 10 miles of excellent, downhill singletrack through tall pine and aspen trees along beautiful Tesuque Creek. The ride starts at a staggering 10,300 feet above sea level and drops 3,400 feet in 10 miles to County Road 72A near the small town of Tesuque. The trail follows along the picturesque Tesuque Creek, starting out in dense pines and dropping down through stands of tall aspens into a small, open meadow filled with willows and wildflowers and ending in the piñon and juniper hills near Tesuque. The ride is popular as a downhill run and for good reason. Excellent singletrack; long downhills on smooth, fast tread; creek crossings; short technical sections; and did I mention you lose 3,400 feet of elevation in 10 miles! With popularity comes heavy use, and the Windsor Trail is starting to show signs of erosion and abuse. As a mountain biker you should be aware of your actions and how they affect other trail users. Keep your speed in check, stay on the main trail, give the right-of-way to the uphill hiker and cyclist, and

▶ Santa Fe, the capital of New Mexico, is the oldest capital city in the United States.

show respect to other trail users. This was a hiking trail way before people started to mountain bike on it. If at all possible do the ride during the week and try to start in early morning or late afternoon.

From the lower parking area at the ski area, look west for the Windsor Trail sign and a bathroom. Access the trail and cross a small bridge to a trail junction. Turn left (going right leads into the Pecos Wilderness), cross a second small bridge, and continue down to a fence and gate covered with downfall. The trail drops down to the Rio en Medio Trail just past a gate. Reach the Rio en Medio and stay right on the Windsor Trail. Cross a small drainage and begin climbing up through the dense conifer forest. Crank up a steep section and reach a small parking area on NM 475 at the 0.9-mile mark. Don't worry; the downhill is coming. Ride through the parking area and turn right onto the singletrack trail leading down a rocky trail into the woods. The singletrack trail soon reaches a gate and the first of several switchbacks. The switchbacks are steep, rocky, and eroded. If you not sure of your skills, it's best to walk this section. Past the switchbacks the trail glides downhill on nice tread to a series of tight switchbacks that dump you on Forest Road 102 at the 2.7-mile mark. Turn left onto FR 102 and travel about 100 feet to a singletrack trail on the right leading into the woods. Go right onto this trail (Windsor Trail) and drop down and cross a small stream on tight singletrack. This is great riding through this section. At the 3.7-mile mark arrive at a junction with the Borrego Trail on the right. Continue straight and drop down a nice, long open meadow filled with willows and bright wildflowers during the summer months. Past the meadow you'll descend a series of switchbacks and arrive at a junction with Borrego Trail on the left. Continue straight and drop down the wide trail on very loose tread. Use caution and watch your speed through this section. Arrive at a junction with the Bear Wallow Trail on the left at the 5.3-mile mark. This is a good spot to take a rest and get some blood back into those forearms. Some tricky riding on tight tread leads into another open meadow filled with tall aspen trees and willows. The trail crosses Tesuque Creek and then turns to wide doubletrack. At the end of the meadow, you arrive at a junction with the Chamisa Trail on the left at the 6.3-mile mark. The trail stays wide and then quickly turns to tight singletrack that drops steeply and crosses Tesuque Creek. Don't even try to stay dry. For almost the next 2 miles, the trail crosses Tesuque Creek at least thirteen times on tight and sometimes rocky singletrack. This is fun stuff here! Reach a junction with San Juan Trail at the 8.9-mile mark and bear to the right and down on wide, rocky tread. Reach a gate and bear right into a riparian area and reach a three-way intersection. Continue straight and then head right along a small stream and fence line to a small bridge. Cross the bridge and arrive at CR 72A and continue straight to the parking area and hopefully your car.

This ride does require a shuttle. You can easily have someone drop you off at the ski area, do the Windsor Trail, and pedal the 4.1 miles back to Santa Fe on New Mexico Highway 590.

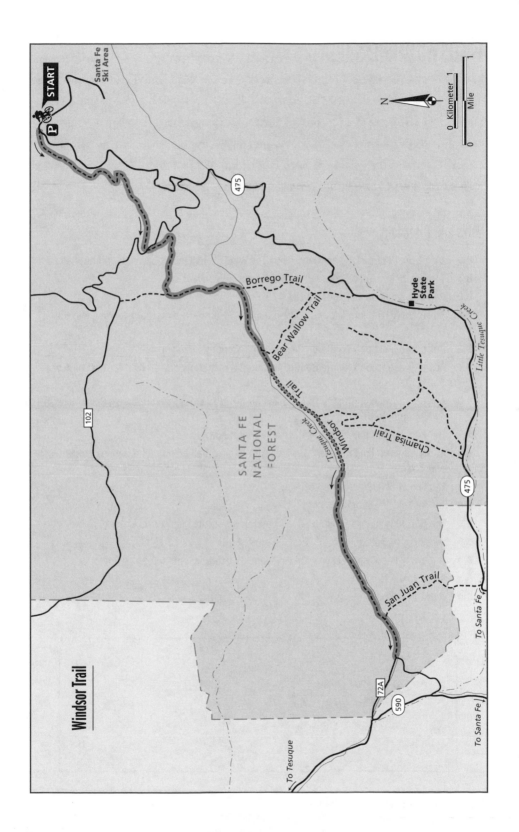

Windsor Trail

START

P

Santa Fe
Ski Area

475

Borrego Trail

Bear Wallow Trail

102

SANTA FE
NATIONAL
FOREST

Tesuque Creek

Windsor Trail

Chamisa Trail

Hyde
State
Park

Little Tesuque Creek

475

San Juan Trail

To Santa Fe

72A

590

To Tesuque

To Santa Fe

To Santa Fe

N

0   Kilometer   1

0   Mile   1

PECOS WILDERNESS AREA
While you're in the area, check out (by foot) the diverse and beautiful Pecos Wilderness Area. There are more than 222,000 acres of protected ponderosa pine, Engelmann spruce, Douglas fir, aspen, and diverse riparian and alpine tundra. Elevation ranges from 8,400 feet to a towering 13,102 feet at Truchas Peak. There are more than 445 miles of trails that are well marked and well maintained and that allow for a number of back-country excursions from short day hikes to extended backpack trips. New Mexico's longest trail, the 50-mile Skyline Trail, lies within the wilderness boundary.

Miles and Directions

0.0   START from the parking area and follow the Windsor Trail into the woods and turn left.

0.3   The Rio en Medio Trail goes left. Bear right on the Windsor Trail.

0.9   Reach a small parking area on NM 475.

2.7   Arrive at FR 102. Turn left and make a quick right onto the singletrack leading into the woods.

3.2   Arrive at a junction with the Big Tesuque Trail. Continue straight.

3.7   Arrive at a junction with the Borrego Trail on the right. Continue straight on the Windsor Trail.

4.5   Arrive at a junction with the Borrego Trail on the left across Tesuque Creek. Continue straight and down.

5.3   The Bear Wallow Trail is on the left. Continue straight.

6.3   At the end of a long meadow, arrive at the Chamisa Trail on the left. Continue straight and down.

6.8   The first of several stream crossings.

8.6   The last of the stream crossings.

8.9   The San Juan Trail goes left. Bear right and down on the Windsor Trail.

9.1   Pedal past a gate.

9.4   Three-way intersection. Follow the singletrack along a stream and fence line.

9.8   Arrive at CR 72A.

10.0   Arrive at the parking area.

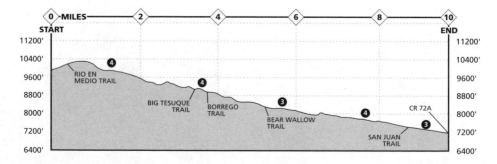

Ride Information

Local Information

Santa Fe Convention & Visitors Bureau, P.O. Box 909, Santa Fe, NM 87504-0909; (505) 984-6760 or (800) 777-2489; www.santafe.org.

Accommodations

Bishop's Lodge, Bishop's Lodge Road, Santa Fe; (800) 732-2240; www.bishopslodge.com; more than 1,000 acres encompass the Bishop's Lodge and resort in the rolling foothills near the town of Tesuque. Expensive, but worth the dough if you want to be catered to.

New Mexico Bed & Breakfast Association, P.O. Box 2925, Santa Fe, NM 87505; (505) 983-4554; www.nmhotels.com.

Restaurants

Maria New Mexican Kitchen, 555 West Cordova Road, Santa Fe; (505) 983-7929.

Organizations

New Mexico Touring Society, P.O. Box 1261, Albuquerque, NM 87103; (505) 237-9700; www.swcp.com/-russells/nmts.

Other Resources

Public Lands Information Center, 1474 Rodeo Road, Santa Fe; (505) 438-7542

23 Dale Ball Trails North

Start: From the trailhead and parking area just off New Mexico Highway 475.
Distance: 3.7-mile loop.
Approximate riding time: 30 to 45 minutes.
Difficulty: Easy with a couple of short, steep climbs.
Trail surface: Singletrack trails.
Lay of the land: Through the rolling piñon- and juniper-covered foothills just north of Santa Fe.
Other trail users: Very popular with hikers and runners.
Canine compatibility: Bring the pooch.

Wheels: Front suspension will work just fine.
Land status: City of Santa Fe, national forest, and private.
Nearest town: Santa Fe.
Fees and permits: No fees or permits required.
Schedule: Dawn to dusk, year-round.
Maps: USGS maps: Santa Fe County; Dale Ball Trails map; Map of the Mountains of Santa Fe, Drake Mountain Maps 2001.
Trail contacts: Santa Fe County Open Space, P.O. Box 276, Santa Fe, NM 81504; (505) 995-2704.

Finding the trailhead: From Santa Fe: From Saint Francis Drive and Paseo de Peralta in Santa Fe, go east on Paseo de Peralta to Washington Avenue. Go north (left) onto Washington Avenue for 0.1 mile to New Mexico Highway 475 (Hyde Park Road). Turn right onto NM 475 and travel 2.1 miles to Sierra Del Norte. Turn left onto Sierra Del Norte and make a quick right into a large parking area. The ride starts here. *DeLorme: New Mexico Atlas & Gazetteer:* Page 24, C-2.

The Ride

This short little ride is on a new trail system located just north of town off NM 475. Numerous private individuals and public organizations are responsible for the creation of these fine trails. The Dale Ball Trails are multiuse trails designed for hikers, runners, and mountain bikers. Numerous man-hours, lots of planning, and a lot of hard work went into the development of these fine multiuse trails. I love these trails for their ease of access from downtown Santa Fe and the option they offer of extending your mileage on a whim. The trails are rideable almost year-round, and they stay dry while trails higher up in elevation retain snow. During the summer months the temperature can soar during midday, so try riding in early morning or late afternoon. There are more than 21 miles of trails in the Dale Ball Trail system with more to come in the future. The trails have become extremely popular and can get very congested on weekend days. For a more enjoyable ride and far more solitude, try mid-week. The trails are well marked and have a trail marker at almost all intersections. The trails are easy to follow, and you should have no problem finding your way around this wonderful area.

► The Spanish controlled New Mexico for almost 300 years, twice as long as the United States.

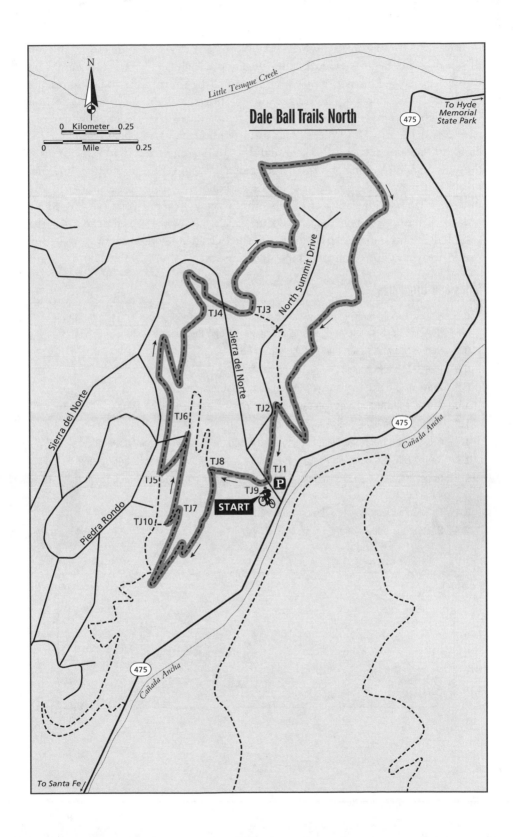

N

0   Kilometer   0.25

0   Mile   0.25

Little Tesuque Creek

Dale Ball Trails North

475

To Hyde
Memorial
State Park

North Summit Drive

TJ4

TJ3

Sierra del Norte

TJ2

475

Cañada Ancha

Sierra del Norte

TJ6

TJ8

TJ1

P

TJ5

TJ9

START

TJ7

TJ10

Piedra Rondo

475

Cañada Ancha

To Santa Fe

From the parking area cross Sierra del Norte and access Trail Junction 9 just left of the dog run. Begin a gradual climb on smooth, tight singletrack that climbs up through piñon and juniper trees. Climb for more than a half mile and soon reach a ridge and a trail junction. The ride cuts to the north, and you enjoy a long section of fun, tight singletrack. Pass a bench on the right and begin a nice, fast downhill run to Sierra del Norte. Cross Sierra del Norte (with caution) and begin an extended climb on fantastic singletrack up through the rounded hills and piñon trees. This is the best section of riding and the hardest. After a long section in the trees, the trail breaks out onto a ridgeline with open views. Follow the ridge for a short run and then begin a fast downhill run back to the parking area and your car. For added mileage reverse your direction and do the ride again or see the directions for the Dale Ball Trails Central ride. Kudos for all the folks who worked on these trails and thanks for your efforts in maintaining them.

Miles and Directions

0.0 START from the parking area and cross Sierra del Norte and access TJ 9 just left of the dog run. Begin riding on tight singletrack up through the piñon trees.

0.2 Reach TJ 8 and go left and continue to climb.

0.6 Reach TJ 7 and continue straight.

0.8 Arrive at TJ 6 and continue straight on somewhat rocky tread.

1.0 At TJ 5 go right and enjoy an extended run of excellent singletrack riding.

1.3 Bench on the right, good views to the west.

1.7 Cross Sierra Del Norte (with caution) and reach the singletrack trail on the other side.

1.9 Reach TJ 3 and continue straight. Beautiful singletrack riding through this section.

3.2 Reach the top of a hill and enjoy good views. Begin a nice downhill run back to the parking area.

3.4 TJ 2. Go left and down to the parking area.

3.7 Back at the parking area.

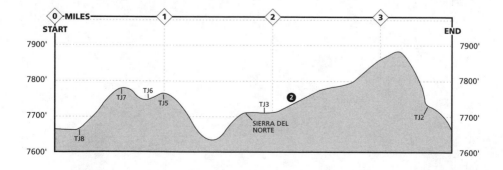

Ride Information

Local Information

Santa Fe Convention & Visitors Bureau, P.O. Box 909, Santa Fe, NM 87504-0909; (505) 984-6760 or (800) 777-2489; www.santafe.org.

Local Events and Attractions

Taste of Santa Fe, Sweeney Convention Center, Santa Fe; (505) 983-4823; early May; feast on some of the best food Santa Fe has to offer from local chefs.

Museum of Indian Arts and Culture, 710 Camino Lejo, Santa Fe; (505) 476-1250; www.museumofnewmexico.org; the "Here, Now and Always" interactive exhibit takes visitors through thousands of years of Native American history. The best museum of Native American art and life in the Southwest!

Accommodations

Guadalupe Inn, 604 Agua Fria, Santa Fe; (505) 989-7422; www.guadalupeinn.com.

Restaurants

Ore House on the Plaza, 50 Lincoln Avenue, Santa Fe; (505) 983-8687; great food and wonderful margaritas.

24 Dale Ball Trails Central

Start: From the trailhead and parking area just off New Mexico Highway 475.
Distance: 6.3-mile loop.
Approximate riding time: 1.0 to 1.5 hours.
Difficulty: Moderate with a couple of short, steep climbs.
Trail surface: Mostly singletrack trails with a short section of dirt road.
Lay of the land: Through the rolling piñon- and juniper-covered foothills just north of Santa Fe.
Other trail users: Very popular with hikers and runners.
Canine compatibility: Bring the pooch.
Wheels: Front suspension will work just fine.

Land status: City of Santa Fe, county of Santa Fe, and private.
Nearest town: Santa Fe.
Fees and permits: No fees or permits required.
Schedule: Dawn to dusk, year-round.
Maps: USGS maps: Santa Fe County; Dale Ball Trails map; Map of the Mountains of Santa Fe, Drake Mountain Maps 2001.
Trail contacts: Santa Fe County Open Space, P.O. Box 276, Santa Fe, NM 87504; (505) 995-2704.
Santa Fe National Forest, 1474 Rodeo Road, Santa Fe, NM 87501; (505) 438-7840; www.fs.fed.us/r3/sfe.

Finding the trailhead: From Santa Fe: From Saint Francis Drive and Paseo de Peralta in Santa Fe, go east on Paseo de Peralta to Washington Avenue. Go north (left) onto Washington Avenue for 0.1 mile to New Mexico Highway 475 (Hyde Park Road). Turn right onto NM 475 and travel 2.1 miles to Sierra Del Norte. Turn left onto Sierra Del Norte and make a quick right into a large parking area. The ride starts here. *DeLorme: New Mexico Atlas & Gazetteer:* Page 24, C-2.

The Ride

The Dale Ball Trails Central are a collection of connecting singletrack trails bordered on the north by NM 475 (Hyde Park Road) and on the south by Cerro Gordo Road. The trails cut through the piñon-covered hills, cross through several arroyos, and offer a great mountain bike outing just minutes from downtown Santa Fe. The trails are well marked and well maintained and marked with signs at every trail junction. Most of the riding is on tight singletrack with a few sections of wide doubletrack and dirt roads. This is one of the best trail systems close to Santa Fe for mountain biking. The trails are popular with hikers, runners, and other cyclists, so maintain a safe speed and yield to the uphill hiker and cyclist.

▶ My son and mountain bike buddy, Jeremy, was born October 3, 1976, in Santa Fe, New Mexico.

From the parking area turn left onto Sierra de Norte and drop down to NM 475 (Hyde Park Road). Cross NM 475 and access a singletrack trail marked Trail Junction 13 just to the right of Cerros Colorados Road. Turn right into the arroyo and pedal on nice singletrack. The trail climbs out of the arroyo and enters into the piñon-covered hills, climbing up to TJ 12. Continue straight, pass TJ 11, and follow

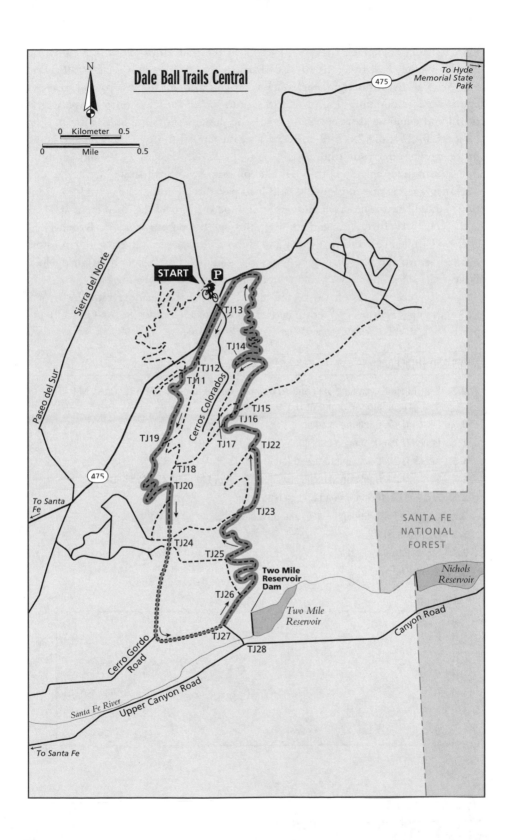

nice, twisting singletrack to TJ 19. Past TJ 19 the trail drops and winds down on excellent singletrack to TJ 20. Make a sharp right and enter into what I call "Dead Car Arroyo." Beautiful, tight singletrack takes you through the arroyo and past several dead cars, dumping you on Cerro Gordo Road. Turn left onto Cerro Gordo Road and climb up past several houses. Drop down a short hill and at the bottom look for TJ 27 at the 2.6-mile mark near a gate. Go left through the gate and climb up the steep, loose, rutted hill past TJ 26 to TJ 25. Go right at TJ 25 and climb on tight, beautiful singletrack through the piñons. At the 3.5-mile mark the trail becomes steep, rocky, and loose. Crank hard past this section and reach TJ 23. Continue straight at this junction and glide on good tread to TJ 22. Turn right at TJ 22 and reach TJ 16. Turn right and climb up through the piñons to TJ 15. Reach TJ 15 at the 4.7-mile mark and turn right and climb a short, steep hill. Drop down into a narrow arroyo and pass through a rocky section, then climb steeply to a ridgeline. Follow the steep line down past a couple of switchbacks where the trail dumps you back onto NM 475. Look to the left and follow the trail leading into the arroyo. Enjoy one last section of sweet singletrack to Cerros Colorados Road. Go right and pedal back to the parking area. What a great little ride!

Miles and Directions

0.0 START from the parking area and go down Sierra del Norte to NM 475. Cross NM 475 and go right into the arroyo at TJ 13.

0.6 Reach TJ 12. Continue straight.

1.1 Reach TJ 19. Continue straight.

1.5 Reach TJ 20. Go right into "Dead Car Arroyo."

1.7 Reach TJ 24. Continue straight, staying in the arroyo to Cerro Gordo Road.

2.1 Arrive at Cerro Gordo Road and go left and up.

2.7 Go left at TJ 27 through a gate and up a steep hill.

3.3 Go right at TJ 25.

3.5 Steep, loose, rocky hill.

3.7 Go straight at TJ 23.

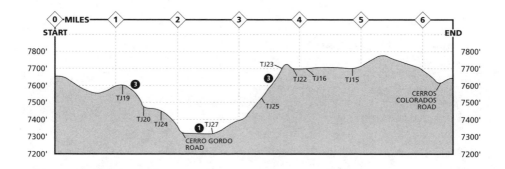

3.8 Turn right at TJ 22.

4.1 Go right at TJ 16.

4.7 Turn right at TJ 15.

5.8 Go left into the arroyo.

6.2 Turn right onto Cerros Colorados Road.

6.3 Back at the trailhead.

Ride Information

Local Information

Santa Fe Convention & Visitors Bureau, P.O. Box 909, Santa Fe, NM 87504-0909; (505) 984-6760 or (800) 777-2489; www.santafe.org.

Local Events and Attractions

Ten Thousand Waves, Hyde Park Road (NM 475); (505) 982-9304; Japanese-style health spa that's right up the road and great for relaxing.

Santa Fe Children's Museum, 1050 Old Pecos Trail, Santa Fe; (505) 989-8359; a small climbing wall, a one-acre garden, and numerous other fascinating things for the kids; admission is $4.00 for adults and $3.00 for kids.

25 San Juan and Chamisa Trails

Start: From the parking area at the Chamisa Trail trailhead.

Distance: 7.5-mile loop.

Approximate riding time: 1.5 to 2.5 hours.

Difficulty: Moderate with a few short hills and rocky sections on tight singletrack.

Trail surface: Paved road, doubletrack and singletrack trails.

Lay of the land: Great riding in the foothills just north of downtown Santa Fe.

Other trail users: This trail is popular with horseback riders, hikers, and joggers.

Canine compatibility: Leave the pooch at home for this one.

Wheels: Front suspension will work just fine on this ride.

Land status: Santa Fe National Forest.

Nearest town: Santa Fe.

Fees and permits: No fees or permits required.

Schedule: Late March to early November.

Maps: USGS maps: Santa Fe County; Map of the Mountains of Santa Fe, Drake Mountain Maps 2001.

Trail contacts: Santa Fe National Forest, 1474 Rodeo Road, Santa Fe, NM 87501; (505) 438–7840; www.fs.fed.us/r3/sfe.

Finding the trailhead: From Santa Fe: From Saint Francis Drive and Paseo de Peralta in Santa Fe, go east on Paseo de Peralta to Washington Avenue. Go north (left) onto Washington Avenue for 0.1 mile to New Mexico Highway 475 (Hyde Park Road). Turn right onto NM 475 and travel 5.6 miles to parking and the Chamisa trailhead on the left. *DeLorme: New Mexico Atlas & Gazetteer:* Page 24, C-2.

The Ride

This is a great mountain bike outing that offers up a variety of technical sections with a little road riding to start the ride. The first section of singletrack is steep, loose, and rocky and climbs for almost a mile. The first downhill section is tight, steep, and rocky, leading down into and across a small drainage. The trail then follows excellent, twisting singletrack through tall cottonwood trees and willows. The riding is absolutely beautiful through this section. The trail then meets up with the Windsor Trail and begins an uphill grunt, crossing Tesuque Creek several times before meeting the Chamisa Trail. The ride then follows the popular Chamisa Trail and climbs up through a beautiful mature pine forest along a small mountain stream. At the top of the hill, a long and sometimes narrow singletrack run will quickly take you back to the parking area and your car. The Chamisa Trail is an extremely popular trail that sees a lot of traffic by different trail users. Remember this and always keep your speed in check and always give the right-of-way to the uphill hiker or cyclist.

From the parking area travel back down NM 475 toward Santa Fe. At the 1.2-mile mark look for a trail on the right at a guardrail. Go right at this trail along Little Tesuque Creek. The trail quickly forks, and you follow the right fork up a rocky

Pedaling uphill near the junction with the Chamisa Trail

hill. Begin an extended climb up to the piñon trees, reaching a fence line at the 1.9-mile mark. Go left at the gate and drop down extremely tight singletrack and cross a small drainage at the bottom. Go left at the bottom of the hill and head into a dry arroyo filled with willows and tall cottonwood trees. Enjoy a mile of beautiful riding and reach a junction with the Windsor Trail at the 3-mile mark. Turn right onto the Windsor Trail (Forest Road 254) and begin climbing with Tesuque Creek on your left. Cross Tesuque Creek for the first time and enjoy tight and sometimes rocky singletrack up to another creek crossing. Hope you're not trying to keep your feet dry. You are going to wade across Tesuque Creek at least ten more times in the next 1.2 miles. At the 5.1-mile mark you cross Tesuque Creek for the last time and climb up a short, steep hill to reach a junction with the Chamisa Trail at a small, beautiful meadow at the 5.5-mile mark. A nice spot for a short break! Go right onto the Chamisa Trail and climb along a small drainage through a wonderful, dense forest of towering pine trees. The trail becomes rocky and climbs steeply to a four-way trail junction. Continue straight on the narrow singletrack with a few steep drop-offs on your left. Past a short technical section, the trail becomes wider and the canyon quickly opens up with a fast descent back to the parking area. Watch out for hikers and other trail users on this section and keep your speed under control!

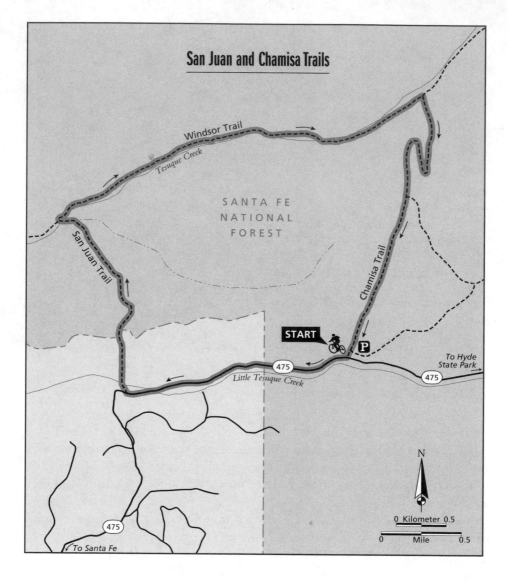

San Juan and Chamisa Trails

Windsor Trail

Tesuque Creek

SANTA FE
NATIONAL
FOREST

San Juan Trail

Chamisa Trail

START

P

475

Little Tesuque Creek

To Hyde
State Park

475

475

To Santa Fe

N

0 Kilometer 0.5

0 Mile 0.5

Miles and Directions

0.0 START from the parking area and head back down NM 475.

1.2 At a guardrail go right down rocky tread.

1.3 The trail forks. You go right up the steep, loose singletrack.

1.5 Power up past a very rocky section following tight singletrack through the piñon trees.

1.9 Go left just past the gate down very steep, tight, rocky singletrack.

2.1 Go left at the bottom of the hill. Enjoy a mile of fantastic singletrack riding through a dry arroyo.

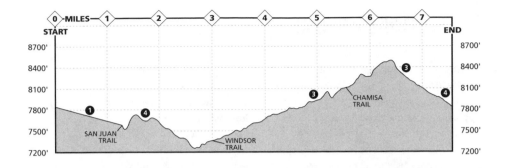

3.0 Come to a junction with FR 254 (Windsor Trail). Go right onto FR 254, following Tesuque Creek on the left.

3.5 Cross Tesuque Creek.

3.9 Cross Tesuque Creek. For the sake of being repetitious, you will cross the stream at least ten more times in the next 1.2 miles.

5.1 The end of the stream crossings, but here comes a short, steep, rocky hill. Continue straight up to a trail junction.

5.5 Go right onto Forest Road 183 (Chamisa Trail). This is wonderful uphill singletrack riding through a drainage and dense, mature pine forest.

6.4 Arrive at a four-way trail junction. Continue straight on FR 183 down to the parking area. This is a popular section of the trail, and there are a couple of steep drop-offs. Watch your speed.

7.5 Arrive back at the parking area.

Ride Information

Local Information

Santa Fe Convention & Visitors Bureau, P.O. Box 909, Santa Fe, NM 87504-0909; (505) 984-6760 or (800) 777-2489; www.santafe.org.

Local Events and Attractions

Feast Day, Santa Clara Pueblo; second week in August; (505) 753-7330.

Accommodations

Open Sky, 134 Turquoise Court, Santa Fe; (505) 471-3475; www.openskynm.com.

26 Chamisa Trail Loop

Start: From the parking area at the Chamisa Trail trailhead.
Distance: 8.6-mile loop.
Approximate riding time: 1.5 to 2.5 hours.
Difficulty: Moderate with a few extended climbs and rocky sections on tight singletrack.
Trail surface: Paved road, doubletrack and singletrack trails.
Lay of the land: Great riding in the foothills just north of downtown Santa Fe.
Other trail users: This trail is popular with horseback riders, hikers, and joggers.
Canine compatibility: Leave the pooch at home for this one.

Wheels: Front suspension will work just fine on this ride.
Land status: Santa Fe National Forest.
Nearest town: Santa Fe.
Fees and permits: No fees or permits required.
Schedule: April to early November.
Maps: USGS maps: Santa Fe County; Map of the Mountains of Santa Fe, Drake Mountain Maps 2001.
Trail contacts: Santa Fe National Forest, 1474 Rodeo Road, Santa Fe, NM 87501; (505) 438–7840; www.fs.fed.us/r3/sfe.

Finding the trailhead: From Santa Fe: From Saint Francis Drive and Paseo de Peralta in Santa Fe, go east on Paseo de Peralta to Washington Avenue. Go north (left) onto Washington Avenue for 0.1 mile to New Mexico Highway 475 (Hyde Park Road). Turn right onto NM 475 and travel 5.6 miles to parking and the Chamisa trailhead on the left. *DeLorme: New Mexico Atlas & Gazetteer:* Page 24, C-2.

The Ride

This is a wonderful ride that takes in the best sections of three different trails to make a great loop through tall pine trees to open, flower-filled meadows along the Tesuque Creek drainage. It's a popular ride that sees a lot of foot and mountain bike traffic. You can avoid the crowds by riding during the weekdays. The loop makes for a great night ride during the late spring, summer, and early fall months. The ride starts on the ever popular Chamisa Trail and enters into a narrow canyon surrounded by tall pine trees. It then drops down to Tesuque Creek and joins the Windsor Trail. You'll climb along the creek and then climb out of the Tesuque Creek drainage on the Borrego Trail to NM 475 and a quick 3 miles on the road back to the Chamisa trailhead. There are a few stiff climbs and enough technical sections to keep you on your toes and a few stream crossings to keep you honest. Watch out for traffic on NM 475 and always remember to yield to the uphill hiker or cyclist.

Pedal up the wide gravel road leading into a narrow canyon. Do not take the Chamisa Trail on the right marked by a sign. Where the canyon becomes narrow, the

Near the start of the Chamisa Trail

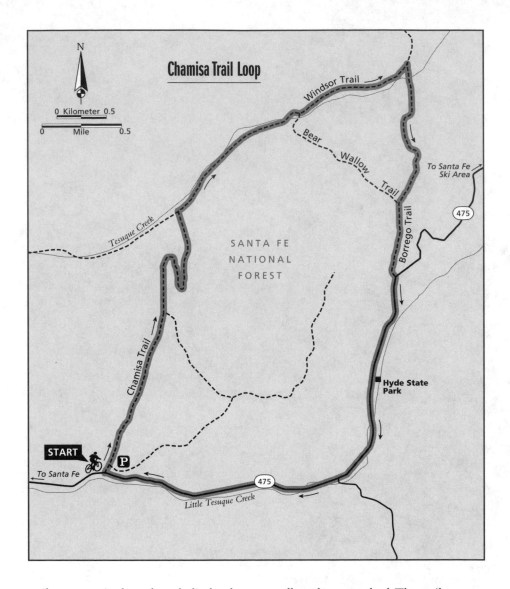

Chamisa Trail Loop

trail turns to singletrack and climbs along a small, rocky streambed. The trail crosses the streambed and reaches a short, steep pitch. Crank up this short section and climb up to another steep section with the streambed falling away to your right. At the 1 mile mark the trail veers to the right and away from the canyon bottom, climbing through the tall pines to a small ridge and four-way trail junction. Arrive at the four-way intersection at the 1.2-mile mark and continue straight and down tight single-track, making a tight left turn along a small drainage and picking up speed through the trees. There's great riding through this section, with a few rocky drop-offs to keep you on your toes. The trail enters into an open meadow at the 2.1-mile mark and soon reaches Tesuque Creek and a junction with the Windsor Trail. Turn right onto the Windsor Trail, pedal through the willows on a wide, hard-packed trail, and cross Tesuque Creek at the 2.8-mile mark. As the trail slices through the willows, it turns to tight singletrack, climbing up to a tight, narrow section. Crank through rocky singletrack on narrow tread with a drop-off to your right. Don't end up in the creek! At the 3.1-mile mark look right across the creek to Bear Wallow Trail. Continue straight up through a small, beautiful meadow on nice singletrack. Past the meadow the trail climbs on wide, rocky tread and soon

▶ Santa Fe is 7,000 feet above sea level and surrounded by the Jemez and Sangre de Cristo Mountains. The highest point near Santa Fe is Santa Fe Baldy, at 12,622 feet above sea level.

comes to a junction with the Borrego Trail on the right at the 4-mile mark. Cross Tesuque Creek via a log bridge and follow the Borrego Trail down and then up along a small drainage. At the 4.3-mile mark the trail cuts right up the first of several switchbacks through the tall pines. Crank hard and reach a small ridge at the top of the climb at the 4.8-mile mark. This is a nice spot to get some air back into those lungs. Then drop steeply down the somewhat rocky tread, making a few tight turns and passing the Bear Wallow Trail on the right. Past the Bear Wallow Trail, you begin one last climb past several log steps and reach NM 475 at the 5.6-mile mark. Turn right onto NM 475 and zoom down the paved road to the Chamisa trailhead and your car.

Miles and Directions

0.0 START from the trailhead and pedal up the wide gravel road into the canyon.

0.3 Trail turns to tight singletrack.

1.2 Reach a four-way intersection. Continue straight and down.

2.1 Reach an open meadow.

2.2 Arrive at Tesuque Creek and the junction with the Windsor Trail. Go right onto the Windsor Trail.

2.9 Narrow section with a steep drop-off to Tesuque Creek.

3.1 Bear Wallow Trail is on the right. Continue straight.

4.0 Turn right across Tesuque Creek and reach the Borrego Trail.

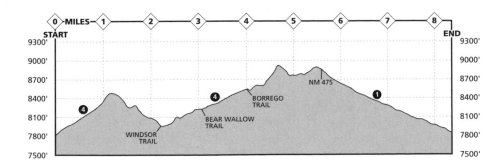

4.3 The first of several steep switchbacks.

4.8 The end of the switchbacks and nice downhill ahead.

5.2 Pass the Bear Wallow Trail on the right.

5.6 Arrive at NM 475. Go right and down the fast, paved road.

8.6 Arrive back at the parking area.

Ride Information

Local Information

Santa Fe Convention & Visitors Bureau, P.O. Box 909, Santa Fe, NM 87504-0909; (505) 984-6760 or (800) 777-2489; www.santafe.org.

Local Events and Attractions

Fourth of July Pancake Breakfast on the Plaza, The Plaza, downtown Santa Fe.

Accommodations

El Rey Inn, 1862 Cerrillos Road, Santa Fe; (505) 982-1931 or (800) 521-1349.

New Mexico Bed & Breakfast Association, P.O. Box 2925 Santa Fe; (505) 983-4554; www.nmhotels.com.

Restaurants

Blake's Lota Burger; great green-chile burgers, with various locations around Santa Fe.

Organizations

New Mexico Touring Society, P.O. Box 1261, Albuquerque, NM 87103; (505) 237-9700; www.swcp.com/~nmts.

27 Aspen Vista

Start: From the parking area at the Aspen Vista Picnic Area.

Distance: 12.1-mile out-and-back.

Approximate riding time: 2.0 to 3.5 hours.

Difficulty: Strenuous with a long climb up to Tesuque Peak.

Trail surface: Dirt road and doubletrack.

Lay of the land: A high-alpine ride up to the summit of Tesuque Peak (12,045 feet).

Other trail users: This trail is popular with hikers and runners.

Canine compatibility: Leave the pooch at home for this one.

Wheels: Front suspension will work just fine on this ride.

Land status: Santa Fe National Forest.

Nearest town: Santa Fe.

Fees and permits: No fees or permits required.

Schedule: Late May to late October.

Maps: USGS maps: Santa Fe County; Map of the Mountains of Santa Fe, Drake Mountain Maps 2001.

Trail contacts: Santa Fe National Forest, 1474 Rodeo Road, Santa Fe, NM 87501; (505) 438-7840; www.fs.fed.us/r3/sfe.

Finding the trailhead: From Santa Fe: From Saint Francis Drive and Paseo de Peralta in Santa Fe, go east on Paseo de Peralta to Washington Avenue. Go north (left) onto Washington Avenue for 0.1 mile to New Mexico Highway 475 (Hyde Park Road). Turn right onto NM 475 and travel 12.9 miles to the Aspen Vista Picnic Area on the right. The ride starts here. *DeLorme: New Mexico Atlas & Gazetteer:* Page 24, C-2.

The Ride

This ride holds a special place in my heart. Back in the early 1970s my wife, Laurel, and I would spend numerous hours taking trips up Aspen Vista Road to hike, ski tour, and snowshoe. Aspen Vista Road (Forest Road 150) starts at an elevation of 10,000 feet and climbs up through a large stand of beautiful aspen and pine trees to the summit of Tesuque Peak at a elevation of 12,045 feet. This is not a ride for the faint of heart, legs, or lungs. Summer is a wonderful time to ride Aspen Vista Road, as various wildflowers grow profusely along the several small streams and open meadows. Mid- and late summer bring violent afternoon thunderstorms, and it's best to plan to reach Tesuque Peak by noon. Fall, with the changing of the aspen trees, is an absolutely spectacular time to enjoy the foliage and stable weather. The views up to and once on Tesuque Peak are nothing short of spectacular and extend in all directions.

From the parking area ride past the large gate and begin climbing on a wide dirt road. The road drops to the south and then crosses the North Fork of Tesuque Creek at the 0.8-mile mark. Past the creek the road climbs steeply through an area of tall, stately aspen trees. Around the 1.8-mile mark you'll cross two small streams and enjoy an open view south to the Ortiz and Sandia Mountains and west to the Jemez Mountains. A large aspen forest extends east and south across the Santa Fe Mountains, a spectacular sight during the fall foliage. At the 2.6-mile mark cross a branch

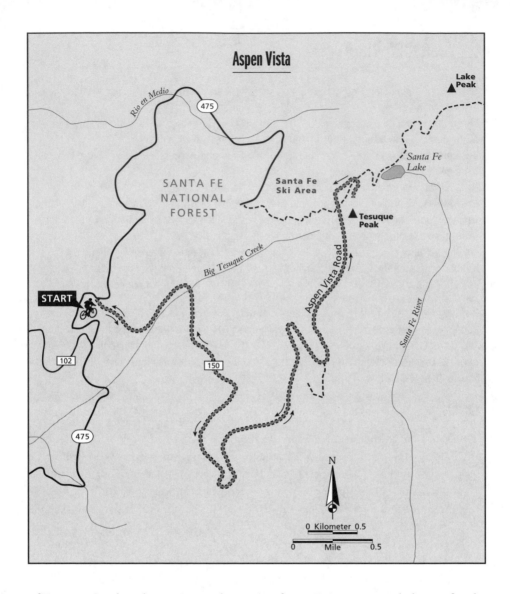

Aspen Vista

of Tesuque Creek and enter into a dense pine forest. Enjoy an extended run of mellow climbing through the trees. Around the 3.7-mile mark you reach a large open meadow with great views to the north and west. The road cuts steeply across the meadow and climbs through a rocky switchback. The air is getting thinner! Keep those legs pumping! The trail quickly reaches another steep switchback with a steep climb beyond that. Around the 5.4-mile mark the trail enters a high-alpine meadow with a good view to the Santa Fe Ski Area. The trail drops down a short pitch and then begins the final steep climb to the summit. Pass through a wooden fence and bear right up to the final summit switchback. Crank for all you're worth and reach

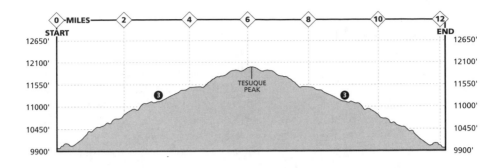

the radio towers and the summit of Tesuque Peak. Great views north to Lake Peak (12,409 feet) and Penitente Peak (12,249 feet), plus open views south, west, and east down to Santa Fe Lake await you. If the weather permits, take a break and enjoy the open views before retracing your route back to the parking area.

Miles and Directions

0.0 START from the parking area, ride past the gate, and begin climbing on FR 150.

0.8 Cross the North Fork of Tesuque Creek.

1.8 Cross two small streams.

2.6 Cross a branch of Tesuque Creek.

3.7 Reach a large open meadow.

5.4 Enter a high-alpine meadow.

5.6 Pass through a wooden fence line.

6.0 Reach the summit of Tesuque Peak.

12.1 Arrive back at the parking area.

Ride Information

Local Information

Santa Fe Convention and Visitors' Bureau, P.O. Box 909, Santa Fe, NM 87504-0909; (505) 984-6760 or (800) 777-2489; www.santafe.org.

Local Events and Attractions

Annual Plaza Arts & Crafts Festival, The Plaza, downtown Santa Fe; (505) 988-7621.

Accommodations:

Adobe Abode, 202 Chapelle, Santa Fe; (505) 983-3133; www.adobeabode.com.

Restaurants

Rancho de Chimayo, County Road 98, Chimayo; (505) 351-4444; great New Mexican cuisine in a lovely setting near the village of Chimayo.

28 Atalaya Mountain

Start: From the trailhead near the Ponderosa Estates.

Distance: 6-mile out-and-back.

Approximate riding time: 1.5 to 2.5 hours.

Difficulty: Strenuous with a major gain in elevation for such a short ride.

Trail surface: The majority of the ride is on narrow singletrack. There is a short section of dirt roads through Ponderosa Estates.

Lay of the land: Extreme technical riding through the rocky, piñon-studded foothills to the summit of Atalaya Mountain (9,121 feet).

Other trail users: Hikers and runners.

Canine compatibility: Leave the pooch at home for this one.

Wheels: Front suspension will work just fine on this ride.

Land status: Santa Fe National Forest and private.

Nearest town: Santa Fe.

Fees and permits: No fees or permits required.

Schedule: Late March to early November.

Maps: USGS maps: Santa Fe County; Map of the Mountains of Santa Fe, Drake Mountain Maps 2001.

Trail contacts: Santa Fe National Forest, 1474 Rodeo Road, Santa Fe, NM 87501; (505) 438-7840; www.fs.fed.us/r3/sfe.

Finding the trailhead: From Santa Fe: At the intersection of Cordova Road and St. Francis Drive, follow Cordova Road and cross Old Pecos Trail. Continue straight on Cordova Road for 1.5 miles. Cordova Road will change to Arenta Street and come to a three-way intersection. Turn left onto Camino Corrales and cross the Old Santa Fe Trail, bearing right onto Garcia Street. Follow Garcia Street to another three-way intersection. Turn right onto Camino del Monte Sol and make a quick left onto Camino de Cruz Blanca, passing St. Johns College on the right. In half a mile you'll reach a small parking area and an information kiosk. The ride starts here. *DeLorme: New Mexico Atlas & Gazetteer:* Page 24, D-1 to D-2.

The Ride

Don't even attempt this ride unless you are an expert cyclist with skills to handle extreme, rocky climbs and descents on narrow singletrack. The trail up to Atalaya Mountain gains a staggering 1,600 feet in 3 miles, and most of that comes in the final 2-mile grunt to the summit. The trail is extremely popular and can be quite crowded during weekends. There is the real danger of getting hurt on this ride, so use caution and don't hesitate to walk the tougher sections of the trail. The trail is best ridden during the early-morning or late-afternoon hours when foot traffic is low. Avoid the ride during the peak midday hours to ensure a more pleasant experience for other trail users and yourself. Show respect and always yield the right-of-way to the uphill hiker or cyclist.

One of the few smooth sections of the ride ▶

From the information board and parking spaces, follow the road past the pillars of Ponderosa Estates. Make the first left just past the pillars and climb up the road, passing several homes to a set of stairs. Dismount and carry your bike up the stairs and follow the nice singletrack into the piñons. The trail climbs gently up to a junction with Trail #174 on the right. Trail #174 cuts back west to St. Johns College. Continue straight up the wider trail into tall ponderosa trees. Don't let the riding through this section fool you: Things are about to get ugly real fast. At the 1.4-mile mark a private road comes in from the right and the trail curves left and begins a steep climb on loose, babyhead-size rocks. Relief arrives for the moment in a short downhill run as you come to a trail shooting sharply to the left.

▶ No fewer than twenty-four performing-arts groups call Santa Fe home. Quite impressive for a city of 65,000 residents.

Ignore that trail and continue straight to a fork in the trail at the 1.8-mile mark. Take the right fork and climb at a reasonable grade on smooth tread. Bear right at another fork at the 2.2-mile mark and then go straight at the 2.3-mile mark and the start of a series of steep, rocky switchbacks. Having fun yet? Just past the switchbacks at the 2.4-mile mark, two trails take a line across the steep hill. Take the lower trail and crank for all you're worth through a rocky section up to the summit ridge. Reach the ridge and sign for Trail #174. Take a breather; it's not over yet. Follow the rocky trail climbing along the ridgeline and through stands of beautiful ponderosa pine trees to the summit of Atalaya Mountain. Before you know it you are at the summit. Enjoy the spectacular views west to the Santa Fe and Jemez Mountains and north to Glorieta Baldy. For the descent retrace your route back to the information board and your car. Keep in mind that the trail down is just as hard, if not harder, than the ascent. Use caution on the steep sections and walk your bike to avoid any mishaps. Again, yield to uphill hikers and cyclists and don't cut any switchbacks.

When I lived in Santa Fe this used to be one of my favorite trail runs. I loved the solitude and the steep nature of the trail. I can tell you this much—the trail is much harder to bike than run.

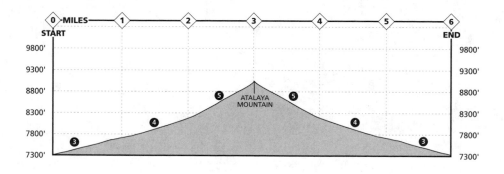

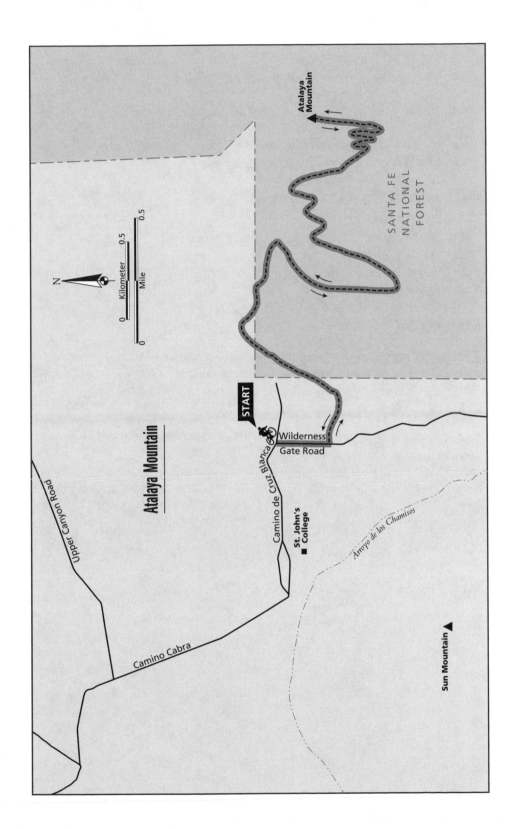

START

Atalaya Mountain

Atalaya
Mountain

SANTA FE
NATIONAL
FOREST

N

Kilometer
0   0.5

Mile
0   0.5

Upper Canyon Road

Camino Cabra

Camino de Cruz Blanca

St. John's
College

Wilderness
Gate Road

Arroyo de los Chamisos

Sun Mountain

Miles and Directions

0.0 START from the parking area, pedal through the pillars of the entrance of Ponderosa Estates, and make the first left.

0.4 Reach a set of stairs at a cul-de-sac. Climb the stairs and follow the singletrack trail into the woods.

0.6 Come to a junction with Trail #174 on the right. Continue straight.

1.4 Pass a private road on the right. The trail curves left.

1.7 The trail forks. Take the right fork.

1.8 The trail forks again. Follow the right fork.

2.3 The switchbacks begin.

2.4 Take the lower of the two trails that cut across the steep hillside.

2.6 Reach a sign and the summit ridgeline. Go left and up.

3.0 The summit of Atalaya Mountain.

6.0 Back at the parking area.

Ride Information

Local Information

Santa Fe Convention & Visitors Bureau, P.O. Box 909, Santa Fe, NM 87504-0909; (505) 984–6760 or (800) 777-2489; www.santafe.org.

Local Events and Attractions

Rodeo de Santa Fe, 3237 Rodeo Road, Santa Fe; (505) 471-4300; if you think mountain biking is tough, watch these guys ride the bulls.

Restaurants

Tomasita's Café, 500 South Guadalupe Street, Santa Fe; (505) 983-5721; great northern New Mexican food. Back in the mid-1970s Tomasita's was a little, funky place off Agua Fria where we used to bring our own beer. Things change!

Organizations

New Mexico Touring Society, P.O. Box 1261, Albuquerque, NM 87103; (505) 237-9700; www.swcp.com/~nmts.

29 Glorieta Mesa

Start: At the boundary of Santa Fe National Forest on Glorieta Mesa.

Distance: 10-mile out-and-back.

Approximate riding time: 1 to 2 hours.

Difficulty: Easy with a few gradual climbs and big views.

Trail surface: Mostly doubletrack trails and dirt roads.

Lay of the land: Through the gentle rolling hills northeast of Santa Fe on Glorieta Mesa.

Other trail users: Popular with bovines, wood-cutters, and four-wheel-drive traffic.

Canine compatibility: Leave the pooch at home.

Wheels: Front suspension will work just fine.

Land status: Santa Fe National Forest.

Nearest town: Pecos.

Fees and permits: No fees or permits required .

Schedule: Can be ridden year-round.

Maps: USGS maps: Santa Fe County.

Trail contacts: Santa Fe National Forest, 1474 Rodeo Road, Santa Fe, NM 87501; (505) 438-7840; www.fs.fed.us/r3/sfe.

Finding the trailhead: From Santa Fe: Travel southeast on Interstate 25 to exit 290 and U.S. Highway 285. Go left from the exit onto Frontage Road to County Road 51. Turn right onto CR 51 and travel 3.7 miles to Forest Road 326. Go left onto FR 326 for a little over a mile to the boundary of the SANTA FE NATIONAL FOREST sign at a fence line. The ride starts here. *DeLorme: New Mexico Atlas & Gazetteer:* Page 24, E-2.

The Ride

Sometimes it's just nice to take your mountain bike, jump on a nice dirt road, and be able to spin in your middle or big chain ring and crank like the devil. Glorieta Mesa is just that place. The wide-open vistas, smooth dirt roads, and beautiful riding through a high-desert environment make this a great choice for cyclists of all abilities. Novice cyclists will enjoy the nontechnical nature of the mesa while the more-advanced cyclists will enjoy the opportunity to really crank on the miles in an area that stays free of snow for most of the winter months.

From the parking area follow FR 326 north, climbing up a gradual hill. Reach the top of the hill and drop down into an open meadow and reach a road on the right at the 0.7-mile mark. Continue straight and climb up the mild hill to the top and open views extending south. From the top of the hill the road rolls down an open, flat area and passes a road on the right at the 2.8-mile mark. Continue straight as the road contours around a small drainage to the right. Continue straight into a wide-open area and arrive at Forest Road 612 at the 4.2-mile mark. Turn left onto FR 612 and climb up a short-lived rocky hill. Drop down into a narrow canyon and reach the turnaround point. This is a good spot to enjoy expansive views north to the high peaks of the Pecos Wilderness and east to the high plains. For the return trip just retrace your path back to the boundary of Santa Fe National Forest and your car.

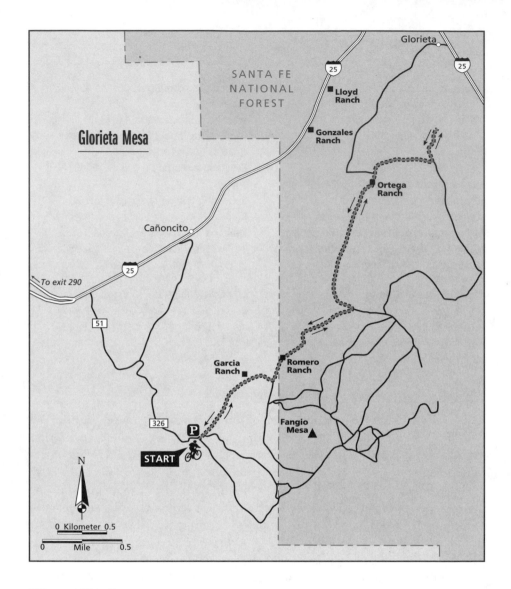

Miles and Directions

0.0 START from the fence line and boundary sign of Santa Fe National Forest and follow FR 326 north into the high plains.

0.4 Reach the top of the hill.

0.7 Reach a road junction. Continue straight.

2.8 Reach a road junction. Continue straight.

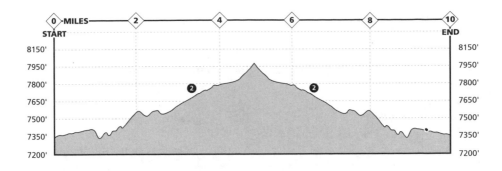

4.2 Arrive at a junction with FR 612. Go left onto FR 612 to the boundary of Santa Fe National Forest. **Option:** For those looking to add a few more miles to the ride, you can continue south on FR 326 past the junction with FR 612 for 2.8 miles to a three-way intersection. Turn around from this point and you've added 5.6 more miles to your ride.

5.0 Reach the edge of the Mesa and the turnaround point.

5.8 Turn right onto FR 326.

10.0 Arrive back at your car.

Ride Information

Local Information
Sante Fe Convention & Visitors Bureau, P.O. Box 909, Santa Fe, NM 87504-0909; (505) 984-6760 or (800) 777-2489; www.santafe.org.

Local Events and Attractions
Santa Fe Convention & Visitors Bureau, P.O. Box 909, Santa Fe, NM 87504-0909; (505) 984-6760 or (800) 777-2489; www.santafe.org.
Museum of Fine Arts, 107 West Palace, Santa Fe; (505) 476-5072; a must-stop on the Santa Fe museum tour. Admission is $5.00 for adults.

Accommodations
El Farolito B&B, 514 Galisteo Street, Santa Fe; (505) 988-4589 or (888) 634-8472.

Restaurants
Old Mexico Grill, 2434 Cerrillos Road, Santa Fe; (505) 473 0338; enjoy authentic cuisine from Mexico. Great food at a reasonable price.

Mountain Bike Tours
Sun Mountain Bike Company, 107 South Washington Avenue, Santa Fe; (505) 820-2902; bike rentals and mountain bike tours.

30 Glorieta Baldy

Start: From the ski and bike shop at Glorieta Baptist Center.
Distance: 21.1-mile loop.
Approximate riding time: 3 to 5 hours.
Difficulty: Strenuous with a big climb up to Glorieta Baldy.
Trail surface: Paved roads, gravel roads, singletrack and doubletrack trails.
Lay of the land: The ride climbs up through La Cueva Canyon to the 10,199-foot summit of Glorieta Baldy.
Other trail users: The trail down from the summit is popular with hikers.
Canine compatibility: Leave the pooch at home for this one.
Wheels: Front suspension will work just fine on this ride.

Land status: Santa Fe National Forest and private.
Nearest town: Pecos.
Fees and permits: No fees or permits required.
Schedule: Dawn to dusk, late April to late October.
Maps: USGS maps: Santa Fe County; Map of the Mountains of Santa Fe, Drake Mountain Maps 2001.
Trail contacts: Southwest Regional Office of the Forest Service, 517 Gold Avenue, Albuquerque, NM 87102; (505) 842–3800; www.fs.fed.us/r3.
Santa Fe National Forest, 1474 Rodeo Road, Santa Fe, NM 87501; (505) 438–7840; www.fs.fed.us/r3/sfe.

Finding the trailhead: From Santa Fe: Travel southeast on Interstate 25 to exit 299. Go left over the interstate and make another left, following the signs for Glorieta Baptist Center. Travel past the entrance (let them know your plans), turn right, and drive 1.2 miles to the trailhead and parking at the ski and bike shop. The ride starts here. *DeLorme: New Mexico Atlas & Gazetteer:* Page 24, D-2.

The Ride

This is a big ride with a long and arduous uphill grunt to the top of Glorieta Baldy, 10,199 feet above sea level. The ride starts in Glorieta Baptist Center and cruises down New Mexico Highway 50 for a few miles to County Road 63A (Forest road 375). Remember that the center is private property and please respect all rules while on their grounds. The ride then travels up La Cueva Canyon on FR 375 through the small village of La Cueva and makes a wide loop to the summit of Glorieta Baldy. The final 2 miles to the summit are steep and rocky. The altitude doesn't help things, as the thin air and rocky tread will turn the final half mile to the summit into a push-a-bike for most cyclists. This is a big uphill climb for just 5 miles of downhill singletrack, but you get 5 miles of exceptional singletrack! The downhill takes a steep and technical line down from the summit into Ruiz Canyon on tight singletrack through dense pine forest. The trail loses more than 2,100 feet from the summit back to the conference center. Quite the drop! The ride up is quite enjoyable for most of the climb and offers good views to the south and west. FR 375 for the

The fire tower on the summit of Glorieta Baldy

most part is fairly smooth and free of rocks. The last 2 miles to the summit are rocky and somewhat rutted.

From the ski and bike shop, head back out toward the entrance and NM 50. Turn left onto NM 50 and enjoy a nice downgrade to CR 63A at the 3.7-mile mark. Turn left onto CR 63A and begin the climb up La Cueva Canyon. Pass by a number of interesting rock cairns and climb up a short hill that ends at a cattle guard. The trail crosses the cattle guard and drops quickly to the small, quaint village of La Cueva, with great views to the north and west. You'll pass another cattle guard at the 7-mile mark and begin to climb through a forest of ponderosa pines. At the 8.9-mile mark an old forest road shoots in from the right. Continue straight and climb steeply up through a cut area. Enjoy a short downhill run as the road curves to the left and begins to climb away from La Cueva Canyon and into the tall pines. At the 10.9-mile mark a road goes right into Alamitos Canyon. Continue straight and reach another old road on the right. Continue straight on FR 375 and reach an open meadow with a road on the right leading into it at the 12.2-mile mark. This is a good spot to take a break before the next 2 miles of steep climbing. Continue straight, crossing La Cueva Creek and traveling up a steep, rocky section that cuts through a dense pine forest. Things are about to get ugly. Pass a memorial on the left and try to keep those legs pumping. The grade becomes steeper and the tread

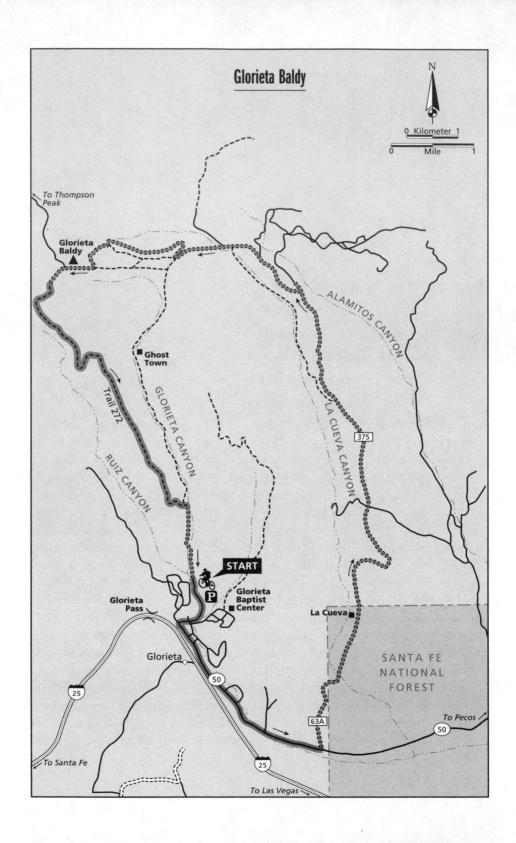

A memorial shrine along the Glorieta Baldy trail

becomes rockier up through this narrow canyon. At the 14.1-mile mark pedal up through steep switchbacks and past a singletrack on the left that leads down into Glorieta Canyon. The road cuts through a small, open meadow filled with tall aspen trees, and the final grunt to the summit begins. Reach a gate, bathrooms, and a picnic area at the 15.4-mile mark. Pedal around the gate and crank up the short hill to the summit and the old lookout tower. Finally, you are at the summit and the end of the climbing. Reward yourself—take a rest and enjoy the views that extend in all directions. Some folks climb the old lookout tower but by the looks of it, I wouldn't recommend it. Time to get ready for the downhill.

Take the obvious trail down to just past the kiosk and make a left onto Trail 272. The trail on the right leads to Thompson Peak. The trail drops steeply on tight singletrack and soon becomes extremely steep and rutted. If you value your life, walk this section. At the 16.5-mile mark the fun begins. Enjoy sweet singletrack that cuts through a beautiful lodgepole-pine forest. The trail becomes wide and extremely fast. Numerous quartz rocks litter the trail and riding is almost too much fun. At the 19.1-mile mark the trail forks. Take either fork and drop down a steep, rocky hill on narrow singletrack. At the 19.7-mile mark the trail forks again. Bear right and you'll soon pass a trail marked by a sign on the left that leads to Broken Arrow Lookout. Use caution here, as the trail becomes steep, loose, and rocky. At the 20.4-mile mark the trail cuts through a boulder field and a short section of slickrock. A great spot to play! Past the slickrock the trail reaches a gate. Continue straight through the gate and then cut left up through the rocks at a sign. The trail then drops steeply on cool riding into Glorieta Canyon. Go right and pass through the RV park. Arrive back at the trailhead and your car. What a great ride!

After your ride if you still have the time and energy, make a little side trip and travel 7 miles down NM 50 to the village of Pecos. This quaint little town is well off the beaten track and is home to Pecos Pueblo, located 2 miles south of town off New Mexico Highway 63. Pecos Pueblo, part of Pecos National Historical Park, contains the ruins of a fifteenth-century pueblo and two missions built in the seventeenth and eighteenth centuries. The pueblo at one time had 660 rooms and several kivas. It was home to more than 2,000 Native Americans who farmed the fields and hunted for game in the surrounding hills. War, sickness, and natural disasters took a huge toll, and by the early 1800s only a handful of Native Americans remained at the pueblo. By 1840 only twenty Pecos families remained at the pueblo, and they eventually moved west to Jemez Pueblo and lived with family there.

Pecos National Historical Park is open daily Memorial Day to Labor Day from 8:00 A.M. to 6:00 P.M., the rest of the year from 8:00 A.M. to 5:00 P.M., and closed December 25 and January 1. Admission is $3.00 per person.

Miles and Directions

0.0   START at the entrance and NM 50.

1.2   Go left onto NM 50 and cruise down the paved highway. Watch out for car traffic.

3.7   Go left onto CR 63A.

4.4   Cruise past the rock cairns and climb a hill.

5.4   Reach a cattle guard and drop down to La Cueva.

8.9   A road goes right. Continue straight.

9.6   Steep climbing through a cut area.

10.4   A short downhill run.

10.9   A road goes right into Alamitos Canyon. Continue straight.

11.8   An old logging road goes right. Continue straight.

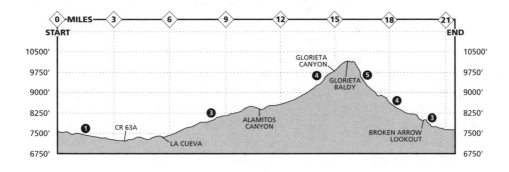

12.2 Arrive at an open meadow with a road entering on the right. Continue straight and begin to climb.

12.8 Climb a steep, rocky hill with a drainage on the left.

14.1 The first of three steep switchbacks.

15.0 A singletrack trail on the left leads into Glorieta Canyon. Continue straight and up.

15.4 Reach a gate, picnic area, and bathrooms.

15.5 Reach the lookout tower and summit of Glorieta Baldy.

15.6 Reach a junction with the Thompson Peak Trail on the right. Go left on TR #272. Things begin to heat up.

16.3 The switchbacks are steep, rocky, and loose. Walk this section if you want to live.

16.5 The fun begins. Cross a small drainage and travel through a lodgepole-pine forest on tight singletrack.

18.2 Smooth sailing on level treads.

19.2 The trail drops down a steep, loose, rocky section.

19.7 Keep to the right.

19.8 Pass a sign and trail on the left leading to Broken Arrow Lookout.

19.9 Pedal through an extremely rocky section. Use caution.

20.4 Slickrock.

20.5 Pedal past the gate.

20.6 Turn left at the sign.

20.8 Go right past the gate and through the RV park.

21.1 Back at the trailhead and your car.

Ride Information

Local Information

Santa Fe Convention & Visitors Bureau, P.O. Box 909, Santa Fe, NM 87504-0909; (505) 984-6760 or (800) 777-2489; www.santafe.org.

Local Events and Attractions

Pecos National Historical Park, NM 63, Pecos.

Restaurants

Santa Fe Baking Co. and Cafe, 504 West Cordova Road, Santa Fe; (505) 988-4292; for a big ride like this, you need good coffee and baked goods—this is the spot!

Mountain Bike Tours

New Mexico Mountain Bike Tours, 49 Main Street, Cerrillos; (505) 474-0074.

Organizations

New Mexico Touring Society, P.O. Box 1261, Albuquerque, NM 87103; (505) 237-9700; www.swcp.com/~nmts.

31 Arroyo de los Chamisos Trail

Start: From the trailhead at the intersection of Saint Frances Drive and Zia Road.
Distance: 7.4-mile out-and-back.
Approximate riding time: 30 minutes to 1 hour.
Difficulty: Easy.
Trail surface: Paved path.
Lay of the land: The path follows along Arroyo de los Chamisos, a major drainage system in the southeast part of town.
Other trail users: The trail is popular with walkers and runners.

Canine compatibility: Leave the pooch at home for this one.
Wheels: Front suspension will work just fine on this ride.
Land status: City of Santa Fe.
Nearest town: Santa Fe.
Fees and permits: No fees or permits required.
Schedule: Dawn to dusk, March to November.
Maps: USGS maps: Santa Fe County.
Trail contacts: Santa Fe National Forest, 1474 Rodeo Road, Santa Fe, NM 87501; (505) 438–7840; www.fs.fed.us/r3/sfe.

Finding the trailhead: From Santa Fe: From the intersection of Saint Francis Drive and Cerrillos Road, travel south on Saint Francis Drive for 2.2 miles to Zia Road. Turn right onto Zia Road, cross the railroad tracks, and make a quick right into a large parking area and the trailhead. *DeLorme: New Mexico Atlas & Gazetteer: Page 24, D-1.*

The Ride

The Arroyo de los Chamisos Trail is a nice little outing on a smooth paved surface that follows the arroyo of the same name south for 3.7 miles. This is a great ride for novice cyclists and for those who want to jump on the mountain bike during the winter months when most of the bike trails are snowed in. The trail is popular with walkers and runners and sees a lot of foot traffic during the weekend days. Keep your speed in check and always show courtesy to other users.

From the parking area follow the paved path across the railroad tracks and then turn left. The path crosses a footbridge and then takes a gentle grade to Siringo Road. At Siringo Road the path crosses the tracks and then goes left and down toward Arroyo de los Chamisos. The path goes through two tunnels and soon reaches Yucca Street at the 1.4–mile mark. Cross Yucca Street (with caution) and make a quick sprint up to Camino Carlos Rey, again crossing with caution. Another short sprint brings you to Avenida de los Campanas and a small park on the other side of the road. There is a small kiosk beside the path that offers some information about the area and path. The path travels over a second footbridge and the arroyo is now on your left. Enjoy more than a mile of nice cruising along the arroyo, which brings you to Rodeo Road, a Sam's Club on the left, and the turnaround point of the ride. Take a short break and then retrace your route back to the trailhead and your car.

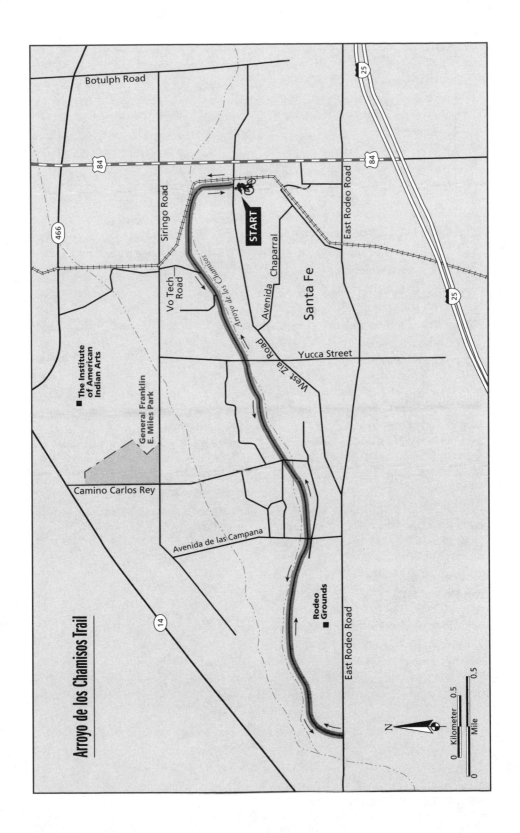

Arroyo de los Chamisos Trail

Botulph Road

84

466

84

25

Siringo Road

Vo Tech Road

Arroyo de los Chamisos

START

Avenida Chaparral

East Rodeo Road

Santa Fe

West Zia Road

Yucca Street

25

The Institute
of American
Indian Arts

General Franklin
E. Miles Park

Camino Carlos Rey

Avenida de las Campana

14

Rodeo
Grounds

East Rodeo Road

N

0   Kilometer   0.5

0   Mile   0.5

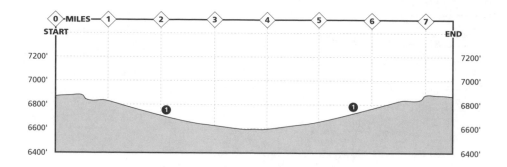

Miles and Directions

0.0 START from the parking area, cross the railroads tracks, and follow the paved path south.

0.2 Cross a wooden footbridge.

1.4 With caution, cross Yucca Street.

2.0 With caution, cross Camino Carlos Rey.

2.4 With caution, cross Avenida de las Campana.

3.7 Arrive at Rodeo Road and the turnaround point.

7.4 Cruise into the parking area.

Ride Information

Local Information
Santa Fe Convention & Visitors Bureau, P.O. Box 909, Santa Fe, NM 87504-0909; (505) 984-6760 or (800) 777-2489; www.santafe.org.

Local Events and Attractions
Cristo Rey, Upper Canyon Road, Santa Fe; (505) 983-8528; a beautiful church in classic adobe style.

Accommodations
Best Western Santa Fe, 3650 Cerrillos Road, Santa Fe; (505) 438-3795 or (800) 528-1234; clean and simple.

Restaurants
Tortilla Flats, 3139 Cerrillos Road, Santa Fe; (505) 471-8685; one of my favorite restaurants, with great green chile.

Mountain Bike Tours
New Mexico Mountain Bike Tours, 49 Main Street, Cerrillos; (505) 474-0074.

32 Los Cerrillos to Waldo

Start: From the village of Los Cerrillos.

Distance: 13.6-mile out-and-back.

Approximate riding time: 1 to 2 hours.

Difficulty: Easy with a few gradual climbs and wonderful views.

Trail surface: Dirt road.

Lay of the land: Through the gentle rolling hills just south of Santa Fe near the small village of Los Cerrillos.

Other trail users: Motorists.

Canine compatibility: Leave the pooch at home.

Wheels: Front suspension will work just fine.

Land status: Santa Fe County.

Nearest town: Los Cerrillos.

Fees and permits: No fees or permits required.

Schedule: Can be ridden year-round.

Maps: USGS maps: Santa Fe County.

Trail contacts: New Mexico Mountain Bike Adventure, P.O. Box 447, Los Cerrillos, NM 87010; (505) 474-0014.

Finding the trailhead: From Santa Fe: Travel south on Cerrillos Road to New Mexico Highway 14. Follow NM 14 south for 19 miles to the village of Los Cerrillos. Turn right off of NM 14 and then make a right at the only stop sign in town. Park near the railroad tracks. The ride starts here. *DeLorme: New Mexico Atlas & Gazetteer:* Page 23, F-10.

The Ride

This gem of a ride takes you from the small, quaint village of Los Cerrillos along Galisteo Creek, past the old railroad station of Waldo, up through Waldo Canyon, and ends just before reaching Interstate 25. The route travels along County Road 57, which is a maintained dirt road. The town of Cerrillos was once the site of several mines that were rich in turquoise and lead deposits. Native Americans mined the area for turquoise centuries before the town was settled and continued to do so until the white miners took over in the 1800s. Los Cerrillos as a town reached its peak in the 1800s and supported twenty-one saloons and four hotels. Things have settled down since then and the town, with its old adobe church, dirt streets, quaint little adobe houses, and nice little shops, is a wonderful place to hang out after your ride.

To start the ride cross the railroad tracks and turn left onto County Road 57. Cross a cattle guard and begin to climb up to the Devils Throne on the left at the 0.7-mile mark. The Devils Throne is a large lava flow, one of the many that are fairly common in the Cerrillos Hills. At the 1-mile mark reach the top of the hill and then drop down, crossing a cattle guard. Look to the left at the 1.9-mile mark for some cottonwood trees and a few old cement foundations, remnants of all that's left of Waldo. The road parallels Galisteo Creek, and a few coke ovens can be seen on the

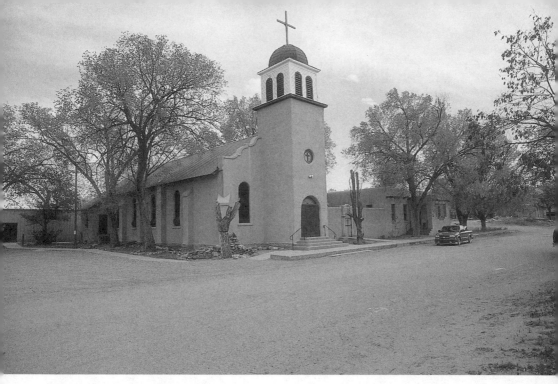

The church in Los Cerrillos

left. The coke ovens were built sometime in the 1920s and were used to produce smelting coke. The road pulls away from the railroad tracks and Galisteo Creek and rolls through the Los Cerrillos Hills with a great view south to the Ortiz Mountains. Cross a cattle guard at the 4.1-mile mark and begin a long gradual climb toward the interstate. At the 6-mile mark climb a steep hill and then reach an intersection with a stop sign. This is the turnaround point. Retrace the route back to Cerrillos.

For a great driving tour, follow NM 14 (Turquoise Trail) south through the old mining towns of Madrid and Golden and then on to Sandia Park, Cedar Crest, and Tijeras. The road travels through the piñon-covered foothills of the Ortiz Mountains and is a designated Scenic and Historical Byway. For more information on the Turquoise Trail, log on to www.turquoisetrail.org or call (888) 263–0003. For an added plus, most of the galleries along NM 14 are open on the first Saturday of each month.

Miles and Directions

0.0   START at the railroad tracks. Cross the tracks and turn left, following CR 57.

0.7   Devils Throne.

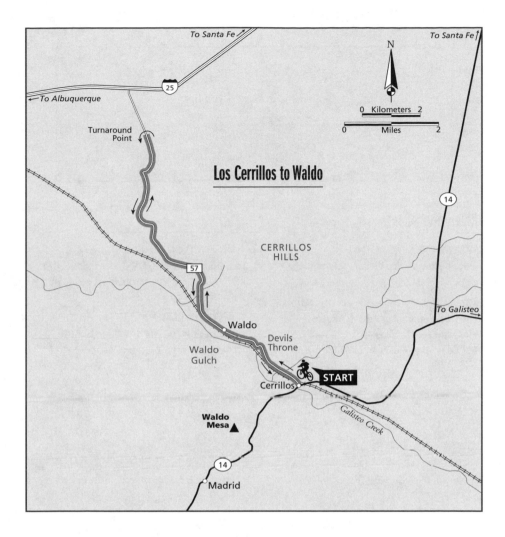

Los Cerrillos to Waldo

1.0 Top of the hill

1.9 The old site of Waldo on the left.

2.6 The road begins to pull away from Galisteo Creek and the railroad tracks.

4.1 Reach a cattle guard.

6.0 Climb a steep hill.

6.8 Reach an intersection at a stop sign. The turnaround point.

13.6 Back in Cerrillos.

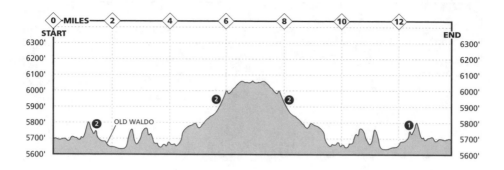

Ride Information

Local Information
Madrid New Mexico Visitors Information,
www.mad-rid.com.

Local Events and Attractions
**Casa Grande Trading Post & Turquoise
Museum,** Los Cerrillos.
Old Coal Mine Museum, Madrid; (505)
438–3780.

Accommodations
Java Junction B & B, NM 14, Madrid; (505)
438–2772; my pick for the best coffee in this
neck of the woods.

Restaurants
Back Road Pizza, NM 14, Madrid; (505)
474–5555; great pizza and beer.

Albuquerque Area

New Mexico's largest city with a population of 700,000, Albuquerque is situated in a fertile river valley almost dead center in the middle of the state. The Rio Grande slowly flows through Albuquerque, giving a constant source of water and bringing life to a vast area of Upper Sonoran Desert. The original site of downtown Albuquerque was an Indian pueblo that was settled sometime in the early 1300s. Evidence of early human inhabitants reaches far back to a limestone cave on the north side of the Sandia Mountains. In 1934 a few simple spear points and a sloth's claw were found inside, giving proof that humans hunted saber-toothed tigers and elephants in the area almost 27,000 years ago. The cave was used as shelter for the nomadic hunters who more than likely followed the path of game to survive.

Francisco Vasquez de Coronado, with his expedition on its fabled search for the lost cities of gold, in 1540 came upon Pueblo people living in simple stone houses along the Rio Grande. These people were farmers, who worked the fertile soils along the river as their ancestors had for the previous 1,000 years. Thus started a hundred years of Spanish domination and mistreatment. The Pueblo people, peaceful by nature, revolted against the Spanish, with freedom coming after the bloody Pueblo Revolt of 1680. Freedom was short-lived for the Pueblo people as the Spanish regained control of the area in 1696. The town of Albuquerque was founded in 1706 by a number of Spanish families who were granted land by King Felipe V. The town's unusual name comes from Don Francisco Fernandez de la Cueva Enrique, Duke of Albuquerque and viceroy of Spain. The main plaza was built sometime in the late 1700s, and the town began to grow from this humble beginning.

Downtown Albuquerque is situated in a fertile river valley, and as you travel farther away from the river the environment is classic Upper Sonoran Desert. The Upper Sonoran life zone is filled with a variety of desert grasses; cacti; yucca; and piñon, juniper, and oak trees. Traveling toward the summit of Sandia Crest, you can pass through three other life zones (Transition, Canadian, and Hudsonian) and a variety of terrain. The Sandia Mountains border Albuquerque to the east and provide a beautiful backdrop and buffer zone to an ever-expanding city. A large section of the Sandia Mountains is designated "wilderness area," giving easy access to a beautiful wild area.

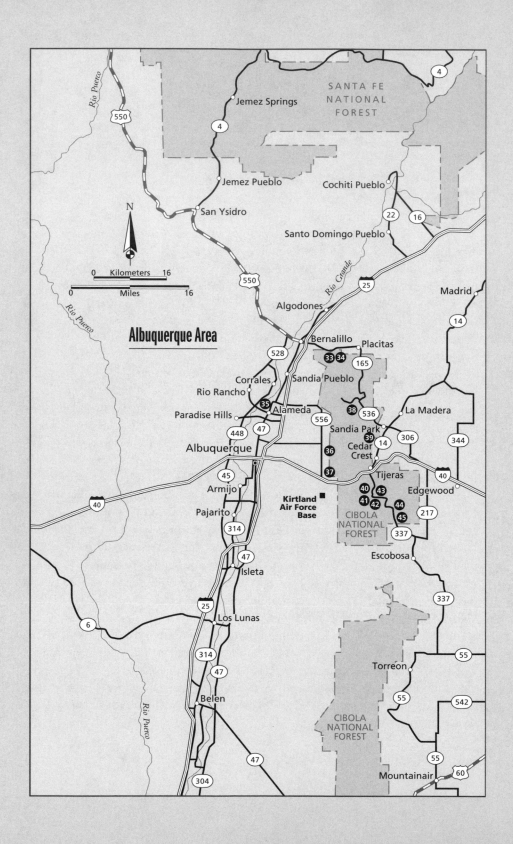

Albuquerque, like most of New Mexico, is blessed with an abundant amount of stable weather and sunshine. Rainfall comes in the summer during the thunderstorm season (July and August); summer can be quite warm. Fall brings cooler temperatures and stable conditions and is a wonderful time to ride in the mountains to view the changing of the aspens. Winters are mild and most snowfall happens above the 8,000-foot level. Spring brings warmer weather and some moisture. The high desert is absolutely beautiful during the spring months as many trees, flowers, and cacti begin to bloom, adding color and beauty to a seemingly stark environment.

The great thing for mountain bikers in the Albuquerque area is that you can ride year-round. Most of the low-lying trails (the Foothills Trails) stay dry for most of the winter. In the summer months the upper slopes of the Sandias are popular with mountain bikers and give cool relief from the hot and dry conditions at lower elevations. Some of the best singletrack in the state can be found in the Tijeras area. Miles and miles of beautiful singletrack surround the Cedro Peak area, giving cyclists in the Albuquerque area some of the most accessible and finest mountain biking in the Southwest.

Albuquerque is the financial and educational center of New Mexico. The University of New Mexico is located here, as are many high-tech companies. There is a major downtown rejuvenation in the works, and the future for Albuquerque as a major city looks bright. With a city the size of Albuquerque, you can find all the amenities and more. There is an active nightlife with many bars, clubs, and restaurants to choose from. Those who are so inclined can go to the theater, opera, ballet, or symphony. Museums abound and, as with the arts, are multicultural. Old Route 66 cuts through town and right through the University of New Mexico district, an area of hip cafes, restaurants, and shops. So if you are visiting the area on a mountain bike trip, check out the many activities this great city has to offer.

33 10K Trail

Start: From the fee station just off New Mexico Highway 165.
Distance: 5.9-mile loop.
Approximate riding time: 45 minutes to 1.5 hours.
Difficulty: Moderate.
Trail surface: Doubletrack and dirt roads.
Lay of the land: Located in the northern foothills 20 miles north of Albuquerque.
Other trail users: Motorists.
Canine compatibility: Bring the dog.

Wheels: Front suspension will work just fine on this ride.
Land status: Cibola National Forest.
Nearest town: Placitas.
Fees and permits: $2.00 fee required.
Schedule: Dawn to dusk.
Maps: USGS maps: Bernalillo County; Cibola National Forest.
Trail contacts: Cibola National Forest, Sandia Ranger District, Star Route Box 174, Tijeras, NM 87059; (505) 281-3304; www.fs.fed.us/r3/cibola.

Finding the trailhead: From Albuquerque: From the intersection of Interstate 25 and Interstate 40, travel 20 miles north on I-25 to exit 242. Travel east on NM 165 for 3 miles to the second entrance to Forest Road 442 on the right. Turn right onto FR 442 and pay the fee. Park at the first parking area on the left just after the fee station. The ride starts here. *DeLorme: New Mexico Atlas & Gazetteer:* Page 23, G-8.

The Ride

This is a great little ride on mostly smooth doubletrack roads in the northern foothills near the small town of Placitas. The ride follows FR 442 for the entire ride. There are excellent views to the Sandia Mountains and west to the Rio Grande Valley and beyond. The riding is quite pleasant, and the road makes a nice loop through stands of piñon and juniper trees. I like the ease of access from I–25 and that the trail stays free of snow for most of the winter. The trail borders the Sandia Wilderness Area and several trails shoot into (no bikes) this urban wilderness. You could easily turn this ride into a hike-a-bike by bringing some hiking shoes and a bike lock to secure your bike while hiking. I did this and followed the Piedra Lisa Trail at the 1.8-mile mark of the ride into the wilderness. It is about 4.5 miles to the Juan Tabo Picnic Area and 2.5 miles one way to Ricon Saddle. The trail dips in and out of two major valleys and offers great views and excellent hiking.

From the parking area head south (straight ahead) and begin a very gentle climb on the smooth doubletrack road. At the 0.8-mile mark pass the Stripmine Trail on the left and pedal up to a parking area on the left. The road forks at the 1.8-mile mark, where the Piedra Lisa Trail heads into the Sandia Wilderness Area and where bikes are not allowed. The trail contours through the hills and reaches the power lines at the 2.3-mile mark. Here the trail turns to the west with wide-open vistas to the north, south, and west. At the 3.2-mile mark the trail reaches a fence line with

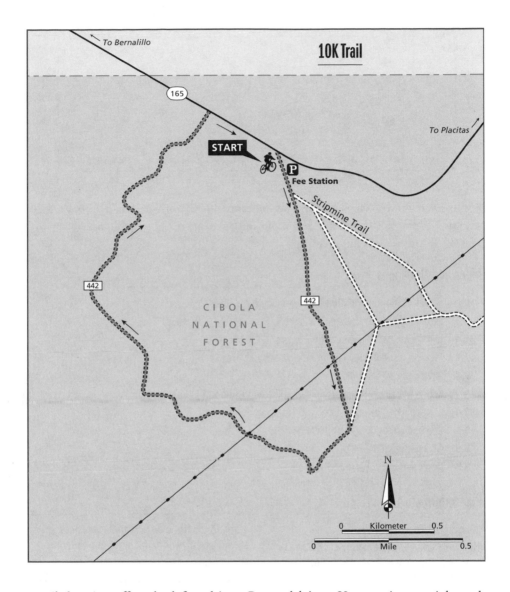

a trail shooting off to the left and into Canon del Agua. You continue straight and enjoy nice riding through stands of piñon and old-desert juniper trees. Numerous cacti line the road and desert flowers bloom in the spring and early summer months. The views to the west are open and are quite spectacular during evening sunsets.

Reach the west fee station on FR 442 and continue straight to NM 165. Turn right onto NM 165 (watch for car traffic) and pedal to the east entrance to FR 442. Turn right and pedal to the parking area and your car.

The village of Placitas has become a haven for artists in the last twenty years. Attracted by the beauty and solitude of the area, many craftspeople now call Placitas

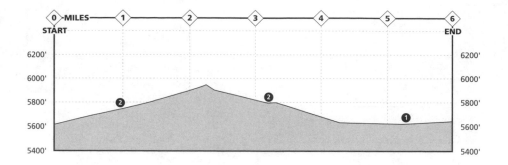

home. Each year on Mother's Day and sometime in November, the artists open their studios for free to the public. For more information on these events, contact the Placitas Chamber of Commerce.

Miles and Directions

0.0 START at the parking area and head south on FR 442.

0.8 Stripmine Trail on the left.

1.4 Large parking area on the left.

1.8 Piedra Lisa Trail goes left into the wilderness area.

2.3 Reach the power lines.

3.2 Fence line and road on the left leading into Canon del Agua.

5.4 Large parking area.

5.5 Fee station, trailhead, and NM 165.

5.8 Go right onto FR 442.

5.9 Back at the trailhead and your car.

Ride Information

Local Information

Placitas Chamber of Commerce, 46 Sandia Lane, Placitas, NM 87001; (505) 867-3011; www.placitaschamber.org.

Local Events and Attractions

Coronado State Monument, U.S. Highway 550 (PO 95), Bernalillo; (505) 867-5351; the big attraction is the old ruins that have been preserved at this wonderful state monument.

Restaurants

The Pinon Café, 221 NM 165, Placitas; (505) 711-1700; good food and close by.

34 Stripmine Trail

Start: From the fee station just off New Mexico Highway 165.
Distance: 5.2-mile out-and-back.
Approximate riding time: 45 minutes to 1.5 hours.
Difficulty: Moderate.
Trail surface: Singletrack and doubletrack trails.
Lay of the land: Located in the northern foothills 20 miles north of Albuquerque.
Other trail users: Motorists.
Canine compatibility: Bring the dog.
Wheels: Front suspension will work just fine on this ride.

Land status: Cibola National Forest.
Nearest town: Placitas.
Fees and permits: $2.00 fee required.
Schedule: Dawn to dusk.
Maps: USGS maps: Bernalillo County; Cibola National Forest.
Trail contacts: Southwest Regional Office of the Forest Service, 517 Gold Avenue, Albuquerque, NM 87102; (505) 842-3800; www.fs.fed.us/r3.
Cibola National Forest, Sandia Ranger District, Star Route Box 174, Tijeras, NM 87059; (505) 281-3304; www.fs.fed.us/r3/cibola.

Finding the trailhead: From Albuquerque: From the intersection of Interstate 25 and Interstate 40, travel 20 miles north on I-25 to exit 242. Travel east on NM 165 for 3 miles to the second entrance to Forest Road 442 on the right. Turn right onto FR 442 and pay the fee. Park at the first parking area on the left just after the fee station. The ride starts here. *DeLorme: New Mexico Atlas & Gazetteer:* Page 23, G-8.

The Ride

This is an excellent little excursion that uses a short section of FR. 442 to access the Stripmine Trail and some great singletrack riding. After doing the out-and-back Stripmine Trail, you can easily up the mileage of the ride by turning left onto FR 442 and doing the 10K Trail loop. This out-and-back ride cuts through the piñon-covered hills and then along a dry arroyo, hugging it before climbing into the red hills and the turnaround point. I like this ride for its easy access from I–25 and its close proximity to the 10K Trail.

No trip to this area would be complete without a stop at Coronado State Monument. The monument is located on the west bank of the Rio Grande just outside the town of Bernalillo. On his quest for the Seven Cities of Cibola, the Spanish explorer Coronado traveled through the area in the winter of 1540–1541 and discovered the abandoned ruins. Coronado stayed the winter, then moved on in search of wealth for the Spanish crown. The ruins have been excavated and hundreds of rooms, some covered with multicolored murals, have been discovered, leading to a major archaeological find along the Rio Grande. For more information on the monument, call (505) 867–5351. Admission is $3.00 for adults and free for children

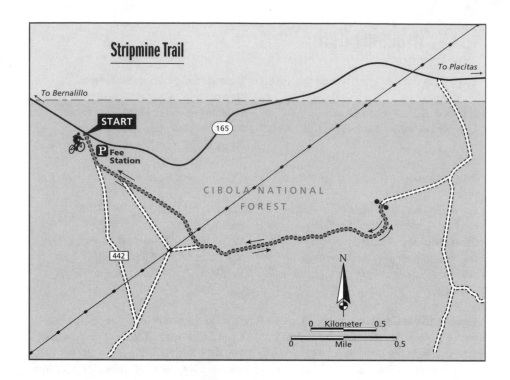

Stripmine Trail

To Placitas →

To Bernalillo ←

START

165

Fee Station

CIBOLA NATIONAL FOREST

442

N

0   Kilometer   0.5

0   Mile   0.5

younger than age 16. It is open daily from 8:00 A.M. to 5:00 P.M. and is closed Easter, Thanksgiving, Christmas, and New Year's Day.

From the parking area follow FR 442 to the south on a smooth dirt road. At the 0.8-mile mark turn left and pass through a fence line and the start of the Stripmine Trail. Drop down and pass a road on the right and enjoy somewhat rocky riding through the rounded, piñon-covered hills. At the 1.5-mile mark climb up a short, steep red hill and drop quickly to a narrow trail with a steep drop-off and arroyo on the left. Use caution here! The angle of the trail becomes steeper and the tread becomes rockier. At the 2.5-mile mark a singletrack trail shoots off to the left. Continue straight and pass some colorful, short cliffs on the right. You soon reach a fence line and the turnaround point at the 2.6-mile mark. A few options exist at this point. I prefer to retrace my route back down the Stripmine Trail and do the 10K Trail, but you can also continue straight past the gate, reach Forest Road 231, and turn left onto NM 165.

Miles and Directions

0.0 START from the parking area and head south on FR 442.

0.8 Turn left through the fence line onto the Stripmine Trail.

1.0 Road on the right. Continue straight.

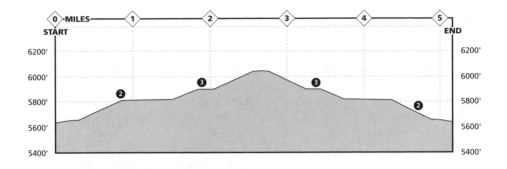

1.7 Use caution. Steep drop-off on the left.

2.5 Singletrack trail heads left. Continue straight.

2.6 Fence line and turnaround point.

5.2 Back at the parking area.

Ride Information

Local Information
Placitas Chamber of Commerce, 46 Sandia Lane, Placitas, NM 87001; (505) 867-3011; www.placitaschamber.org.

Local Events and Attractions
San Felipe Pueblo, P.O. Box 4339, San Felipe; (505) 867-3381; small and conservative, this pueblo is known for dancers. Well worth the visit.

Restaurants
The Merc Deli, 221 NM 165, Placitas; (505) 867-8661; if you're hungry for good deli food, this is the place in Placitas.

35 Corrales Bosque

Start: From the trailhead just off Alameda Boulevard.

Distance: 14.4-mile out-and-back.

Approximate riding time: 1 to 2 hours.

Difficulty: Easy with no hills.

Trail surface: Singletrack and doubletrack trail and short section of dirt roads.

Lay of the land: The trail follows the Rio Grande north and south and starts near the village of Alameda.

Other trail users: Hikers and runners use these trails. Show respect to other trail users.

Canine compatibility: Leave the dog at home for this ride.

Wheels: Front suspension will work just fine on this ride.

Land status: Rio Grande State Park, The Nature Conservancy, and Albuquerque Open Space.

Nearest town: Alameda.

Fees and permits: No fees or permits required.

Schedule: Dawn to dusk, year-round.

Maps: Albuquerque Open Space/River Trail.

Trail contacts: Albuquerque Open Space Division, P.O. Box 1293, Albuquerque, NM 87103; (505) 873-6620.
Two Wheel Drive, 1706 Central Avenue Southeast, Albuquerque, NM 87106; (505) 243-8443.

Finding the trailhead: From Albuquerque: Travel north on Interstate 25 to exit 233. Turn left onto Alameda Boulevard and travel 3.6 miles to a parking area on the left marked Alameda/Rio Grande Open Space. The ride starts from the parking area. *DeLorme: New Mexico Atlas & Gazetteer:* Page 23, H-6.

The Ride

This is a beautiful ride along the Rio Grande through a "bosque," a cottonwood-covered river bottom filled with water-loving plants and animals. The trail winds through partially wooded areas to open sand flats alongside the Rio Grande and is a wet oasis surrounded by dry desert. Along with stately cottonwood trees, the wet areas along the river are filled with willows, box elders, various shrubs, tall prairie grasses, and beautiful wildflowers during the late spring and early summer months. There are great views east to the Sandia Mountains and west to the high mesas surrounding Albuquerque. The riding is quite pleasant and never really technical, and it should be taken at a leisurely pace so as to enjoy the peaceful surroundings that the bosque offers. This is also a great ride in the winter and offers a great opportunity to get out in the middle of winter and put some miles on those winter legs.

From the parking area go right on a paved path under Alameda Boulevard. Follow the trail across a ditch via a small bridge. The trail goes over the Rio Grande via a large bridge and then goes right and passes through a red gate to reach the ditch road. At the 0.4-mile mark turn right onto a singletrack trail. Ignore a trail on the right at the 0.7-mile mark and continue straight to a ramp at the 1-mile mark. Turn right and take the first trail on the left. The trail goes over a ramp and follows the ditch for a short

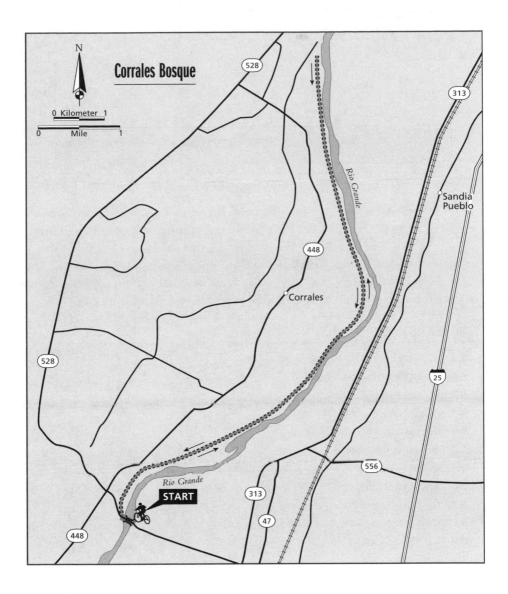

section before leading back into the bosque. Enjoy pleasant riding through the tall cottonwood trees before reaching a ramp at the 3.6-mile mark. Bear right at the ramp and pass through the first of several metal gates in the next mile. Around the 4.8-mile mark pass through the last gate and look to the right for access to the river and a nice beach. This is a great spot to take a short break and enjoy the views east to the Sandia Mountains. Around the 6.9-mile mark reach a ramp and turn right toward the river. The trail stays close to the river and then veers toward the ditch. Reach a flood-control channel and the turnaround point. Follow your route back to the parking area and the end of a wonderful ride in a unique river environment.

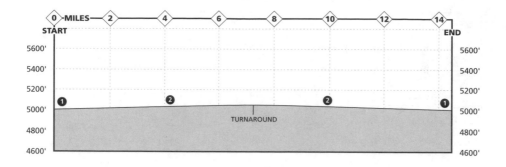

During the fall and winter months, sandhill cranes, Canada geese, and various species of ducks take advantage of this peaceful stopover on their way south to Mexico and beyond. The birds follow the river south, and it's one of the major flyways for migratory birds in the west. Waterfowl are not the only animals that call this beautiful area home. Keep your eyes open and stay alert and you may catch a glimpse of a passing coyote, a fox, a rabbit, various songbirds, and maybe even a beaver!

Miles and Directions

0.0   START by turning right out of the parking area.

0.1   Follow the trail across a bridge.

0.3   Go right through the gate.

0.4   Go right onto a singletrack trail.

0.7   Continue straight.

1.0   Go right at the ramp.

1.4   Ride over a ramp.

3.6   Bear right at the ramp.

3.7   The first of several metal gates.

4.9   River access and an inviting beach.

6.9   Turn right just after a ramp.

7.2   Turnaround point.

14.4   Back at the parking area.

Ride Information

Local Information
Albuquerque Convention & Visitors Bureau, P.O. Box 26866, 401 Second Street Northwest, Albuquerque, NM 87125; (505) 842-9918 or (800) 284-2282; www.abqcvb.org.

Organizations
New Mexico Touring Society, P.O. Box 1261, Albuquerque, NM 87103; (505) 237-9700; www.swcp.com/-russells/nmts.

36 North Foothills Trails

Start: From the Embudito trailhead.
Distance: 9.7-mile loop.
Approximate riding time: 1 to 2 hours.
Difficulty: Moderate with a couple of short, steep climbs.
Trail surface: Doubletrack and singletrack trails.
Lay of the land: Beautiful riding on excellent trails in the foothills of the Sandia Mountains.
Other trail users: This trail is popular with hikers and other trail users.
Canine compatibility: The trail can be crowded, so leave the pooch at home.

Wheels: Front suspension will work just fine on this ride.
Land status: Albuquerque Open Space.
Nearest town: Albuquerque.
Fees and permits: No fees or permits required.
Schedule: Dawn to dusk, year-round.
Maps: Albuquerque Open Space/North Foothills Trails.
Trail contacts: Albuquerque Open Space Division, P.O. Box 1293, Albuquerque, NM 87103; (505) 873-6620.
Two Wheel Drive, 1706 Central Avenue Southeast, Albuquerque, NM 87106; (505) 243-8443.

Finding the trailhead: From Albuquerque: From the junction of Interstate 40 and Interstate 25 in Albuquerque, travel north on I-25 to exit 228. Travel east on Montgomery Boulevard for 6.6 miles to Tramway Boulevard. Continue straight on Montgomery Boulevard past the intersection for 0.5 mile to a four-way stop. Go left onto Glenwood Hills Road and travel 0.5 mile to Trailhead Road. Turn right onto Trailhead Road and cruise into the large Embudito trailhead parking area and the start of the ride. *DeLorme: New Mexico Atlas & Gazetteer:* Page 31, H-8.

The Ride

How lucky are locals in the Albuquerque area to have such a great system of trails right out their back door! The Foothills Trail System is the result of a lot of hard work by a number of individual activists and several government agencies. The trails are well marked and well maintained and they offer a fantastic opportunity for outdoor enthusiasts to enjoy the beauty of the piñon- and cactus-covered foothills below the rocky and rugged Sandia Mountains. The trail system sees a lot of use on weekends and holidays, so be careful and show respect to other trail users.

From the trailhead pass through a gate and follow the tight singletrack trail through large granite boulders and stands of beautiful cholla cactus. The trail is mostly hard-packed with brief sections of rocky tread and climbs at a gentle grade up to a trail junction at 1.1 miles. Continue straight at the trail junction and reach another junction at the 1.2-mile mark. Turn left onto Trail 365 and begin a section of beautiful singletrack riding up to a road. Cross the road and soon reach a trail junction at the 1.9-mile mark. Stay left on Trail 365 and soon reach the paved Simms Park Road at the 2.8-mile mark. Cross Simms Park Road and pick up the trail on the other side. Get ready for a great section of beautiful singletrack riding through

Prickly pear cactus along the trail

stands of desert juniper and piñon trees. Views extend north and east to the Sandia Mountains and west to the city. The trail slices through a small, beautiful arroyo and then cuts up through a section of very rocky tread. At the 4.4-mile mark you reach a junction, with Trail 365 veering to the left. Go right onto Trail 230 and climb up loose, rocky singletrack to a gate. Reach the gate, turn right, and drop into an arroyo with several technical moves through large granite boulders. Regroup and cruise to a trail junction at the 5.6-mile mark. This is a good spot for a short break. There are great views east to the various rocky outcrops that hover high above the surrounding foothills.

Turn right onto Trail 230 and then left onto Trail 341 at the 5.8-mile mark. Cruise through the nature-walk area on a wide doubletrack trail and reach a trail junction at the 6.4-mile mark. There are excellent views to the south and west. This ride rocks! Go right onto Trail 342 and you'll soon reach a junction with Trail 305A. Go left onto Trail 305A and enjoy twisting tight singletrack through the trees. Doesn't get much better than this! Pass through a gate and reach Trail 305 at the 7.2-mile mark. I biked this trail on a late fall afternoon, and the sun was just setting in the west. This section of the ride was simply beautiful! The hillsides had a soft, mellow glow and the rocks were turning a light pink. The air was cool, fresh, and a pleasure to breathe. It was easy to understand how the Sandias got their name (watermelon).

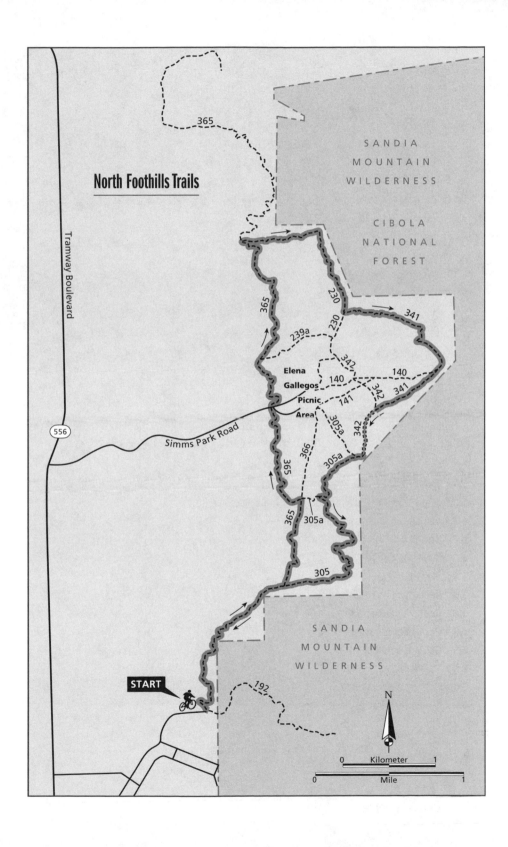

North Foothills Trails

Tramway Boulevard

SANDIA
MOUNTAIN
WILDERNESS

CIBOLA
NATIONAL
FOREST

365

365

230

230

341

239a

342

140

140

Elena
Gallegos

342

341

Picnic
Area

141

342

305a

342

556

Simms Park Road

366

305a

365

305a

365

305a

305

SANDIA
MOUNTAIN
WILDERNESS

START

192

N

0   Kilometer   1

0   Mile   1

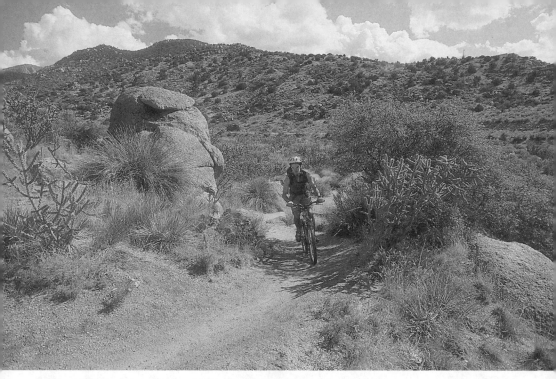

Classic high-desert terrain on the North Foothills Trails

Go left onto Trail 305 and enjoy an extended run on smooth singletrack up to a familiar trail junction. Reach Trail 365 and cruise back to the parking area.

Miles and Directions

0.0 START from the trailhead and follow the singletrack trail.

1.1 Trail junction, continue straight.

1.2 Go left onto Trail 365.

1.6 Cross the road.

1.9 Stay on Trail 365.

2.8 Reach Simms Park Road.

4.4 Reach a trail junction. Go right onto Trail 230.

5.0 Go right at the gate.

5.6 Go right onto Trail 230.

5.8 Go left onto Trail 341.

6.4 Go right onto Trail 342.

6.5 Go left onto Trail 305A.

7.2 Turn left onto Trail 305.

8.5 Back at Trail 365.

9.7 Back at the parking area.

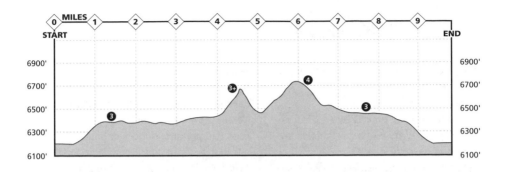

Ride Information

Local Information

Albuquerque Convention & Visitors Bureau, P.O. Box 26866, 401 Second Street Northwest, Albuquerque, NM 87125; (505) 842-9918 or (800) 284-2282; www.abqcvb.org.

Local Events and Attractions

Indian Pueblo Cultural Center, 2401 Twelfth Street, Albuquerque; (505) 843-7270 or (800) 766-4405; admission is $4.00 for adults and $3.00 for children. Owned and operated by nineteen pueblos of New Mexico.

37 South Foothills Trail

Start: From the trailhead at the dead end of Copper Road.
Distance: 5.4-mile loop.
Approximate riding time: 1.0 to 1.5 hours.
Difficulty: Moderate with a couple of short, steep climbs.
Trail surface: Doubletrack and singletrack trails.
Lay of the land: Beautiful riding on excellent trails in the foothills of the Sandia Mountains.
Other trail users: This trail is popular with hikers and other trail users.
Canine compatibility: The trail can be crowded, so leave the pooch at home.

Wheels: Front suspension will work just fine on this ride.
Land status: Albuquerque Open Space.
Nearest town: Albuquerque.
Fees and permits: No fees or permits required.
Schedule: Dawn to dusk, year-round.
Maps: Albuquerque Open Space/South Foothills Trails.
Trail contacts: Albuquerque Open Space Division, P.O. Box 1293, Albuquerque, NM 87103; (505) 873-6620.
Two Wheel Drive, 1706 Central Avenue Southeast, Albuquerque, NM 87106; (505) 243-8443.

Finding the trailhead: From Albuquerque: From the Intersection of Interstate 25 and Interstate 40, travel east on I-40 for 8.2 miles to exit 167 (Tramway Boulevard). Go north onto Tramway Boulevard for 0.7 mile to Copper Road. Turn right onto Copper Road and drive to a parking area on the left where Copper Road dead-ends. The ride starts here. Lock your car and don't leave any valuables exposed. *DeLorme: New Mexico Atlas & Gazetteer:* Page 31, A-8.

The Ride

Not as long as its big brother to the north, the South Foothills Trail offers a great short workout on excellent singletrack and a few technical sections that will keep most cyclists on their toes. The riding is mostly on hard-packed singletrack trails that form a loop around the cacti-, yucca-, and piñon-covered hills below the rugged Sandia Mountains.

From the parking area reach the trailhead and go right on tight singletrack at a large boulder, heading in a southern direction toward a big hill (U-Mound). Reach U-Mound on excellent tight tread climbing up a short, steep hill. The trail bears left and becomes rocky and technical. Pedal hard through a rocky section and reach the crest of a hill. Drop down on excellent singletrack through the cacti and piñon and juniper trees. At the 1.4-mile mark reach a junction with Trail 400 on the left. Continue straight and climb up a series of short, steep switchbacks. There are good views west to the city and West Mesa. Reach the top of the hill and continue straight to a trail junction at the 2-mile mark. Go right onto buffed-out singletrack, passing a trail marker to a trail junction at the 2.4-mile mark. Turn left onto Trail 365 and drop

Catching some air on the South Foothills Trail

down to another trail junction. Continue straight on Trail 365, cross a small bridge, and climb steeply to a trail junction at the 2.9-mile mark. Go right onto Trail 365 to another trail junction. Go left onto Trail 365A, cross a wooden footbridge, and climb up to a trail junction at the 3.5-mile mark. Go right up a short, steep hill then drop steeply on rough singletrack to Indian School Road and a trail junction. Go left onto Trail 401 and enjoy a great run on twisting, tight singletrack, staying right at a fence line. Awesome riding brings you to a viaduct, where you turn left and follow the viaduct to a trail junction. Reach the trail junction, turn right, and head down toward the parking area. Reach the parking area at the 5.4-mile mark. Ready for another lap?

Miles and Directions

0.0 START from the trailhead and follow the singletrack trail toward U-Mound.

0.5 Reach U-Mound

0.7 Steep, rocky section.

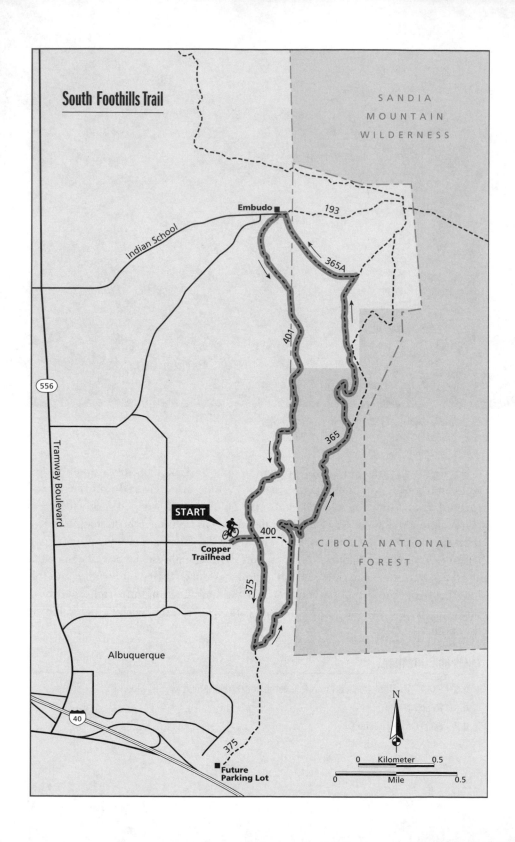

South Foothills Trail

SANDIA
MOUNTAIN
WILDERNESS

Embudo
193
365A
401
365

Indian School

556

Tramway Boulevard

START
400
Copper
Trailhead

375

CIBOLA NATIONAL
FOREST

Albuquerque

40

375

Future
Parking Lot

N

0   Kilometer   0.5
0   Mile   0.5

Leading the way on the South Foothills Trail

1.4 Junction with Trail 400. Continue straight.

2.0 Go right.

2.2 Trail marker, continue straight.

2.4 Go left and down.

2.6 Continue straight on Trail 365.

2.9 Go right onto Trail 365.

3.1 Go left onto Trail 365A.

3.5 Go right and up.

3.7 Reach Trail 401 and Indian School Road. Go left onto Trail 401.

4.1 Go right along the fence line.

4.4 Go right.

4.8 Go left at the viaduct.

5.2 Go right.

5.3 Go right.

5.4 Back at the parking area.

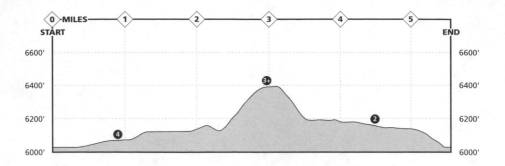

Ride Information

Local Information

Albuquerque Convention & Visitors Bureau, P.O. Box 26866, 401 Second Street Northwest, Albuquerque, NM 87125; (505) 842-9918 or (800) 284-2282; www.abqcvb.org.

Local Events and Attractions

New Mexico Museum of Natural History and Science, 1801 Mountain Road Northwest, Albuquerque; (505) 841-2800; twelve billion years of natural history in one building!

Accommodations

Hacienda Antigua, 6708 Tierra Drive Northwest, Albuquerque; (505) 345-5399 or (800) 201-2986.

New Mexico Bed & Breakfast Association, P.O. Box 2925, Santa Fe; (505) 983-4554; www.nmhotels.com.

Restaurants

Sadie's, 6230 Fourth Street Northwest, Albuquerque; (505) 345-9440; still, after all these years, one of the best restaurants for New Mexican cuisine.

Organizations

New Mexico Touring Society, P.O. Box 1261, Albuquerque, NM 87103; (505) 237-9700; www.swcp.com/-russells/nmts.

38 Sandia Peak Ski Area

Start: From the base of the ski area just off New Mexico Highway 536.
Distance: More than 24 miles of varying difficulty.
Approximate riding time: 30 minutes to 4 hours.
Difficulty: Easy, moderate, and as hard as you want to make it.
Trail surface: Single and doubletrack trails.
Lay of the land: Located northeast of Albuquerque at the Sandia Peak Ski Area.
Other trail users: Hikers; keep your speed under control on the steep downhills.
Canine compatibility: Leave Fido at home.
Wheels: Front suspension will work just fine on this ride.
Land status: Cibola National Forest.

Nearest town: Cedar Crest.
Fees and permits: Call Sandia Peak Ski Area, (505) 242-9133, for details.
Schedule: Memorial Day to Labor Day.
Maps: Sandia Peak Trails.
Trail contacts: Southwest Regional Office of the Forest Service, 517 Gold Avenue, Albuquerque, NM 87102; (505) 842-3800; www.fs.fed.us/r3.
Cibola National Forest, Main Headquarters, 2113 Osuna Road, Suite A, Albuquerque, NM 87107; (505) 761-8700; www.fs.fed.us/r3/cibola.
Two Wheel Drive, 1706 Central Avenue Southeast, Albuquerque, NM 87106; (505) 243-8443.

Finding the trailhead: From Albuquerque: Travel east on Interstate 40 to exit 175 and the town of Tijeras. Follow New Mexico Highway 14 (Turquoise Trail) north for 6 miles to NM 536 (Crest Highway). Turn left onto NM 536 and travel 6.1 miles to the Sandia Peak Ski Area on the left. Pull into the large parking area. The rides start here. *DeLorme: New Mexico Atlas & Gazetteer:* Page 23, H-8.

The Ride

The Sandia Peak Ski Area is not so much a single ride as it is a number of well-maintained trails that go up, across, and down through the ski area. There are 24 miles of trails that range from bone-jarring downhill runs to smooth buffed-out singletrack and steep, lung-busting climbs. The ski area is a great place to hang out, to take the lift up and ride down all day, or to ride the steep and technical "King of the

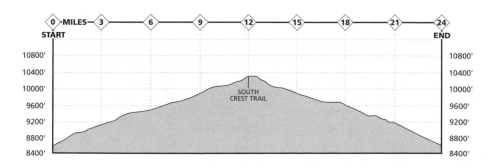

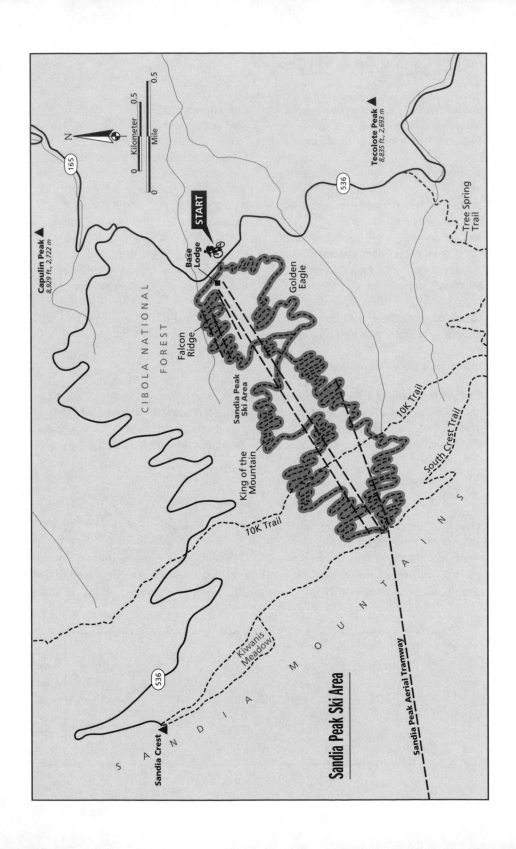

Sandia Peak Ski Area

Capulin Peak
8,929 ft., 2,722 m

Tecolote Peak
8,835 ft., 2,693 m

CIBOLA NATIONAL FOREST

Base Lodge

START

Falcon Ridge

Golden Eagle

Sandia Peak Ski Area

King of the Mountain

10K Trail

10K Trail

Tree Spring Trail

South Crest Trail

Sandia Crest

Kiwanis Meadow

SANDIA MOUNTAINS

Sandia Peak Aerial Tramway

N

Kilometer

Mile

165

536

536

Mountain" race course that makes a loop up to the top of the ski area and back down to the base. The trails at the ski area are well marked, so it is quite difficult to get lost.

For those of you without a bike, don't worry. Sandia Peak has a full-service shop and a rental fleet of more than forty bikes. The views from the top are quite spectacular and stretch out in all directions. The lifts are in operation on holidays and weekends from Memorial Day through Labor Day. The ski area also has a series of four mountain bike races throughout the summer months. Plan to spend the day and enjoy the services (restaurants, etc.) that the ski area has to offer. For more information, contact www.sandiapeak.com/biking.

Ride Information

Local Information

Sandia Peak Ski Area, 10 Tramway Loop Northeast, Albuquerque, NM 87122; (505) 242-9052; www.sandiapeak.com.

Restaurants

Double Eagle 11 Outdoor Grill, Ski Area Base Lodge, Sandia Peak Ski Area; (505) 242-9133.

39 Faulty Trail

Start: From the trailhead just off New Mexico Highway 337.
Distance: 12.9-mile loop.
Approximate riding time: 2.5 to 4.0 hours.
Difficulty: Moderate with some steep, technical sections on loose tread.
Trail surface: Singletrack trails and paved roads.
Lay of the land: Located northeast of Albuquerque near the quaint town of Cedar Crest.
Other trail users: Hikers and runners use these trails.
Canine compatibility: Leave the dog at home for this one.
Wheels: Front suspension will work just fine on this ride.

Land status: Cibola National Forest.
Nearest town: Cedar Crest.
Fees and permits: No fees or permits required.
Schedule: Dawn to dusk, year-round.
Maps: USGS maps: Bernalillo County; Sandia Ranger District Map.
Trail contacts: Southwest Regional Office of the Forest Service, 517 Gold Avenue, Albuquerque, NM 87102; (505) 842-3800; www.fs.fed.us/r3.
Cibola National Forest, Main Headquarters, 2113 Osuna Road, Suite A, Albuquerque, NM 87107; (505) 761-8700; www.fs.fed.us/r3/cibola.

Finding the trailhead: From Albuquerque: Travel west on Interstate 40 to exit 175 and the town of Tijeras. Stay to the right and reach a four-way stop. Turn left onto New Mexico Highway 14 and travel north to Cedar Crest. Turn left onto Forest Road 299 just past the post office and travel 0.5 mile to a fork in the road. Take the left fork and travel 1.2 miles to the Cole Springs Picnic Area and the start of the ride. *DeLorme: New Mexico Atlas & Gazetteer:* Page 31, A-8 to 23, H-8.

The Ride

This is one of the harder trails in the Albuquerque area and should be attempted by strong intermediate and expert cyclists only. Those lacking the skills are really not going to have a pleasant time and would be better off just hiking the trail.

Sections of steep rocky uphills, technical stream crossings, and extended sections of technical riding make this a course for cyclists with strong legs, lungs, and skills.

From the Cole Springs Picnic Area, access the Canoncito Trail and begin riding into the forest along the stream. Around the 0.6-mile mark the trail comes close to the stream with a series of pretty pools. Push your bike up a steep section and reach a small open area where the trail splits to both sides of the stream. Take either fork up to Canoncito Spring and a fork in the trail marked with a wooden sign. Go right onto the Faulty Trail and enjoy excellent singletrack riding through the pine trees. Reach the creek crossing and, in my case, push up to a small ridgeline. Make several more stream crossings and reach an open area at a small rock cliff with excellent views. The trail drops steeply past the rocks, crosses the Cienega Trail, and climbs up a steep, technical section to a junction with an old trail on the right. Past the trail

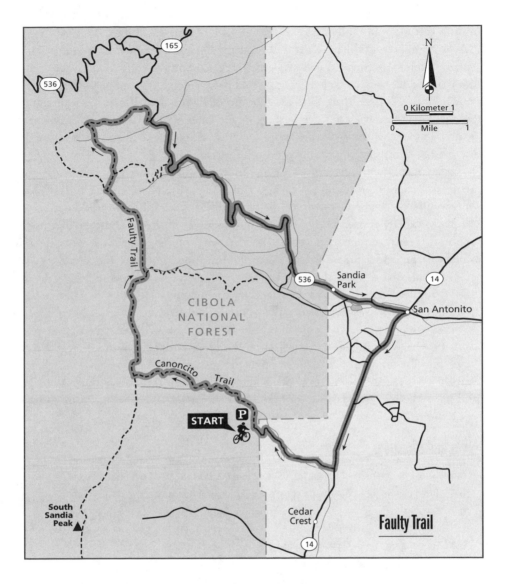

Faulty Trail

the Faulty Trail drops again, crosses the Sulphur Trail, and begins an extended run up and then down on extremely rocky, technical riding. This is the crux of the ride and it doesn't let up until you reach the Oso Corredor Trail at the 4.8-mile mark. Continue straight on the Faulty Trail on smoother tread to where the Faulty Trail changes to the Bill Spring Trail at the 5.2-mile mark. Follow the trail down fast, awesome tread along the stream and through tall, towering oak trees to a paved path along the Doc Long Picnic Area. Follow this straight to New Mexico Highway 536. Turn right onto NM 536 and zoom down the Crest Highway to a junction with NM 14. This section is quite fast and NM 536 does see some heavy traffic. Use caution on this section of the ride. When you reach NM 14, turn right toward Cedar Crest. Travel 2.4 miles on NM 14 to FR 299 and turn right and follow it back to the Cole Springs Picnic Area and the end of the ride. It's no problem if you don't want to do the road riding back to Cole Springs Picnic Area. At the 6.1-mile mark where the trail reaches the paved path near the Doc Long Picnic Area, just turn around and retrace your route back to Cole Springs Picnic Area via the Faulty and Canoncito Trails. I prefer this way as it adds more technical singletrack riding and reverses all the hard sections that you encounter on the way up.

The Faulty Trail received its name due to its location almost dead center along a geological fault line running east to west along East Mountain. The Faulty Trail also runs parallel along the boundary of the beautiful Sandia Mountain Wilderness. The Sandia Mountain Wilderness is 37,232 acres located in a diverse landscape of Upper Sonoran Desert, rounded, beautiful hills filled with piñon and juniper trees, dense ponderosa pine and spruce-fir forest with cool mountain streams, and Precambrian granite walls that seem to shoot up to the sky. It is an area of intense beauty just a mere 15 miles from downtown Albuquerque, giving easy access to solitude that can be found only in a wilderness area free of motorized travel.

The wilderness area has a number of beautiful and easily accessible trails, especially on the western side. La Luz Trail is the most popular. The trail starts at the Juan Tabo Picnic Area, climbs up through the foothills, and gains almost a mile of vertical relief before ending at the Sandia Tram 7.8 miles later. So do yourself a favor and leave the bike at the car or at home and take a relaxing hike into this "urban wilderness."

Miles and Directions

0.0   START on the marked Canoncito Trail on the right. Do not go left onto Barts Trail.

0.6   Reach some nice pools and a short push up along the stream.

0.7   Reach the top of the hill and follow either trail along the stream to the Faulty Trail. Go right onto the Faulty Trail.

1.3   Reach a trail on the right. Continue straight.

1.8   The first of several stream crossings.

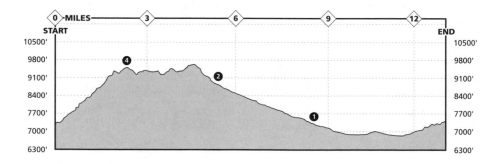

3.0 Small rock band and good views. Good spot for a break.

3.2 Cross Cienega Trail.

3.5 Cross Sulphur Trail. A long section of technical riding lies ahead.

4.8 Reach a junction with the Oso Corredor Trail on the left. Continue straight.

5.2 The Faulty Trail becomes the Bill Spring Trail.

6.1 Reach a paved path along the Doc Long Picnic Area. Continue on the path.

7.0 Cross a ditch and turn right onto NM 536.

8.8 Turn right onto NM 14.

11.2 Go right onto FR 299.

11.7 The road forks. Go left and climb back up to Cole Springs Picnic Area and your car.

12.9 Back at your car.

Ride Information

Local Information:

Albuquerque Convention & Visitors Bureau, P.O. Box 26866, 401 Second Street Northwest, Albuquerque, NM 87125; (505) 842-9918 or (800) 284-2282; www.abqcvb.org.

Local Events and Attractions

Albuquerque Biological Park: Aquarium and Botanic Garden, 2601 Central Avenue Northwest, Albuquerque; (505) 764-6200; admission is $5.00 for adults and $3.00 for children age twelve and younger. A lot of bang for the buck! Take the kids and enjoy.

Accommodations

Elaine's A Bed & Breakfast, Cedar Crest; (505) 281-2467 or (800) 821-3092; www.elainesbnb.com; beautiful accommodations in a three-story log home.

Restaurants

Kokopelli's Kafe & Bakery, NM 14, Cedar Crest; (505) 281-2002; great place for breakfast or lunch.

40 Tunnel Canyon

Start: From the trailhead just off New Mexico Highway 337.
Distance: 4.2-mile loop.
Approximate riding time: 45 minutes to 1 hour.
Difficulty: Moderate with some steep, technical sections on loose tread.
Trail surface: Singletrack trails and paved roads.
Lay of the land: Located east of Albuquerque near the quaint town of Tijeras.
Other trail users: Hikers and runners use these trails. Show respect to other trail users.
Canine compatibility: Leave the dog at home; there is very little water and the limestone rocks are extremely painful on paws.

Wheels: Front suspension will work just fine on this ride.
Land status: Cibola National Forest.
Nearest town: Tijeras.
Fees and permits: No fees or permits required.
Schedule: Dawn to dusk, year-round.
Maps: USGS maps: 7.5 Sedillo; The Trails of Cedro Peak and Otero Canyon by Two Wheel Drive.
Trail contacts: Southwest Regional Office of the Forest Service, 517 Gold Avenue, Albuquerque, NM 87102; (505) 842-3800; www.fs.fed.us/r3.
Cibola National Forest, Sandia Ranger District, Star Route Box 174, Tijeras, NM 87059; (505) 281-3304; www.fs.fed.us/r3/cibola.

Finding the trailhead: From Albuquerque: Travel east on Interstate 40 to exit 175 and the town of Tijeras. Stay right and pass through a four-way stop and reach NM 337. Travel for 2.5 miles on NM 337, pass the Tijeras Ranger station on the left, and reach a small parking area on the right marked with a TRAIL 14 sign. The ride starts here. *DeLorme: New Mexico Atlas & Gazetteer:* Page 31, A-8.

The Ride

This is a sweet little gem of a ride that travels up and above picturesque Tunnel Canyon on excellent tight singletrack. There are excellent views to the Sandias and great exposure as you sidehill it to Otero Canyon. The ride is short and makes for a good warm-up for the longer rides in the area. Folks who are new to the area might want to do this ride to get a good feel for the area and the type of riding you experience in the tree-covered hills.

From the parking area the trail heads into Tunnel Canyon on smooth singletrack and cuts through the tall meadow grass. There is a Forest Service sign marked 14. The trail becomes narrow and somewhat rockier as you enter into a dry streambed. The trail cuts through the piñon trees and stays to the left of the streambed. At the 0.9-mile mark make a sharp left and begin to climb out of Tunnel Canyon. Great views to the Sandias take your mind off the climb and you quickly gain a ridge. A

Looking fashionable on the Tunnel Canyon Trail ▶

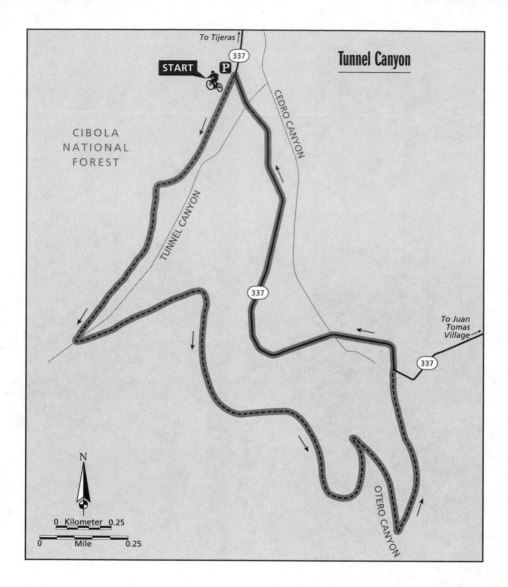

little exposure on the left makes the riding harder than it should be. Lean to the right and reach a trail junction at the top of the climb. Continue straight and then drop down on tight singletrack past several limestone steps and a few tight switchbacks. The trail dumps you into Otero Canyon, where you make a left down the dry streambed, cross a small stream, and reach a paved road. Continue straight to NM 337. Turn left and zoom down the highway back to the trailhead and your car.

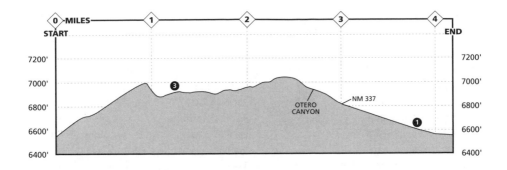

Miles and Directions

0.0 START at the parking area and travel up Tunnel Canyon on Trail 14.

0.9 Reach a trail junction and go left.

2.0 Arrive at a trail junction. Continue straight and down.

2.6 Arrive at Otero Canyon.

3.0 Reach NM 337. Go left.

4.2 Back at the parking area.

Ride Information

Local Information:

Albuquerque Convention & Visitors Bureau, P.O. Box 26866, 401 Second Street Northwest, Albuquerque, NM 87125; (505) 842-9918 or (800) 284-2282; www.abqcvb.org.

Local Events and Attractions

American International Rattlesnake Museum, 202 San Felipe Street Northwest, Albuquerque; (505) 242-6569; admission is $2.00 for adults. More than thirty species of rattlesnakes and a short film on the contributions of this wonderful reptile.

41 Otero Canyon West

Start: From the trailhead just off New Mexico Highway 337.
Distance: 7.8-mile loop.
Approximate riding time: 1 to 2 hours.
Difficulty: Moderate with some steep, technical sections on loose tread.
Trail surface: Singletrack trails and a short section of paved road.
Lay of the land: Located east of Albuquerque near the quaint town of Tijeras.
Other trail users: Hikers and runners use these trails. Show respect to other trail users.
Canine compatibility: Leave the dog at home; there is very little water and the limestone rocks are extremely painful on paws.

Wheels: Front suspension will work just fine on this ride.
Land status: Cibola National Forest.
Nearest town: Tijeras.
Fees and permits: No fees or permits required.
Schedule: Dawn to dusk, year-round.
Maps: USGS maps: 7.5 Sedillo; The Trails of Cedro Peak and Otero Canyon by Two Wheel Drive.
Trail contacts: Southwest Regional Office of the Forest Service, 517 Gold Avenue, Albuquerque, NM 87102; (505) 842-3800; www.fs.fed.us/r3.
Cibola National Forest, Sandia Ranger District, Star Route Box 174, Tijeras, NM 87059; (505) 281-3304; www.fs.fed.us/r3/cibola.

Finding the trailhead: From Albuquerque: Travel west on Interstate 40 to exit 175 and the town of Tijeras. Stay right and pass through a four-way stop and reach NM 337. Travel for 3.7 miles on NM 337, pass the Tijeras Ranger station on the left, and reach a small parking area on the right marked with a TRAIL 56 sign. The ride starts here. *DeLorme: New Mexico Atlas & Gazetteer:* Page 31, A-8.

The Ride

Just like its sister ride to the east, Otero Canyon West offers up a wide variety of great singletrack riding on buffed-out trails. The downhill through Otero Canyon is almost 3 miles long on some of the best singletrack in the area. The climb up to the ridge is rocky, steep, and technical. Once on the ridge you are rewarded with a long stretch of smooth singletrack and great views to the Sandias. This is a must-do ride!

From the parking area pedal down the paved road and turn left onto a singletrack trail. Cross a small stream and pedal up to a trail junction at 0.4 mile. Go right onto the Tunnel Canyon Trail and climb up steep switchbacks to a trail junction at the 1.1-mile mark. The Tunnel Canyon Trail continues straight; you go left and up some extremely rocky tread to a ridgeline. The crux of the ride lies here, and picking the right line through the rocks is crucial to staying on the bike. The steep section is short-lived and you soon gain the ridge and arrive at a trail junction. The seas become calm again! Turn left and enjoy a beautiful, extended run through the piñon and juniper trees on tight, twisting singletrack. This is classic Tijeras singletrack. Enjoy!

At the 3.6-mile mark you arrive at a three-way trail junction. Turn left and enjoy more singletrack riding through the trees. Continue straight, ignoring a trail on the

Nala, the super lab, leading the way (as always) on the Otero Canyon West Trail

right, at the 4.4-mile mark and ride down into a rock-strewn dry creek bed. Heavy seas lie ahead. Get ready for 2 miles of fast, twisting downhill on rocky tread into the mouth of Otero Canyon. Is this great riding or what! The downhill winds and twists through the trees and past several small limestone cliffs and steps. This is one of my favorite trails in the Tijeras area. Before you know it you are back at the mouth of Otero Canyon and a familiar trail junction. Continue straight back to the parking area and your car.

Miles and Directions

0.0 START from the parking area and pedal down the paved road.

0.4 Turn right onto the Tunnel Canyon Trail.

1.1 Go left and up.

1.3 Reach the ridgeline and a trail junction. Go left on excellent singletrack.

3.6 Go left at a three-way junction.

4.3 Continue straight.

4.4 Continue straight down the dry creek bed.

7.4 Back at the mouth of the canyon.

7.8 Cruise into the parking area.

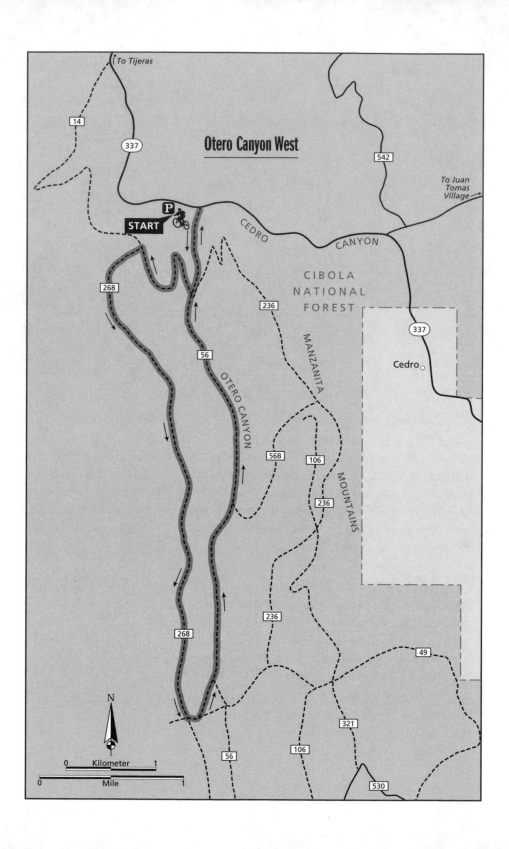

Otero Canyon West

To Tijeras

14

337

542

To Juan
Tomas
Village

P

START

CEDRO

CANYON

CIBOLA
NATIONAL
FOREST

268

236

337

Cedro

56

OTERO CANYON

MANZANITA

56B

106

236

MOUNTAINS

236

268

49

N

321

56

106

530

0   Kilometer   1

0   Mile   1

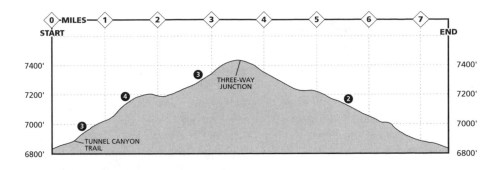

Ride Information

Local Information:

Albuquerque Convention & Visitors Bureau, P.O. Box 26866, 401 Second Street Northwest, Albuquerque, NM 87125; (505) 842-9918 or (800) 284-2282; www.abqcvb.org.

Local Events and Attractions

Albuquerque Museum, 2000 Mountain Road Northwest, Albuquerque; (505) 243-7255; admission is $2.00 for adults and $1.00 for seniors and children. The largest collection of Spanish colonial artifacts in the United States.

Restaurants

Maria Teresa, 618 Rio Grande Boulevard Northwest, Albuquerque; (505) 242-3900; great outdoor patio and wonderful food to match.

Accommodations

Jazz Inn B & B, 111 Walter Northeast, Albuquerque; (505) 242-1530 or (888) JAZZINN; more than 5,000 jazz CDs and albums, plus a piano and great jazz-theme rooms. This place is cool!

42 Otero Canyon East

Start: From the trailhead just off New Mexico Highway 337.
Distance: 7.9-mile loop.
Approximate riding time: 1 to 2 hours.
Difficulty: Moderate with some steep, technical sections on loose tread.
Trail surface: Singletrack trails and a short section of paved road.
Lay of the land: Located east of Albuquerque near the quaint town of Tijeras.
Other trail users: Hikers and runners use these trails. Show respect to other trail users.
Canine compatibility: Leave the dog at home; there is very little water and the limestone rocks are extremely painful on paws.

Wheels: Front suspension will work just fine on this ride.
Land status: Cibola National Forest.
Nearest town: Tijeras.
Fees and permits: No fees or permits required.
Schedule: Dawn to dusk, year-round.
Maps: USGS maps: 7.5 Sedillo; The Trails of Cedro Peak and Otero Canyon by Two Wheel Drive.
Trail contacts: Southwest Regional Office of the Forest Service, 517 Gold Avenue, Albuquerque, NM 87102; (505) 842–3800; www.fs.fed.us/r3. Cibola National Forest, Sandia Ranger District, Star Route Box 174, Tijeras, NM 87059; (505) 281–3304; www.fs.fed.us/r3/cibola.

Finding the trailhead: From Albuquerque: Travel west on Interstate 40 to exit 175 and the town of Tijeras. Stay right and pass through a four-way stop and reach NM 337. Travel for 3.7 miles on NM 337, pass the Tijeras Ranger station on the left, and reach a small parking area on the right marked with a TRAIL 56 sign. The ride starts here. *DeLorme: New Mexico Atlas & Gazetteer:* Page 31, A-8.

The Ride

This ride offers up the whole package and then some! It has excellent tight single-track through beautiful piñon and juniper trees; an extended cruise on level, buffed-out singletrack; a long, twisting downhill through Otero Canyon with technical steps and switchbacks that will challenge the best of cyclists; and views out to the picturesque Sandia Mountains. Welcome to the wild and wonderful world of mountain biking, Tijeras style!

From the parking area follow the old paved road into Otero Canyon and make a quick left onto a singletrack trail. Follow the trail across the small stream and climb gently up to a trail junction. The Tunero (Tunnel) Trail goes right, but you go left across Otero Canyon and make a left onto Trail 236 (Blue Ribbon Trail). Things are about to get a little ugly. This is the start of almost a mile of steep climbing past several tight switchbacks that will test your ability to make hard moves on loose, rocky trail. Reach the first of the switchbacks at the 0.6-mile mark and climb up to the second. Crank through the second switchback and hit the third one hard. This is the

Sweet Tijeras singletrack, just awesome!

hardest of the three and is followed by a steep, rocky climb to gain a ridgeline. Reach the ridgeline and relax. Things get a lot easier now. Enjoy an extended run on level singletrack through an open meadow that is filled with downed brush. Cross a doubletrack at the 2.1-mile mark and enjoy beautiful riding through the trees. Things get ugly again at the 3-mile mark as you are forced to walk (in my case) or pedal up through a very rocky staircase. At the 3.2-mile mark a doubletrack trail shoots in from the right. Continue straight to a three-way junction and cruise through it, riding under a canopy of tall pine trees on tight, cool singletrack. At the 4-mile mark go right on a doubletrack trail that quickly turns to singletrack that slices through a small, open meadow. Reach a trail junction at the 4.5-mile mark and go right. Here is where the fun begins. Go right and quickly reach another trail junction at the 4.6-mile mark. Turn right at this junction and travel down some rocky tread into Otero Canyon. Fast, winding singletrack takes you through the trees and down some of the best downhill in the area. Be on the lookout for other trail users and watch out for the limestone steps that sneak up on you. Enjoy more than 2 miles of awesome downhill that dumps you into the mouth of Otero Canyon. Boy, was that fun or what? Pedal to a familiar trail junction and retrace the first 0.4 mile of the ride back to the parking area.

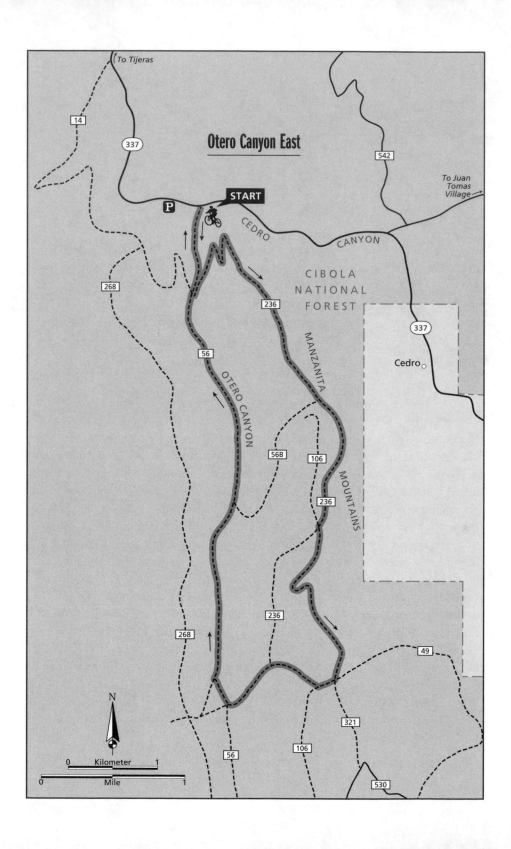

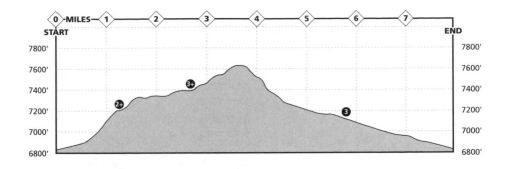

Miles and Directions

0.0 START from the parking area and pedal up the paved road.

0.5 Go left across Otero Canyon and left again onto Trail 236.

0.6 The first of the switchbacks.

1.2 The third and most technical of the switchbacks.

1.5 Reach the ridge and level tread. Great views to the Sandias.

2.1 Cross an old doubletrack trail.

3.0 Very technical staircase.

3.2 Pass a doubletrack trail on the right.

4.0 Go right on the doubletrack, which quickly turns to singletrack.

4.5 Go right.

4.6 The trail forks. Go right and down rocky tread.

7.5 Back at a familiar trail junction.

7.9 Cruise up to the parking area.

Ride Information

Local Information

Albuquerque Convention & Visitors Bureau, P.O. Box 26866, 401 Second Street Northwest, Albuquerque, NM 87125; (505) 842–9918 or (800) 284–2282; www.abqcvb.org.

Local Events and Attractions

National Atomic Museum, 1905 Mountain Road Northwest, Albuquerque; (505) 245–2137; admission is $4.00 for adults and $3.00 for children younger than age sixteen. Learn about the race to build the first nuclear weapon in a fifty-one-minute film: *Ten Seconds That Shook the World.*

43 Chamisoso and Coyote Trails

Start: From the parking lot on Forest Road 462 just off New Mexico Highway 337.
Distance: 9.9-mile loop.
Approximate riding time: 1.5 to 2.5 hours.
Difficulty: Moderate with some steep, technical sections on loose tread.
Trail surface: Singletrack and doubletrack trails.
Lay of the land: Located east of Albuquerque near the quaint town of Tijeras.
Other trail users: Hikers and runners use these trails. Show respect to other trail users.
Canine compatibility: Leave the dog at home; there is very little water and the limestone rocks are extremely painful on paws.

Wheels: Front suspension will work just fine on this ride.
Land status: Cibola National Forest.
Nearest town: Tijeras.
Fees and permits: No fees or permits required.
Schedule: Dawn to dusk, year-round.
Maps: USGS maps: 7.5 Sedillo; The Trails of Cedro Peak and Otero Canyon by Two Wheel Drive.
Trail contacts: Southwest Regional Office of the Forest Service, 517 Gold Avenue, Albuquerque, NM 87102; (505) 842–3800; www.fs.fed.us/r3.
Cibola National Forest, Sandia Ranger District, Star Route Box 174, Tijeras, NM 87059; (505) 281–3304; www.fs.fed.us/r3/cibola.

Finding the trailhead: From Albuquerque: Travel west on Interstate 40 to exit 175 and the town of Tijeras. Stay right, pass through a four-way stop, and reach NM 337. Travel for 1.3 miles on NM 337, pass the Tijeras Ranger Station on the left and reach FR 462 on the left. The ride starts at the dirt parking area at the start of FR 462. *DeLorme: New Mexico Atlas & Gazetteer:* Page 31, A-8.

The Ride

For my money the area around Tijeras has some of the best singletrack riding to be found in the state of New Mexico, if not the whole Southwest. The Coyote and Chamisoso Trails are at the top of my list for pure singletrack fun. Expect tight singletrack, awesome downhills, technical rocky sections, and beautiful scenery through the piñon-studded hills. Do this ride!

From the parking area begin a gentle climb up FR 462. Continue straight past the Chamisoso Trail on the right (the loop ends here) and climb up to a fork in the road. FR 462 goes to the right; go straight, heading for a gate. Just before the gate take the singletrack trail on the right and enjoy some smooth singletrack riding. Around the 1.3-mile mark the trail climbs and bears to the left through a small meadow. An old jeep road continues straight. Stay on the singletrack and drop down quickly along a pretty little canyon. At the end of the downhill, cross a small arroyo on a wooden plank (use caution) and pedal through rocky tread and several staircases. Things are about to get nasty. At the 2.2-mile mark the trail forks: either way is steep, loose, and strenuous. At the top reach a small, open meadow and drop down

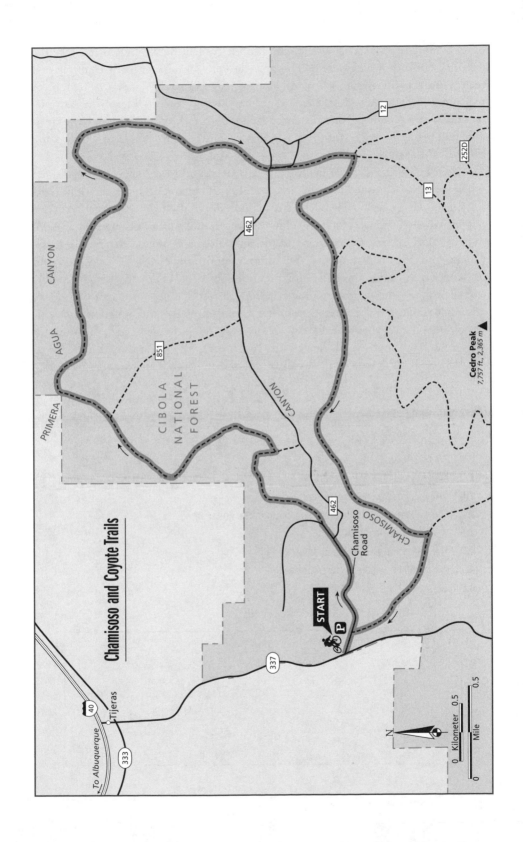

Chamisoso and Coyote Trails

on beautiful, smooth singletrack to a fork in the trail at the 2.9-mile mark. Take the left fork and begin an extended climb on loose, rocky tread. Keep cranking and reach a beautiful open meadow with wide-open views to the Sandias. A great place to hang and regroup. Pedal through the meadow and reach a fork at the 4.6-mile mark. Go right and begin another extended climb on rocky tread through the trees. The trail begins to descend at the 5.5-mile mark and soon reaches Four Corners and FR 462 at 6.2 miles.

Cross FR 462 and travel up Trail 13, a wide gravel road. Stay to the right and when the road begins to loop back left, look for a singletrack trail on the right leading into the trees at the 6.3-mile mark. Tighten down the helmet and get ready for a wild downhill on steep, rocky tread into beautiful Chamisoso Canyon. Steep, tight switchbacks lead into the canyon and the difficulty eases around the 7-mile mark. Catch your breath and follow the smooth, tight singletrack down Chamisoso Canyon. This is almost too much fun. Be on the lookout for wild flowers during the late spring and early summer months. After almost a mile and a half of smooth downhill riding, a trail comes in from the right. Ignore this trail junction and continue down the canyon toward the power lines. At the power lines make a hard right and enjoy tight singletrack riding to FR 462. Reach FR 462 at the 9.8-mile mark, turn left, and cruise back to the parking area and the end of an awesome mountain bike ride.

Miles and Directions

0.0 START from the parking area and pedal up FR 462.

0.6 FR 462 forks. Continue straight.

1.3 Go left through a small meadow.

2.0 Technical riding on loose, rocky tread.

2.2 The trail forks. Take either fork and climb on technical tread.

2.5 A small, open meadow.

2.9 The trail splits. Go left, climbing up and up.

4.1 A beautiful open area with great views.

4.6 Go right.

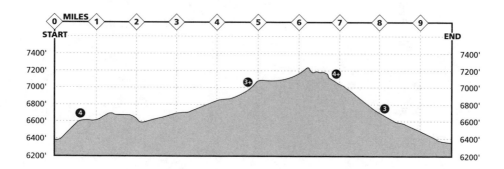

5.5 The trail descends into Four Corners and FR 462.

6.2 Four Corners and FR 462.

6.3 Go right on the Chamisoso Trail.

7.0 Smooth sailing now.

8.5 Continue straight toward the power lines.

9.0 At the power lines make a hard right and travel down the fun singletrack.

9.8 Back at FR 462. Go left and back to the parking area.

9.9 Back at the car. Crack open a cold one.

Ride Information

Local Information

Albuquerque Convention & Visitors Bureau, P.O. Box 26866, 401 Second Street Northwest, Albuquerque, NM 87125; (505) 842-9918 or (800) 284-2282; www.abqcvb.org.

Local Events and Attractions

Midnight Rodeo, 4901 McLeod Road Northeast, Albuquerque; (505) 888-0100; for country music fans, it doesn't get any bigger or better than this.

44 Cedro Peak Loop

Start: From the trailhead near Cedro Peak Campground.
Distance: 9.7-mile loop.
Approximate riding time: 1.5 to 2.0 hours.
Difficulty: Moderate with some steep, technical sections on loose tread.
Trail surface: Singletrack and doubletrack trail and a short section of dirt roads.
Lay of the land: Located east of Albuquerque near the quaint town of Tijeras.
Other trail users: Hikers and runners use these trails. Show respect to other trail users.
Canine compatibility: Leave the dog at home; there is very little water and the limestone rocks are extremely painful on paws.

Wheels: Front suspension will work just fine on this ride.
Land status: Cibola National Forest.
Nearest town: Tijeras.
Fees and permits: No fees or permits required.
Schedule: Dawn to dusk, year-round.
Maps: USGS maps: 7.5 Sedillo; The Trails of Cedro Peak and Otero Canyon by Two Wheel Drive.
Trail contacts: Southwest Regional Office of the Forest Service, 517 Gold Avenue, Albuquerque, NM 87102; (505) 842–3800; www.fs.fed.us/r3.
Cibola National Forest, Sandia Ranger District, Star Route Box 174, Tijeras, NM 87059; (505) 281–3304; www.fs.fed.us/r3/cibola.

Finding the trailhead: From Albuquerque: Travel west on Interstate 40 to exit 175 and the town of Tijeras. Stay right, pass through a four-way stop, and reach New Mexico Highway 337. Travel for 4.7 miles on NM 337, passing the Tijeras Ranger station on the left, and turn left onto Juan Tomas Road (Forest Road 242). Follow Juan Tomas Road for 0.6 mile and turn left onto Forest Road 252. Follow FR 252 for 1.7 miles, passing the Cedro Peak Campground to a parking area on the left. The ride starts here. *DeLorme: New Mexico Atlas & Gazetteer:* Page 31, A-8.

The Ride

I could rave all daylong about the singletrack riding in the Tijeras area. There are long, winding, tight singletrack through the juniper and piñon trees; short technical sections through limestone rocks and staircases; fast downhills on buffed-out singletrack; and views that will take your breath away. This is what you can expect when you ride in the Tijeras area, and the Cedro Peak Loop delivers that and then some. Enjoy, this is a great ride!

From the parking area, head back down FR 252 for 0.2 mile and make a quick left onto Trail 252B. Get ready for 2 miles of continuous singletrack through the piñon and juniper trees on sometimes rocky tread. This is a great run that will put a huge grin on the face of the singletrack connoisseur. Follow the wonderful singletrack up to a junction with Trail 252C and go right for a short way to a three-way intersection. Turn left and drop down some rocky tread to an intersection with Tablazon Trail (Trail 12) and Lone Pine Trail (Trail 11). Turn right onto Lone Pine Trail and climb up a short, steep hill. Reach level ground and start another extended run on some of the finest singletrack in the area. Every time you think it can't get

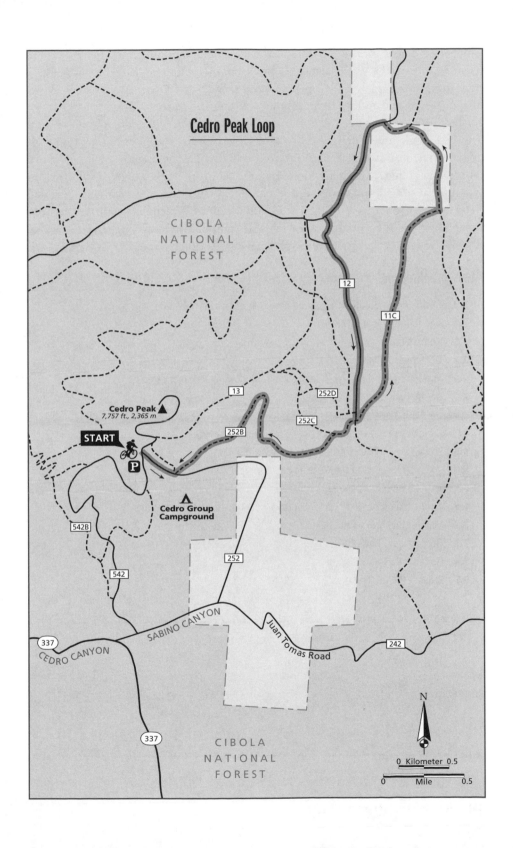

Cedro Peak Loop

CIBOLA
NATIONAL
FOREST

12

11C

13

252D

252C

252B

Cedro Peak ▲
7,757 ft., 2,365 m

START

P

▲ **Cedro Group
Campground**

542B

542

252

337

SABINO CANYON

CEDRO CANYON

Juan Tomas Road

242

337

CIBOLA
NATIONAL
FOREST

N

0   Kilometer   0.5

0   Mile   0.5

any better, it does! At the 3.4-mile mark you reach a trail junction. The trail on the right heads into the woods and onto private property. You continue down the narrow, rocky tread, reaching an open area and a three-way intersection. Go left down the dirt road and follow it to another intersection at the 4.8-mile mark. Travel straight up the rocky tread past a gate to an intersection with some old stone ruins on the left. Continue straight on rocky doubletrack for a mile of bumpy riding. At the 5.8-mile mark turn left onto Tablazon Trail (Trail 12) and enjoy a mile and a half of pleasant riding, passing a windmill on the left. You'll pass Mighty Mule Trail on the right at the 7.1-mile mark and crank up to a familiar trail junction at 7.3 miles. Retrace your route back to the car from this point. Remember to turn right onto Trail 252C and then make a quick left onto Trail 252B. Enjoy singletrack riding in the opposite direction back to the parking area. Another classic Tijeras ride. Enjoy!

Miles and Directions

0.0   START from the parking area and travel back down FR 252.

0.2   Turn left onto Trail 252B.

1.8   Rocky tread.

2.2   Go right onto Trail 252C.

2.3   Turn left at the three-way intersection. Drop down steep, rocky tread.

2.4   Go right and up Lone Pine Trail.

3.4   Go down, bearing left.

4.2   Go left at the three-way junction in the open meadow.

4.8   Lower Pine Trail goes right. Continue straight and up.

5.0   Four-way junction at the ruins. Proceed straight and continue climbing.

5.8   Turn left onto Tablazon Trail (Trail 12).

6.5   A windmill on the left and lots of flowers during the summer months.

7.1   Mighty Mule Trail on the right.

7.3   Go right onto Trail 252C

7.4   Go left onto Trail 252B.

9.7   Back at the parking area.

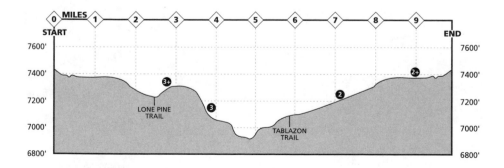

Ride Information

Local Information

Albuquerque Convention & Visitors Bureau, P.O. Box 26866, 401 Second Street Northwest, Albuquerque, NM 87125; (505) 842–9918 or (800) 284–2282; www.abqcvb.org.

Local Events and Attractions

Midnight Rodeo, 4901 McLeod Road Northeast, Albuquerque; (505) 888–0100; for country music fans, it doesn't get any bigger or better than this.

45 Oak Flat Loop

Start: From Oak Flat Picnic Area.
Distance: 7.5-mile loop.
Approximate riding time: 1 to 2 hours.
Difficulty: Moderate with some steep, technical sections on loose tread.
Trail surface: Singletrack and doubletrack trail and a short section of dirt roads.
Lay of the land: Located east of Albuquerque near the quaint town of Tijeras.
Other trail users: Hikers and runners use these trails. Show respect to other trail users.
Canine compatibility: Best to leave the dog at home for this ride.
Wheels: Front suspension will work just fine on this ride.

Land status: Cibola National Forest.
Nearest town: Tijeras.
Fees and permits: No fees or permits required.
Schedule: Dawn to dusk, year-round.
Maps: USGS maps: 7.5 Sedillo; The Trails of Cedro Peak and Otero Canyon by Two Wheel Drive.
Trail contacts: Southwest Regional Office of the Forest Service, 517 Gold Avenue, Albuquerque, NM 87102; (505) 842–3800; www.fs.fed.us/r3.
Cibola National Forest, Sandia Ranger District, Star Route Box 174, Tijeras, NM 87059; (505) 281–3304; www.fs.fed.us/r3/cibola.

Finding the trailhead: From Albuquerque: Travel west on Interstate 40 to exit 175 and the town of Tijeras. Stay right, pass through a four-way stop, and reach New Mexico Highway 337. Travel for 7.6 miles on NM 337, passing the Tijeras Ranger station on the left, and turn left onto Oak Flat Road. Follow Oak Flat Road for 1.1 miles and turn left into the Oak Flat Picnic Area. Turn right at the intersection and park on the right at the first parking area. There is a gate before the first parking area that is locked from October 31 to May 1. For the sake of clarity and a reference point, the mileage starts from the gate. If you are going to do the ride during these times, just park on the side of the road before the gate. *DeLorme: New Mexico Atlas & Gazetteer:* Page 31, A-8.

The Ride

This is a great ride with extended sections of wonderful singletrack riding through the pine- and oak-covered hills near the Oak Flat Picnic Area. The hardest part of this ride for me was finding the start. Read carefully. From the gate continue straight into the parking area. Find a parking spot as close to the gate as possible. Pedal back to the gate and start the mileage from that point.

Pedal back into the parking area and just before the first marked parking space on the right follow a trail into the woods to a singletrack on the left. Take the trail and turn left onto Ponderosa Trail at the 0.4-mile mark. Follow Ponderosa Trail through a cut area to the marked Gamble Trail on the left at 0.9 mile. Go left onto Gamble Trail and down some rocky tread to a trail junction. Continue straight and go right at the next trail junction onto excellent, tight singletrack, reaching Mahogany Trail at the 2-mile mark. Get ready for a great run on excellent singletrack. At the 2.4-mile mark Cut-off Trail comes in from the right. Continue straight

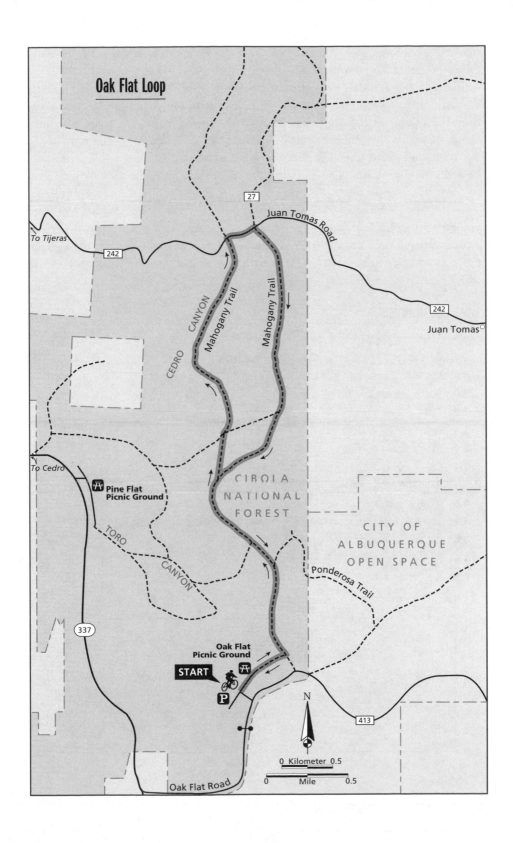

Oak Flat Loop

To Tijeras

242

27

Juan Tomas Road

242

Juan Tomas

CEDRO CANYON

Mahogany Trail

Mahogany Trail

To Cedro

Pine Flat
Picnic Ground

TORO

CANYON

CIBOLA
NATIONAL
FOREST

CITY OF
ALBUQUERQUE
OPEN SPACE

Ponderosa Trail

337

Oak Flat
Picnic Ground

START

P

413

N

Oak Flat Road

0 Kilometer 0.5

0 Mile 0.5

on buffed-out singletrack, reaching a beautiful open meadow at the 3.3-mile mark. During the summer months the meadow is filled with various wildflowers. The colorful Indian paintbrushes are particularly pretty and light up the grass-filled hillsides along the meadow. The trail drops into and across an arroyo and crosses one more time before ending at Juan Tomas Road at the 4-mile mark. Go right onto Juan Tomas Road and climb up a short hill. Look for a doubletrack on the right at the 4.2-mile mark. Turn right and follow the doubletrack into the trees. You are now back on Mahogany Trail. The trail quickly turns to singletrack and winds and twists through the trees on tight singletrack. There's excellent riding through this section with very little climbing. Reach Cut-off Trail on the right at the 5.8-mile mark and continue straight. Climb ever so gently up to a familiar trail junction with Gamble Trail at the 6.6-mile mark. Turn right and retrace your route back to the car. For those looking for some added mileage, turn around and reverse the route. This will add 5 miles to your ride.

Miles and Directions

0.0   START from the parking area and head into the woods.

0.1   Bear to the right and stay left at all trail junctions.

0.4   Reach Ponderosa Trail. Turn left.

0.9   Reach Gamble Trail. Go left and down.

1.2   Continue straight.

1.4   Turn right.

2.0   Reach Mahogany Trail.

2.4   Cut-off Trail is on the right. Continue straight.

3.3   Reach an open meadow.

4.0   Arrive at Juan Tomas Road. Go right.

4.2   Turn right onto Mahogany Trail.

5.8   Cut-off Trail is on the right. Continue straight.

6.6   Back at Gamble Trail. Go right.

7.5   Back at the car.

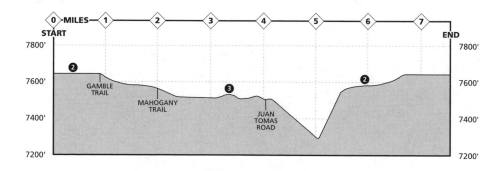

Ride Information

Local Information

Albuquerque Convention & Visitors Bureau, P.O. Box 26866, 401 Second Street Northwest, Albuquerque, NM 87125; (505) 842-9918 or (800) 284-2282; www.abqcvb.org.

Local Events and Attractions

Midnight Rodeo, 4901 McLeod Road Northeast, Albuquerque; (505) 888-0100; for country music fans, it doesn't get any bigger or better than this.

The Art of Mountain Biking

Within the following pages, you will find everything you need to know about off-road bicycling. This section begins by exploring the fascinating history of the mountain bike itself, then goes on to discuss everything from mountain biking etiquette to tips and techniques for bicycling over logs and up hills. Also included are the types of clothing that will keep you comfortable and in style, essential equipment ideas to keep your rides smooth and trouble-free, and descriptions of off-road terrain to prepare you for the kinds of bumps and bounces you can expect to encounter.

The mountain bike, with its knobby tires and reinforced frame, takes cyclists to places once unreachable by bicycle—down rugged mountain trails, through streams of rushing water, across the frozen Alaskan tundra, and even to work in the city. There seem to be few limits on what this fat-tired beast can do and where it can take us. Few obstacles stand in its way; few boundaries slow its progress. Except for one—its own success. If trail closure means little to you now, read on and discover how a trail can be here today and gone tomorrow. With so many new off-road cyclists taking to the trails each year, it's no wonder trail access hinges precariously between universal acceptance and complete termination. But a little work on your part can go a long way to preserving trail access for future use. Nothing is more crucial to the survival of mountain biking itself than to read the examples set forth in the following pages and practice their message.

Without open trails, the maps in this book are virtually useless. Cyclists must learn to be responsible for the trails they use and to share these trails with others. This section addresses such issues as why trail use has become so controversial, what can be done to improve the image of mountain biking, and how to have fun and ride responsibly. You'll also find the worldwide-standard Rules of the Trail.

Mountain Bike Beginnings

It seems the mountain bike, originally designed for lunatic adventurists bored with straight lines, clean clothes, and smooth tires, has become globally popular in as short a time as it would take to race down a mountain trail.

Like many things of a revolutionary nature, the mountain bike was born on the West Coast. But unlike in-line skates, purple hair, and the peace sign, the concept of the off-road bike cannot be credited solely to the imaginative Californians—they were just the first to make waves.

The design of the first off-road–specific bike was based on the geometry of the old Schwinn Excelsior, a one-speed, camelback cruiser with balloon tires. Joe Breeze was the creator behind it, and in 1977 he built ten of these "Breezers" for himself and his Marin County, California, friends at $750 apiece—a bargain.

Breeze was a serious competitor in bicycle racing, placing thirteenth in the 1977 U.S. Road Racing National Championships. After races, he and friends would scour local bike shops hoping to find old bikes they could then restore. It was the 1941 Schwinn Excelsior, for which Breeze paid just five dollars, that began to shape and change bicycling history forever. After taking the bike home, removing the fenders, oiling the chain, and pumping up the tires, Breeze hit the dirt. He loved it.

His inspiration was not altogether unique. On the opposite end of the country, nearly 2,500 miles from Marin County, East Coast bike bums were also growing restless. More and more old, beat-up clunkers were being restored and modified. These behemoths often weighed as much as eighty pounds and were so reinforced they seemed virtually indestructible. But rides that take just forty minutes on today's twenty-five-pound featherweights took the steel-toed-boot-and-blue-jean-clad bikers of the late 1970s and early 1980s nearly four hours to complete.

Not until 1981 was it possible to purchase a production mountain bike, but local retailers found these ungainly bicycles difficult to sell and rarely kept them in stock. By 1983, however, mountain bikes were no longer such a fringe item, and large bike manufacturers quickly jumped into the action, producing their own versions of the off-road bike. By the 1990s the mountain bike had firmly established its place with bicyclists of nearly all ages and abilities, and it now commands nearly 90 percent of the U.S. bike market.

There are many reasons for the mountain bike's success in becoming the hottest two-wheeled vehicle in the nation. They are much friendlier to the cyclist than traditional road bikes because of their comfortable upright position and shock-absorbing fat tires. And because of the health-conscious, environmentalist movement, people are more activity minded and seek nature on a closer front than paved roads can allow. The mountain bike gives you these things and takes you far away from the daily grind—even if you're only minutes from the city.

Mountain Biking Etiquette

The Mountain Bike Controversy: Being a Responsible Trail User

Are Off-Road Bicyclists Environmental Outlaws? Do We Have the Right to Use Public Trails?

Mountain bikers have long endured the animosity of folks in the backcountry who complain about the consequences of off-road bicycling. Many people believe that the fat tires and knobby tread do unacceptable environmental damage and that our uncontrollable riding habits are a danger to animals and other trail users. Mountain biking does cause more damage than traveling by foot because the wheels are in contact with the ground all the time, and bicycle tracks can open channels that accelerate erosion. But by riding responsibly it is possible to leave only a minimal impact—something we all must take care to achieve.

Unfortunately, it is often people of great influence who view the mountain bike as the environment's worst enemy. Consequently, we mountain bike riders and environmentally concerned citizens must be educators, impressing upon others that we also deserve the right to use these trails. Our responsibilities as bicyclists are no more and no less than those of any other trail user.

Rules of the Trail

If every mountain biker always yielded the right-of-way, stayed on the trail, avoided wet or muddy trails, never cut switchbacks, always rode in control, showed respect for other trail users, and carried out every last scrap of what was carried in (candy wrappers and bike-part debris included)—in short, if we all did the right things—we wouldn't need a list of rules governing our behavior.

The fact is, most mountain bikers are conscientious and are trying to do the right thing; however, thousands of miles of dirt trails have been closed due to the irresponsible habits of a few riders.

Here are some basic guidelines adapted from the International Mountain Bicycling Association Rules of the Trail. These guidelines can help prevent damage to land, water, plants, and wildlife; maintain trail access; and avoid conflicts with other backcountry visitors and trail users.

1. Only ride on trails that are open. Don't trespass on private land, and be sure to obtain any necessary permits. If you're not sure if a trail is closed or if you need a permit, don't hesitate to ask. The way you ride will influence trail management decisions and policies. Federal and state wilderness areas are always off-limits to cycling.

2. Keep your bicycle under control. Watch the condition of the trail at all times, and follow the appropriate speed regulations and recommendations.

3. Yield to others on the trail. Make your approach well known in advance, either with a friendly greeting or a bell. When approaching a corner, junction, or blind spot, expect to encounter other trail users. When passing others, show your respect by slowing to a walking pace.

4. Don't startle animals. Animals may be easily scared by sudden approaches or loud noises. For your safety—and the safety of others in the area as well as the animals themselves—give all wildlife a wide berth. When encountering horses, defer to the horseback riders' directions and dismount on narrow trails.

5. Zero impact. Be aware of the impact you're making on the trail beneath you. You should not ride under conditions where you will leave evidence of your passing, such as on certain soils or shortly after a rainfall. If a ride features optional side hikes into wilderness areas, be a zero-impact hiker too. Whether you're on bike or on foot, stick to existing trails, leave gates as you found them, and carry out everything you brought in.

6. Be prepared. Know the equipment you are using, the area where you'll be riding, and your cycling abilities and limitations. Avoid unnecessary breakdowns by keeping your equipment in good shape. When you head out, bring spare parts and supplies for weather changes. Be sure to wear appropriate safety gear, including a helmet, and learn how to be self-sufficient.

Like the trails we ride on, the social dimension of mountain biking is very fragile and must be cared for responsibly. We do not want to destroy another person's enjoyment of the outdoors. By riding in the backcountry with caution, control, and responsibility, our presence can be felt positively by other trail users. By adhering to these rules, trail riding—a privilege that can quickly be taken away—will continue to be ours to share.

Soft Cycling

The term "soft-cycling" describes the art of minimum-impact bicycling and should apply to both the physical and social dimensions of the sport. But make no mistake—it is possible to ride fast and furiously while maintaining the balance of soft-cycling. Here are a few more ways to minimize the physical impact of mountain bike riding.

- **Stay on the trail.** Don't ride around fallen trees or mud holes that block your path. Stop and cross over them. When you come to a vista overlooking a deep valley, don't ride off the trail for a better vantage point. Instead, leave the bike and walk to see the view. Riding off the trail may seem inconsequential when done only once, but soon someone else will follow, then others, and the cumulative results can be catastrophic. Each time you wander from the trail you begin creating a new path, adding one more scar to the earth's surface.

- **Do not disturb the soil.** Follow a line within the trail that will not disturb or damage the soil.

- **Do not ride over muddy or wet trails.** After a rain shower or during the thawing season, trails will often resemble muddy, oozing swampland. The best thing to do is to stay off the trails completely. Realistically, however, we're all going to come across some muddy trails we cannot anticipate. Instead of blasting through each section of mud, which may seem both easier and more fun, lift the bike and walk past. Each time a cyclist rides through a soft or muddy section of trail, that part of the trail is permanently damaged. Regardless of the trail's conditions, though, remember always to go over the obstacles across the path, not around them. Stay on the trail.

- **Avoid trails that are considered impassable and impossible.** Don't take a leap of faith down a kamikaze descent on which you will be forced to lock your brakes and skid to the bottom, ripping the ground apart as you go.

Trail Maintenance

Unfortunately, despite all of the preventive measures taken to avoid trail damage, we're still going to run into many trails requiring attention. Simply put, a lot of hikers, equestrians, and cyclists use the same trails—some wear and tear is unavoidable.

But like your bike, if you want to use these trails for a long time to come, you must also maintain them.

Trail maintenance and restoration can be accomplished in a variety of ways. One way is for mountain bike clubs to combine efforts with other trail users (i.e., hikers and equestrians) and work closely with land managers to cut new trails or repair existing ones. This not only demonstrates the commitment cyclists have in caring for and maintaining the land, but also breaks the ice that often separates cyclists from their fellow trail mates. Another good way to help out is to show up, ready to work, on a Saturday morning with a few riding buddies at your favorite off-road domain. With a good attitude, thick gloves, and the local land manager's supervision, trail repair is fun and very rewarding. It's important, of course, that you arrange a trail-repair outing with the local land manager before you start pounding shovels into the dirt. They can lead you to the most needy sections of trail and instruct you on what repairs should be done and how best to accomplish the task.

We must be willing to sweat for our trails in order to sweat on them. Police yourself and point out to others the significance of trail maintenance. "Sweat Equity," the rewards of continued land use won with a fair share of sweat, pays off when the trail is "up for review" by the land manager and he or she remembers the efforts made by trail-conscious mountain bikers.

Rules of the Road

Occasionally, even hard-core off-road cyclists will find they have no choice but to ride the pavement. Laws vary by state, but outlined below are a few rules to follow no matter where you ride.

- Follow the same driving rules as motorists. Be sure to obey all road signs and traffic lights.
- Ride with the traffic and not against it.
- Wear a helmet and bright clothing so you are more visible to motorists. Bright colors such as orange and lime green are also highly visible at night.
- Wear a helmet.
- Equip your bike with lights and wear reflective clothing if you plan on riding at night. When riding at night the bicycle or rider should have a white light visible at least 500 feet to the front and a red light or reflector visible at least 600 feet to the rear.
- Ride single file on busy roads so motorists can pass you safely.
- When stopping, be sure to pull completely off the roadway.
- Use hand signals to alert motorists to what you plan on doing next.
- Follow painted lane markings.
- Make eye contact with drivers. Assume they don't see you until you are sure they do.

- Don't ride out to the curb between parked cars unless they are far apart. Motorists may not see you when you try to move back into traffic.
- Turn left by looking back, signaling, getting into the left lane, and turning. In urban situations, continue straight to the crosswalk and walk your bike across the crosswalk when the pedestrian walk sign is illuminated.
- Never ride while under the influence of alcohol or drugs. DUI laws apply when you're riding a bicycle.
- Avoid riding in extremely foggy, rainy, icy, or windy conditions.
- Watch out for parallel-slat sewer grates, slippery manhole covers, oily pavement, gravel, wet leaves, and ice.
- Cross railroad tracks as perpendicular as possible. Be especially careful when it's wet out. For better control as you move across bumps and other hazards, stand up on your pedals.
- Don't ride too close to parked cars—a person opening the car door may hit you.
- Don't ride on sidewalks. Instead, walk your bike. Pedestrians have the right-of-way on all walkways and crosswalks. By law you must give pedestrians audible warning when you pass. Use a bike bell or announce clearly, "On your left/right."
- Slow down at street crossings and driveways.

Clothing

Just as the original mountain bikers headed off in their jeans to hit the trail, mountain bikers can and do wear just about anything to go riding now. There are a few things in the following list that are absolutely necessary and a few that will make your riding more comfortable and more enjoyable.

Be Prepared—Wear Your Armor

It's crucial to discuss the clothing you must wear to be safe, practical, and—if you prefer—stylish. The following is a list of items that will save you from disaster, outfit you comfortably, and most important, keep you looking cool.

Helmet. A helmet is an absolute necessity because it protects your head from complete annihilation. It is the only thing that will not disintegrate into a million pieces after a wicked crash on a descent. A helmet with a solid exterior shell will also protect your head from sharp or protruding objects.

Shorts. These are necessary if you plan to ride your bike more than twenty to thirty minutes. Padded cycling shorts provide cushioning between your body and the bicycle seat, protecting your derriere against serious saddle soreness. There are two types of cycling shorts you can buy. Touring shorts are good for people who don't want to look like they're wearing anatomically correct cellophane. These look like regular athletic shorts with pockets, but they have built-in padding in the crotch area for protection from chafing and saddle sores. The more popular, traditional cycling shorts are made of skintight material, also with a padded crotch. Cycle shorts also wick moisture away from your body and prevent chafing. Whichever style you prefer, cycling shorts are a necessity for long rides.

Gloves. You may find well-padded cycling gloves invaluable when traveling over rocky trails and gravelly roads for hours on end. When you fall off your bike and land on your palms, gloves are your best friend. Long-fingered gloves may also be useful, as branches, trees, assorted hard objects, and, occasionally, small animals will reach out and whack your knuckles. Insulated gloves are essential for winter riding.

Glasses. Not only do sunglasses give you an imposing presence and make you look cool (both are extremely important), they also protect your eyes from harmful ultraviolet rays, invisible branches, creepy bugs, and dirt.

Shoes. Mountain bike shoes are constructed with stiff soles in order to transfer more of the power from a pedal stroke to the drive train and to provide a solid platform on which to stand, thereby decreasing fatigue in your feet. You can use virtually any good, light, outdoor hiking footwear, but specific mountain bike shoes (especially those with inset cleats) are best. They are lighter, breathe better, and are constructed to work with your pedal strokes instead of the natural walking cadence.

Actual armor. If you ride on very technical trails you may want to consider buying some knee-and-shin guards and elbow pads to protect you from whacking your shins on your handlebars and your elbows on the ground.

Dress for the Weather

Layers. It is best to dress in layers that can be added or removed as weather conditions change. When the air has a nip in it, layers will keep the chill away from your chest and help prevent the development of bronchitis. A polypropylene long-sleeved shirt is best to wear against the skin beneath other layers of clothing. Polypropylene, like wool, wicks away moisture from your skin to keep your body dry. The next layer should be a wool or synthetic insulating layer that helps keep you warm but is also breathable. A fleece jacket or vest works well. The outer layer should be a waterproof, windproof, and breathable jacket and pants. Good cold-weather clothing should fit snugly against your body but not be restrictive. Try to avoid wearing cotton or baggy clothing when the temperature falls. Cotton holds moisture like a sponge, and baggy clothing catches cold air and swirls it around your body.

Tights or leg warmers. These are best in temperatures below 55 degrees Fahrenheit. Knees are sensitive and can develop all kinds of problems if they get cold. Common problems include tendinitis, bursitis, and arthritis.

Wool or synthetic socks. These may be helpful in cold weather conditions. Don't pack too many layers under those shoes, though. You may stand the chance of restricting circulation, and your feet will get very cold, very fast.

Thinsulate or Gore-tex gloves. We may all agree that there is nothing worse than frozen feet—unless your hands are frozen. A good pair of Thinsulate or Gore-tex gloves should keep your hands toasty and warm.

Hat or helmet on cold days. Sometimes, when the weather gets really cold and you still want to hit the trails, it's tough to stay warm. We all know that 130 percent of the body's heat escapes through the head, so it's important to keep the cranium warm. Ventilated helmets are designed to keep heads cool in the summer heat, but they do little to help keep heads warm during rides in subzero temperatures. Cyclists should consider wearing a hat on extremely cold days. Fleece skullcaps are great head and ear warmers that fit snugly over your head beneath the helmet. Head protection is not lost. Another option is a helmet cover that covers those ventilating gaps and helps keep the body heat in. These do not, however, keep your ears warm. Your ears will welcome a fleece headband when it's cold out.

All of this clothing can be found at your local bike shop or outdoor retailer, where the staff should be happy to help fit you into gear for the seasons of the year.

Be Prepared—Supplies and Equipment

The Essentials

Remember the Boy Scout motto: Be Prepared. Here are some essential items that will keep you from walking out a long trail, being stranded in the woods, or even losing your life.

First-Aid Kit

- adhesive bandages
- moleskin
- various sterile gauze and dressings
- white surgical tape
- Ace bandage
- antihistamine
- aspirin
- Betadine solution
- first-aid book
- antacid
- tweezers
- scissors
- antibacterial wipes
- triple-antibiotic ointment
- plastic gloves
- sterile cotton-tip applicators
- syrup of ipecac (to induce vomiting)
- thermometer
- wire splint
- matches
- guidebook (In case all else fails and you must start a fire to survive, this guidebook will serve as excellent fire starter!)

Bicycle Repair Kit

- spare tube
- tire irons
- patch kit
- pump
- spoke wrench
- spare spokes to fit your wheel (tape these to the chain stay)

- chain tool
- Allen keys (bring appropriate sizes to fit your bike)
- duct tape

Water. Without it, cyclists may face dehydration, which may result in dizziness and fatigue. On a warm day, cyclists should drink at least one full bottle during every hour of riding. Remember, it's always good to drink before you feel thirsty—otherwise, it may be too late.

Food. This essential item will keep you rolling. Cycling burns up a lot of calories and is among the few sports in which no one is safe from "bonking." Bonking feels like it sounds. Without food in your system, your blood sugar level plummets, and there is no longer any energy in your body. This instantly results in total fatigue, shakiness, and lightheadedness. So when you're filling your water bottle, remember to bring along some food. Fruit, energy bars, or some other forms of high-energy food are highly recommended. Candy bars are not, however, because they will deliver a sudden burst of high energy, then let you down soon after, causing you to feel worse than before. Energy bars are available at most grocery stores and bike shops and are similar to candy bars, but they provide complex carbohydrate energy and high nutrition rather than fast-burning simple sugars.

Map and compass. Do not rely solely on the maps in this book. A GPS system is also useful (if you know how to use it).

To Have or Not to Have—Other Very Useful Items

There is no shortage of items for you and your bike to make riding better, safer, and easier. We have rummaged through the unending lists and separated the gadgets from the good stuff, coming up with what we believe are items certain to make mountain bike riding more enjoyable.

Tires. Buying a good pair of knobby tires is the quickest way to enhance the off-road handling capabilities of a bike. There are many types of mountain bike tires on the market. Some are made exclusively for very rugged off-road terrain. These big-knobbed, soft rubber tires virtually stick to the ground with magnetlike traction, but they tend to deteriorate quickly on pavement. There are other tires made exclusively for the road. These are called "slicks" and have no tread at all. For the average cyclist, though, a good tire somewhere in the middle of these two extremes should do the trick. Realize, however, that you get what you pay for. Do not skimp and buy cheap tires. As your primary point of contact with the trail, tires may be the most important piece of equipment on a bike. With inexpensive rubber, the tire's beads may unravel or chunks of tread actually rip off the tire. If you're lucky, all you'll suffer is a long walk back to the car. If you're unlucky, your tire could blow out in the middle of a rowdy downhill, causing a wicked crash.

Clipless pedals. Clipless pedals, like ski bindings, attach your shoe directly to the pedal. They allow you to exert pressure on the pedals during both the down- and up-strokes. They also help you to maneuver the bike while in the air or climbing various obstacles. Toe clips may be less expensive, but they are also heavier and harder to use. Clipless pedals take a little getting used to, but they're easier to get out of in an emergency than toe clips and are definitely worth the trouble.

Bar ends. These clamp-on additions to your original straight bar will provide more leverage, an excellent grip for climbing, and a more natural position for your hands. Be aware, however, of the bar end's propensity for hooking trees on fast descents, sending you, the cyclist, airborne. Opinions are divided on the general usefulness of bar ends these days and, over the last few years, bar ends have fallen out of favor with manufacturers and riders alike.

Backpacks and hydration packs. These bags are ideal for carrying keys, extra food and water, guidebooks, foul-weather clothing, tools, spare tubes, a camera, and a cellular phone, in case you need to call for help. If you're carrying lots of equipment, you may want to consider a set of panniers. These are much larger and mount on either side of each wheel on a rack. Keep in mind, however, that with panniers mobility will be severely limited. There are currently a number of streamlined backpacks with hydration systems on the market. Hydration packs are fast becoming an essential item for cyclists pedaling for more than a few hours, especially in hot, dry conditions. Some water packs can carry as much as one hundred ounces of water in their bladder bags. These packs strap on your back with a handy hose running over your shoulder so you can be drinking water while still holding onto the bars with both hands on a rocky descent.

Suspension forks. For off-roaders who want nothing to impede their speed on the trails, investing in a pair of suspension forks can be a good idea. Like tires, there are plenty of brands to choose from, and they all do the same thing—absorb the brutal beatings of a rough trail. The cost of these forks, however, is sometimes more brutal than the trail itself.

Full suspension bikes. Full suspension bikes help smooth out the ride and keep the wheels in contact with the ground. They have been around for a while, but the prices are now falling into a range that the average mountain biker can afford. There are a number of different designs intended for different activities, such as cross-country riding and downhill riding. Be careful when buying and test ride several bikes to determine just what you want.

Bike computers. These are fun gadgets to own and are much less expensive than in years past. They have such features as trip distance, speedometer, odometer, time of day, altitude, alarm, average speed, maximum speed, heart rate, global satellite positioning, etc. Bike computers will come in handy when following these maps or to know just how far you've ridden in the wrong direction.

Types of Terrain

Before roughing it off-road, we may first have to ride the pavement to get to our destination. Please don't be dismayed. Some of the country's best rides are on the road. Once we get past these smooth-surfaced pathways, though, adventures in dirt await us.

Rails-to-Trails. Abandoned rail lines are converted into usable public resources for exercising, commuting, or just enjoying nature. Old rails and ties are torn up and a trail, paved or unpaved, is laid along the existing corridor. This completes the cycle from ancient Indian trading routes to railroad corridors and back again to hiking and cycling trails.

Unpaved roads are typically found in rural areas and are most often public roads. Be careful when exploring, though, not to ride on someone's unpaved private drive.

Forest roads. These dirt and gravel roads are used primarily as access to forestland and are generally kept in good condition. They are almost always open to public use.

Singletrack can be the most fun on a mountain bike. These trails, with only one track to follow, are often narrow, challenging pathways. Remember to make sure these trails are open before zipping into the woods.

Doubletrack. These are usually old Jeep trails or small logging roads where two distinct trails exist parallel to each other. Doubletrack trail can be found almost anywhere and can be as exciting as singletrack.

Open land. Unless there is a marked trail through a field or open space, you should not plan to ride there. Once one person cuts his or her wheels through a field or meadow, many more are sure to follow, causing irreparable damage to the landscape.

Mountain Biking into Shape

If your objective is to get in shape and lose weight, then you're on the right track, because mountain biking is one of the best ways to get started.

One way many of us have lost weight in this sport is the crash-and-burn-it-off method. Picture this: You're speeding uncontrollably down a vertical drop that you realize you shouldn't be on—only after it is too late. Your front wheel lodges into a rut and launches you through endless weeds, trees, and pointy rocks before coming to an abrupt halt in a puddle of thick mud. Surveying the damage, you discover, with the layers of skin, body parts, and lost confidence littering the trail above, that those unwanted pounds have been shed—permanently. Instant weight loss.

There is, of course, a more conventional (and quite a bit less painful) approach to losing weight and gaining fitness on a mountain bike. It's called the workout, and bicycles provide an ideal way to get physical. Take a look at some of the benefits associated with cycling.

Cycling helps you shed pounds without gimmicky diet fads or weight-loss programs. You can explore the countryside and burn nearly ten to sixteen calories per minute or close to 600 to 1,000 calories per hour. Moreover, it's a great way to spend an afternoon.

No less significant than the external and cosmetic changes to your body from riding are the internal changes taking place. Over time, cycling regularly will strengthen your heart as your body grows vast networks of new capillaries to carry blood to all those working muscles. This will, in turn, give your skin a healthier glow. The capacity of your lungs may increase up to 20 percent, and your resting heart rate will drop significantly. The Stanford University School of Medicine reports to the American Heart Association that people can reduce their risk of heart attack by nearly 64 percent if they can burn up to 2,000 calories per week. This is only two to three hours of bike riding!

Recommended for insomnia, hypertension, indigestion, anxiety, and even for recuperation from major heart attacks, bicycling can be an excellent cure-all as well as a great preventive. Cycling just a few hours per week can improve your figure and sleeping habits, give you greater resistance to illness, increase your energy levels, and provide feelings of accomplishment and heightened self-esteem.

Techniques to Sharpen Your Skills

Many of us see ourselves as pure athletes—blessed with power, strength, and endless endurance. However, it may be those with finesse, balance, agility, and grace who get around most quickly on a mountain bike. Although power, strength, and endurance do have their places in mountain biking, these elements don't necessarily form the complete framework for a champion mountain biker.

The bike should become an extension of your body. Slight shifts in your hips or knees can have remarkable results. Experienced bike handlers seem to flash down technical descents, dashing over obstacles in a smooth and graceful effort as if pirouetting in Swan Lake. Here are some tips and techniques to help you connect with your bike and float gracefully over the dirt.

Going Uphill—Climbing Those Treacherous Hills

Shift into a low gear. Before shifting, be sure to ease up on your pedaling so there is not too much pressure on the chain. You can break your chain or bend your derailleur with too much pressure. With that in mind, it's important to shift before you find yourself on a steep slope, where it may be too late. Find the best gear for you that matches the terrain and steepness of each climb.

Stay seated. Standing out of the saddle is often helpful when climbing steep hills on a bike, but you may find that on dirt, standing may cause your rear tire to lose its grip and spin out. Climbing is not possible without traction. As you improve, you will likely learn the subtle tricks that make out-of-saddle climbing possible. Until then, have a seat.

Lean forward. On very steep hills, the front end may feel unweighted and suddenly pop up. Slide forward on the saddle and lean over the handlebars. Think about putting your chin down near your stem. This will add more weight to the front wheel and should keep you grounded. It's all about using the weight of your head to your advantage. Most people don't realize how heavy their noggin is.

Relax. As with downhilling, relaxation is a big key to your success when climbing steep, rocky climbs. Smooth pedaling translates into good traction. Tense bodies don't balance well at low speeds. Instead of fixating grimly on the front wheel, look up at the terrain above, and pick a good line.

Keep pedaling. On rocky climbs, be sure to keep the pressure on, and don't let up on those pedals! You'll be surprised at what your bike will just roll over as long as you keep the engine revved up.

Going Downhill—The Real Reason We Get Up in the Morning

Relax. Stay loose on the bike, and don't lock your elbows or clench your grip. Your elbows need to bend with the bumps and absorb the shock, while your hands should have a firm but controlled grip on the bars to keep things steady. Breathing slowly, deeply, and deliberately will help you relax while flying down bumpy singletrack. Maintaining a death-grip on the brakes will be unhelpful. Fear and tension will make you wreck every time.

Use your eyes. Keep your head up and scan the trail as far forward as possible. Choose a line well in advance. You decide what line to take—don't let the trail decide for you. Keep the surprises to a minimum. If you have to react quickly to an obstacle, then you've already made a mistake.

Rise above the saddle. When racing down bumpy, technical descents, you should not be sitting on the saddle, but hovering just over it or behind it, allowing your bent legs and arms, instead of your rear, to absorb the rocky trail. This will also help keep your weight back to avoid going over the handlebars. Think jockey.

Remember your pedals. Be mindful of where your pedals are in relation to upcoming obstacles. Clipping a rock will lead directly to unpleasantness. Most of the time, you'll want to keep your pedals parallel to the ground.

Stay focused. Many descents require your utmost concentration and focus just to reach the bottom. You must notice every groove, every root, every rock, every hole, every bump. You, the bike, and the trail should all become one as you seek singletrack nirvana on your way down the mountain. But if your thoughts wander, however, then so may your bike, and you may instead become one with the trees!

Braking. Using your brakes requires using your head, especially when descending. This doesn't mean using your head as a stopping block, but rather to think intelligently. Use your best judgment in terms of how much or how little to squeeze those brake levers. The more weight a tire is carrying, the more braking power it has. When you're going downhill, your front wheel carries more weight than the rear. Braking gently with the front brake will help keep you in control without going into a skid. Be careful, though, not to overdo it with the front brakes and accidentally toss yourself over the handlebars. And don't neglect your rear brake! When descending, shift your weight back over the rear wheel, thus increasing your rear braking power as well. This will balance the power of both brakes and give you maximum control. Good riders learn just how much of their weight to shift over each wheel and how to apply just enough braking power to each brake, so not to "endo" over the handlebars or skid down a trail.

Obstacles

Logs. When you want to hop a log, pull up sharply on the handlebars, and pedal forward in one swift motion. This clears the front end of the bike. Then quickly scoot forward and pedal the rear wheel up and over. Keep the forward momentum until you've cleared the log, and by all means, don't hit the brakes, or you may do some interesting acrobatic maneuvers!

Rocks and roots. Worse than highway potholes! Stay relaxed and let your elbows and knees absorb the shock. Staying seated will keep the rear wheel weighted to prevent slipping.

Water. Before crossing a stream or puddle, be sure to first check the depth and bottom surface. There may be an unseen hole or large rock hidden under the water that could wash you up if you're not careful. You should also consider that riding through a mountain stream can cause great damage to the stream's ecosystem. If you still want to try, hit the water at a good speed, pedal steadily, and allow the bike to steer you through. Once you're across, tap the brakes to squeegee the water off the rims and the guilt off your conscience.

Leaves. Be careful of wet leaves. They may look pretty, but a trail or bridge covered with leaves may cause your wheels to slip out from under you. Leaves are not nearly as unpredictable and dangerous as ice, but they do warrant your attention on a rainy day.

Mud. If you must ride through mud, hit it head on and keep pedaling. You want to part the ooze with your front wheel and get across before it swallows you up. Above all, don't leave the trail to go around the mud. This just widens the path even more and leads to increased trail erosion.

Sand. This can be one of the most challenging trail conditions. The basic technique is to get the weight off the front tire by pulling up on the handlebars, getting your weight behind your seat, and pedaling like crazy. Your front tire should float over the surface of the sand. If it dives in, you're walking.

Slickrock. Moab, Utah, is famous for its slickrock, but you may find small sections of exposed rock in many places around the country. Depending on the type of rock, slickrock is very rideable when it's dry but slippery when it's wet.

Curbs are fun to jump, but as with logs, be careful.

Curbside drains. Be careful not to get a wheel caught in the grate. This is a recipe for a pretzeled wheel and a broken collarbone.

Dogs make great pets, but they seem to have it in for mountain bikers. If you think you can't outrun a dog that's chasing you, stop and walk your bike out of its territory. A loud yell to "Get!" or "Go home!" often works, as does a sharp squirt from your water bottle right between the eyes.

Cars are tremendously convenient when we're in them, but dodging irate motorists in big automobiles becomes a real hazard when riding a bike. As a cyclist you must realize most drivers aren't expecting you to be there and often wish you weren't. Stay alert and ride carefully, clearly signaling all of your intentions.

Potholes, like grates and back-road canyons, should be avoided. Just because you're on an all-terrain bicycle doesn't mean you're indestructible. Potholes regularly damage rims, pop tires, and sometimes lift unsuspecting cyclists into a spectacular swan dive over the handlebars.

LAST-MINUTE CHECKOVER

Before a ride, it's a good idea to give your bike a once-over to make sure everything is in working order. Go through the following checklist before each ride to make sure everything is secure and in place.

- **Check the air pressure in your tires to make sure they are properly inflated before each ride.** Mountain bikes require about forty-five to fifty-five pounds per square inch of air pressure. If your tires are underinflated, there is greater likelihood that the tubes may get pinched on a rock, causing the tire to go flat.
- **Pinch the tires to feel for proper inflation.** They should give just a little on the sides but feel very hard on the treads. If you have a pressure gauge, use that.
- **Check your brakes.** Squeeze the rear brake and roll your bike forward. The rear tire should skid. Next, squeeze the front brake and roll your bike forward. The rear wheel should lift into the air. If this doesn't happen, then your brakes are too loose. Make sure the brake levers don't touch the handlebars when squeezed with full force.
- **Check all quick releases on your bike.** Make sure they are all securely tightened. To avoid hooking them on a stick or branch, quick releases should point toward the back of the bike. The front quick release lever should be on the left of the

bike and tightened so it runs parallel to the arm of the fork. The back quick release should be closed so it points toward the back of the bike.

- **Lube up.** If your chain squeaks, apply some lubricant.
- **Check your nuts and bolts.** Check the handlebars, saddle, cranks, and pedals to make sure that each is tight and securely fastened to your bike.
- **Check your wheels.** Spin each wheel to see that they spin through the frame and between brake pads freely.

Have you got everything? Make sure you have your spare tube, tire irons, patch kit, frame pump, tools, food, water, foul-weather gear, and guidebook.

Need more information on mountain biking? Consider reading *Basic Essentials Mountain Biking.* You'll discover such things as choosing and maintaining a mountain bike; useful bike-handling techniques; preparing for long rides; overcoming obstacles such as rocks, logs, and water; and even preparing for competition.

Repair and Maintenance

Fixing a Flat

TOOLS YOU WILL NEED

- Two tire irons
- Pump (either a floor pump or a frame pump)
- No screwdrivers!!! (This can puncture the tube.)

REMOVING THE WHEEL

The front wheel is easy. Simply disconnect the brake shoes, open the quick release mechanism or undo the bolts with the proper sized wrench, then remove the wheel from the bike.

The rear wheel is a little more tricky. Before you loosen the wheel from the frame, shift the chain into the smallest gear on the freewheel (the cluster of gears in the back). Once you've done this, removing and installing the wheel, like the front, is much easier.

REMOVING THE TIRE

Step one: Insert a tire iron under the bead of the tire and pry the tire over the lip of the rim. Be careful not to pinch the tube when you do this.

Step two: Hold the first tire iron in place. With the second tire iron, repeat step one, 3 or 4 inches down the rim. Alternate tire irons, pulling the bead of the tire over the rim, section by section, until one side of the tire bead is completely off the rim.

Step three: Remove the rest of the tire and tube from the rim. This can be done by hand. It's easiest to remove the valve stem last. Once the tire is off the rim, pull the tube out of the tire.

CLEAN AND SAFETY CHECK

Step four: Using a rag, wipe the inside of the tire to clean out any dirt, sand, glass, thorns, etc. These may cause the tube to puncture. The inside of a tire should feel smooth. Any pricks or bumps could mean that you have found the culprit responsible for your flat tire.

Step five: Wipe the rim clean, then check the rim strip, making sure it covers the spoke nipples properly on the inside of the rim. If a spoke is poking through the rim strip, it could cause a puncture.

Step six: At this point, you can do one of two things: replace the punctured tube with a new one, or patch the hole. It's easiest to just replace the tube with a new tube when you're out on the trails. Roll up the old tube and take it home to repair later that night in front of the TV. Directions on patching a tube are usually included with the patch kit itself.

INSTALLING THE TIRE AND TUBE
(This can be done entirely by hand.)

Step seven: Inflate the new or repaired tube with enough air to give it shape, then tuck it back into the tire.

Step eight: To put the tire and tube back on the rim, begin by putting the valve in the valve hole. The valve must be straight. Then use your hands to push the beaded edge of the tire onto the rim all the way around so that one side of your tire is on the rim.

Step nine: Let most of the air out of the tube to allow room for the rest of the tire.

Step ten: Beginning opposite the valve, use your thumbs to push the other side of the tire onto the rim. Be careful not to pinch the tube in between the tire and the rim. The last few inches may be difficult, and you may need the tire iron to pry the tire onto the rim. If so, just be careful not to puncture the tube.

BEFORE INFLATING COMPLETELY

Step eleven: Check to make sure the tire is seated properly and that the tube is not caught between the tire and the rim. Do this by adding about five to ten pounds of air, and watch closely that the tube does not bulge out of the tire.

Step twelve: Once you're sure the tire and tube are properly seated, put the wheel back on the bike, then fill the tire with air. It's easier squeezing the wheel through the brake shoes if the tire is still flat.

Step thirteen: Now fill the tire with the proper amount of air, and check constantly to make sure the tube doesn't bulge from the rim. If the tube does appear to bulge out, release all the air as quickly as possible, or you could be in for a big bang. Place the wheel back in the dropout and tighten the quick release lever Reconnect the brake shoes.

When installing the rear wheel, place the chain back onto the smallest cog (farthest gear on the right), and pull the derailleur out of the way. Your wheel should slide right on.

Lubrication Prevents Deterioration

Lubrication is crucial to maintaining your bike. Dry spots will be eliminated. Creaks, squeaks, grinding, and binding will be gone. The chain will run quietly, and the gears will shift smoothly. The brakes will grip quicker, and your bike may last longer with fewer repairs. Need I say more? Well, yes. Without knowing where to put the lubrication, what good is it?

THINGS YOU WILL NEED
- One can of bicycle lubricant, found at any bike store
- A clean rag (to wipe excess lubricant away)

WHAT GETS LUBRICATED
- Front derailleur
- Rear derailleur
- Shift levers
- Front brake
- Rear brake
- Both brake levers
- Chain

WHERE TO LUBRICATE

To make it easy, simply spray a little lubricant on all the pivot points of your bike. If you're using a squeeze bottle, use just a drop or two. Put a few drops on each point wherever metal moves against metal, for instance, at the center of the brake calipers. Then let the lube sink in.

Once you have applied the lubricant to the derailleurs, shift the gears a few times, working the derailleurs back and forth. This allows the lubricant to work itself into the tiny cracks and spaces it must occupy to do its job. Work the brakes a few times as well.

LUBING THE CHAIN

Lubricating the chain should be done after the chain has been wiped clean of most road grime. Do this by spinning the pedals counterclockwise while gripping the chain with a clean rag. As you add the lubricant, be sure to get some in between each link. With an aerosol spray, just spray the chain while pedaling backwards (counterclockwise) until the chain is fully lubricated. Let the lubricant soak in for a few seconds before wiping the excess away. Chains will collect dirt much faster if they're loaded with too much lubrication.

Ride Index

Sweet Singletrack
5. Goose Lake Loop
8. Devisadaro Peak
10. Talpa Traverse Trail
12. Elliot Barker Trail
13. South Boundary Trail
18. Angostura Trail
22. Windsor Trail
23. Dale Ball Trails North
24. Dale Ball Trails Central
25. San Juan and Chamisa Trails
26. Chamisa Trail Loop
30. Glorieta Baldy
36. North Foothills Trail
37. South Foothills Trail
39. Faulty Trail
40. Tunnel Canyon
41. Otero Canyon West
42. Otero Canyon East
43. Chamisoso and Coyote Trails
44. Cedro Peak Loop
45. Oak Flat Loop

Technical Terrain
5. Goose Lake Loop
8. Devisadaro Loop
9. Ojitos Canyon Loop
13. South Boundary Trail
17. Canon Tio Maes Trail
18. Angostura Trail
22. Windsor Trail
28. Atalaya Mountain
30. Glorieta Baldy
39. Faulty Trail
43. Chamisoso and Coyote Trails
44. Cedro Peak Loop

Epic Rides
5. Goose Lake Loop
13. South Boundary Trail
22. Windsor Trail
30. Glorieta Baldy

Beginner's Luck
1. Red River Fault Loop
2. Rinconada Trail
6. Cebolla Mesa
7. West Rim Trail
14. Rio Grande del Rancho Trail
20. Caja del Rio North
21. Forest Road 24/Caja del Rio
23. Dale Ball Trails North
29. Glorieta Mesa
31. Arroyo de los Chamisos Trail
32. Los Cerrillos to Waldo
33. 10K Trail
35. Corrales Bosque
40. Tunnel Canyon
45. Oak Flat Loop

Great Climbs
4. Middle Fork Lake
5. Goose Lake Loop
8. Devisadaro Peak
9. Ojitos Canyon Loop
11. Capulin Trail
27. Aspen Vista
28. Atalaya Mountain
30. Glorieta Baldy
38. Sandia Peak Ski Area
39. Faulty Trail
43. Chamisoso and Coyote Trails

Great Downhills

4. Middle Fork Lake
5. Goose Lake Loop
8. Devisadaro Peak
13. South Boundary Trail
17. Canon Tio Maes Trail
18. Angostura Trail
22. Windsor Trail
27. Aspen Vista
28. Atalaya Mountain
38. Sandia Peak Ski Area
41. Otero Canyon West
42. Otero Canyon East

Scenic Rides

2. Rinconada Trail
4. Middle Fork Lake
5. Goose Lake Loop
7. West Rim Trail
16. Gallegos Peak/Forest Road 442
22. Windsor Trail
27. Aspen Vista
29. Glorieta Mesa
30. Glorieta Baldy
36. North Foothills Trail
38. Sandia Peak Ski Area
41. Otero Canyon West
42. Otero Canyon East

About the Author

Bob D'Antonio has spent many hours hiking, biking, and climbing throughout the United States. He has written several Falcon Guides on hiking and rock climbing and is the author of seven mountain biking guides. A native of Philadelphia, Pennsylvania, Bob lives in Louisville, Colorado, with his wife Laurel and their three children.